Vital Signs

Velvet, the velvet of your skin (is warm)
bones – the fragment of my death (are cold)
I dye the white cloth red to bathe my ancient bones like a
    taxidermist
in the material of fire and blood
The anatomy lessons of my father mix with the vulnerable
    embroidered tablecloths of my mother
Dehavada traditions join with the skills of old muslim artisans
History sleeps with art on a phenomenological earth-bed

Anita Dube (1997)
Silence (Blood Wedding)

The scapula or shoulder blade: the scapula is a flat triangular shaped bone which lies on the posterior wall superficial to the ribs and separated from them by muscle. .

Shuttered like a fan no-one suspects your shoulder blades of wings. While you lay on your belly I kneaded the hard edges of your flight. You are a fallen angel but still as the angels are; body light as a dragonfly, great gold wings cut across the sun.

   If I'm not careful you'll cut me. If I slip my hand too casually down the sharp side of your scapula I will lift away a bleeding palm. I know the stigmata of presumption. The wound that will not heal if I take you for granted.

Jeanette Winterson (1992)
Written on the Body

Vital Signs

Feminist Reconfigurations of the Bio/logical Body

Edited by
MARGRIT SHILDRICK
and
JANET PRICE

Edinburgh University Press

© The contributors, 1998

Edinburgh University Press
22 George Square, Edinburgh

Typeset in ITC–New Baskerville
by Pioneer Associates, Perthshire, and
printed and bound in Great Britain by
Cromwell Press, Trowbridge, Wiltshire

A CIP record for this book is available from
the British Library

ISBN 0 7486 0962 8 (paperback)
ISBN 0 7486 0963 6 (hardback)

Contents

Acknowledgements

OUR THANKS ARE DUE to all those friends and colleagues who have contributed time and energy towards the completion of this book. We would like to thank especially Jackie Jones of Edinburgh University Press, who commissioned this text, for her enthusiasm and encouragement, and the contributors for their commitment, and their willingness to explore new areas and to take risks. We are grateful to the Department of Primary Care, University of Liverpool, for making various practical facilities available, and to Helene Blankstone and Nicci Jones for their patience in frequently extricating the text from the temperamentality of office technology and from human error. Our thanks also to the International Health Division, Liverpool School of Tropical Medicine for practical help.

Margrit: my special thanks to Jude Lobley for her enthusiastic engagement with every aspect of the project, to Lis Davidson for continuing support, and to Janet for following through on our long-time aspiration.

Janet: Grindl Dockery has provided a constant source of support and love throughout, and has offered much practical assistance, and Gill Price has sustained me with her humour and her shared anger. Finally, my thanks to Margrit for the opportunities of working, writing and laughing with her that this book has afforded.

Introduction

Vital Signs: Texts, Bodies and Biomedicine

MARGRIT SHILDRICK AND JANET PRICE

THE BEATING OF THE HEART, the pulsing of arteries, the flush of the skin, the intake and exhalation of breath, the reflex constriction of the pupil in light – these are the vital signs of the living body, the markers of an intricate interplay of dynamic forces which form what is known as the biological corpus. Though the discourse of biomedicine takes that model as its privileged theme, it is a foreclosure that must be resisted. The vital signs that are explored in this collection move into a more thoroughly discursive field in which texts and practices are every bit as important as, indeed inseparable from, the substance of the body.

It is an academic truism that the body, after decades of perceived neglect, is once again at the forefront of academic discourse, not just in the humanities and social sciences, but more paradoxically in the medical sciences too, where a detached concern with the brute matter of blood, flesh and bones is increasingly challenged and superseded by a notion of constructed and differential embodiment. The renewed interest seems to come from two apparently disparate, even incommensurate, sources, namely feminist and poststructuralist theories. Each has been credited with initiating a deconstruction of the conventional body both as biologically fixed and given, and at the same time absent, or at least irrelevant, to the concerns of the western logos. And yet feminism, despite its own disruptive approach to conventional paradigms,

1

has been deeply suspicious of other non-feminist attempts to radically challenge and rethink the nature of bodies, or to theorise embodiment. The fear is that far from reclaiming bodies, and with them the value of the embodied feminine, the trajectory of such approaches might be to efface the corporeal altogether in favour of the very abstraction that has historically worked against women. It would be frivolous to dismiss such concerns as entirely unfounded, and indeed some practitioners of the postmodern give little ground to materiality in any form. But just as feminist theory is itself now recognised as plural and non-universalisable, so too its counterparts go in many, rather than one direction. It is surely prudent to investigate the multiple possibilities that contemporay theories offer before dismissing them all as the same old masculinist story.

The intention of *Vital Signs* is, then, to offer a set of essays which engage with and mobilise postconventional and, more specifically, what have been grouped together as postmodern modes of inquiry in the field of what we have called the bio/logical body. What is at stake in the most general sense is the essentialist – and characteristically modernist – view of the body as a natural and immanent given that finds a place within the western logos only as the devalued term of the mind/body binary. As such it plays no part in questions of subjectivity, or even of personhood, but serves the transcendent spirit merely as a mundane housing, sometimes all too painfully present and troublesome in degenerative illness or aging, but most often forgotten or disavowed. The entrenched dualism of such a model is most usually ascribed to the distinctions proposed by Descartes between the *res cogitans* – the mind – with its qualities of intelligence, animation and selfhood, and the *res extensa* – the corporeal body – which functions mechanistically according to the logic of a mathematical–causal model. Although the Cartesian split is rather more complex and nuanced than is often allowed, there is little doubt that the notion of embodiment – that is the irreducible imbrication of being-in-a-body – is foreign to it. As Descartes puts it in a famous passage:

Although the whole mind seems to be united to the whole body, nevertheless, were a foot or an arm or any other bodily part amputated, I know that nothing would be taken away from my mind (1979: 97).

Moreover, the relevance of such statements was not limited to the exercise of abstract rationality, but was intended by Descartes to have application to the newly resurgent science of medicine. What was put into play, albeit with complications and digressions, was the so-called medical model of the body, in which a detached and reductionist concentration on the signs and symptoms of health and disease 'serves to dehumanise the "patient" and reduce her to the status of a (mal)functioning machine' (Shildrick 1997: 15). The bio/logical body of modernity is deeply invested in the discourse and practices of biomedicine. It is with that extension – both implicit and explicit – that *Vital Signs* is concerned.

The usual deployment of postmodernist analysis is as a highly abstract tool which generates a series of unsettling insights which may appear to have few immediate material implications. Committed opponents accuse it wholesale – without justification in our view – of being dead-end, of delighting in a relativity that denies the possibility of ethical formulations, and of a lack of recognition of the material and substantive effects of theory, or that theorising is itself a cultural and political practice. Such objections have been particularly evident with regard to writing addressing the body, where it has seemed that the corpus has been dematerialised, rendering it dispersed, fragmented and lacking in specificity. Moreover, questions of embodied sexual difference have been almost universally ignored or elided. In contrast, we want to show postmodernism at work in the substantive field, not just of bodies, but more particularly of what can be broadly termed the clinic, by which we mean all those issues which fall within the biomedical discourse around bodies. And although in many ways the technological capacities of late twentieth-century biomedicine, such as new imaging techniques, may themselves speak to a postmodern age and provide the ground for a reconfigured clinic, our interest is equally firmly directed towards a reworking of the traditional concerns of health care, such as geriatric medicine, heart disease, and disability.

Our focus is motivated by the concern that, despite powerful feminist interests in the areas of both health issues and postmodernist theory, the two have very rarely been brought together.[1] Indeed, the parameters set by liberal humanist conceptions of the binaries of health/disease, whole/broken, normal/abnormal and indeed self/other, remain largely unproblematised in mainstream feminist work on the specifics of biomedical care, bioethics, and the experience of corporeal distress. Such dichotomous thinking reflects an all too easy acceptance of the foundational categories of western thought whereby vulnerability is something that happens to already existent subjects and already existent bodies. In conventional approaches, the integrity of the 'healthy' body must be actively maintained and protected against the threat of disease, degeneration, disability, or lack of control. In consequence, although specific practices may be challenged as more or less adequate to the needs of women, there is little recognition that biomedical discourse is itself constitutive of the embodied subject. Aside from the occasional gesture towards Foucault, feminist writing in this area has hitherto tended to ignore the developments in contemporary theory, and to exhibit instead a belief in foundational facts, in the givenness of biological bodies, and in the transparency of experience. And despite an awareness of the overdetermination of female/feminine malady, there has been little or no attempt to deconstruct the mobilising signifiers of health and disease.

In general, mainstream feminist work around issues of biomedicine has tended to locate itself in an everyday understanding of the body, untroubled by the intricacies of high theory. Ever since the highly instructive *Our Bodies, Ourselves* (Boston Women's Health Book Collective 1976) was first published, much important and influential work has been done in the area of health to improve the specific delivery to women, to widen access, challenge stereotypical notions of 'female' diseases, and to put the issues of agency and choice upfront. The explicitly political agenda of such work drew freely on the nascent women's movement of the 1970s, with its commitment to consciousness-raising, to the acquisition of knowledge about one's own body, and to challenging the institutional structures that influence health. In keeping with the wider movement, women's own experiences served as the inalienable, and unproblematised, ground for analysis and action, summed up by the slogan 'The personal is political'. Feminist activity was directed by an epistemological challenge to both the varying pathological constructions of the female body and the notion that women were inherently sick, and by practical opposition to male-dominated medical control in areas such as pregnancy and childbirth. Many such essentially oppositional campaigns continue to be active today, and undoubtedly women in general have found considerable strength and support in the women's health movement.

Inherent to all such approaches has been an implicit acceptance of the binary structure of biomedical practice, such that doctor/patient for example is recognised as the locus of a regulatory power relationship without being deconstructed as such. Moreover, as Wendi Hadd argues: 'The notion of being entitled to control one's body is formulated within a discourse which accepts as a given the concept of mind/body dualism' (1991: 165). The body is positioned as an object apart – inert property almost – and the aim is to ensure that its 'owner' is the one who exerts control by challenging health-care providers to relinquish their power of definition of, and intervention into, the corporeal. The problematic remains caught up in binary thinking, witness to both the perceived struggle between medical professionals and women for control over the body, and to the struggle that divides woman as agent from her body. As Val Walsh argues, '"(h)aving control" and "being human" are very closely connected', and 'evidence of wear and tear signifies loss of control, accompanied by loss of human status' (1995: 6). What Walsh presumably means by the 'human status' that is forfeit by the out-of-control body is better expressed as an autonomous, rational personhood, the proper site of an intentional agency that operates within fixed boundaries. In contrast, the overflowing of corporeal boundaries – through illness or impairment, and notably through being female, with its inherent potential for the leakiness of menstruation, lactation and childbirth, for example – characteristically signifies not just disruption of the unmarked, universalised body, but disqualification from full personhood.[2]

Within such a framework, no-one – regardless of gender – can exist as a fully embodied subject, for either we must claim the putative ideal of empowerment and autonomy by effecting the separation of mind from body, in order to exercise control over our own materiality; or we must remain tied to the body, and disempowered by our very identification with it. For women, however, and indeed in analogous ways for other others, the essentialist belief in the special immanence of the female body – women *are* their bodies in a way that men are not – has in any case worked to disallow the option of transcendence, with its prize of full personhood in the post-Enlightenment sense. The whole notion of embodiment has, then, been contentious within feminist theory, for to acknowledge the centrality of the corporeal has seemed to mitigate the claim to full equality. In consequence, the women's health movement has, at the same time as focusing on the female body, been constrained to contest the belief that biology is destiny. What has come into play is a notion of a pre-given, biological, sexed body which is nonetheless mediated and changed by social processes. And in addressing some very practical issues, what has become apparent is the extraordinary extent to which biomedicine both authorises and disallows particular representations, and indeed experiences, of the corporeal. It is now widely recognised that medicine and its related sciences, far from being neutral and objective purveyors of fact, have the social and political power to shape and disseminate particular versions of corporeality at the expense of others. The ability of the medical eugenics movement at the beginning of the century to promulgate, for example, a notion of supposedly racial characteristics such as mental inferiority as inheritable is one clear illustration. As Susan Sherwin puts it:

The reality that medicine creates is socially accepted; given the power and authority that are awarded to medical expertise, its reality is generally socially dominating (1992: 191).

However, although functioning as the dominant discourse, biomedicine is constantly under challenge from resistant discourses, from subaltern knowledges which disrupt its totalising claims. The last decade has seen, for example, the emergence of newly constituted knowledges about HIV and AIDS, in and through which people with AIDS and those living with HIV have questioned the type of knowledge that is validated as truth. Their challenge to the primacy and relevance of double-blind placebo-controlled clinical trials in establishing the efficacy of drug treatments is a case in point. Moreover, people with AIDS situate themselves as active subjects within AIDS discourse, querying the distribution and use of biomedical knowledge over their bodies, whilst struggling to renegotiate their place as embodied subjects in the face of an overwhelming exercise of biomedicine's regulatory power.

Important though such struggles and insights are, they are only half the story: the discursive power of biomedicine does not simply direct choice among alternative models of the body, with the probable implication that some are more 'true' to life than others. It actively and continuously constructs the body as a focus of what Foucault calls power/knowledge. Rather than there being any foundational pre-existing corpus which is then variously interpreted and experienced through differential cultural forces – of which biomedicine is pre-eminent – the claim derived from postconventional theory is that the body is materialised *only* insofar as it is always/already mediated. As Liz Grosz remarks:

It is not simply that the body is represented in a variety of ways according to historical, social and cultural exigencies while it remains basically the same; these factors actively produce the body as a body of a 'determinate type' (1994: x).

The issue is not whether or not the body really exists, but how it comes to be present to us. What is at stake is not simply the adequacy of various definitions and descriptions of corporeality in terms of health and disease, normality and abnormality, whole and broken, but the very understanding of the body as 'being there' at all. At very least, postconventional approaches must dispense with any recourse to a naturally given and stable corpus.

What has happened over the last few years, often coincidentally with, and yet non-communicating with, a practical concern for the reform of biomedicine, is that the feminist take-up of post-modernism has produced some exciting new moves in which the reworking of the structures of knowledge and identity has positioned the discursively constructed body as a central concern. In that form – the body as an epistemological text – the project has seemed to foreclose on the capacity to engage with the 'real' body, and to sideline any concern with the substantive issues of biomedicine, or indeed other areas of materialist interest. The body in question has remained a highly abstract construct, contesting the normativities of post-Enlightenment thought, dissolving the categories of the given, but eluding the tangible concerns of the clinic. More recently, several feminist theorists – notably Judith Butler (1993) and Liz Grosz (1994) – have sought to reinstate the materiality of the body, but again without any in-depth engagement with concrete situations. In the face of the dispersal and dematerialisation of the body that emerges from some strands of postmodernist theory, we would insist on the necessary implication of the material body in the very acts of academic production. Writing, thinking, conceptualising, creating images are not the abstract processes of the incorporeal mind; rather theorising is an embodied act, and the making of knowledge an activity, in which the 'creative and disruptive presence of our bodies is a necessary element' (Potts and Price 1995: 103). We write through the/our body. That move indicates that feminist postmodernists at least are prepared to open up new considerations. Moreover, in recent feminist deployments of postconventional (though not necessarily postmodernist) insights, the experiencing 'I', the subject of modernist discourse, is not thereby left all the more bodyless, but on the contrary is restored to her body where both are contingent and provisional constructs.

This is nowhere more apparent than in the use of phenomenology as a tool of analysis. What has made it particularly efficacious is that it constitutes an alternative model to the bio/logical body that gives substance to embodiment without appealing to a fixed and unchanging materiality. The notion of being-in-the-world – or perhaps more appropriately becoming-in-the-world – is an expression of indivisible corporeal subjectivity in which the temporal and spatial are fully operative. The contrast with Descartes' disembodied mind could not be clearer. Nonetheless, although the structure of the self is fully imbricated with its corporeal capacities, the emphasis given to bodily integrity seems to leave too little space to those forms of differential embodiment which blur and confound the boundaries of the normative standard. In this respect, what marks out a specifically feminist methodology has been the move made by theorists such as Iris Marion Young and Ros Diprose to utilise the work of Merleau-Ponty whilst at the same time offering a critique of the universalised and implicity masculine body that stands at the centre of mainstream phenomenology.

It is precisely at this point of specifically feminist interventions into the postmodern/postconventional that the collection, *Vital Signs*, intends to situate itself. We are acutely aware of both the fear of more traditional feminists working in the area of biomedicine that postmodernism will dissolve all meaning and value, and of the exasperation felt by postmodernist feminists towards those for whom the categories of modernity remain unquestioned. Our aim is to overcome that mutual incomprehension and to demonstrate through a variety of perspectives that postmodernism can and should inform, and more importantly transform, the relations of the clinic. As the editors of another collection focused on the interrelationship of feminism and postmodernism put it:

Postmodernism . . . is a name for the way we live now, and it needs to be taken account of, put into practice, and even contested within feminist discourses as a way of coming to terms with our lived situations (Wicke and Ferguson 1994: 1).

Two very specific moments underwrite the project. First, Donna Haraway's tantalising remark that 'it is time to write the death of the clinic' (1991: 245 n. 4) suggests that the critique, launched by Foucault, of the body of modernity and its associated biomedicine should give way to an acknowledgement that the paradigms of that particular epoch are in any case being overtaken by the cybotechnological innovations of postmodernity. And whilst we remain wary of any uncritical turn to periodisation, we endorse the need, as do some of our contributors such as Cathryn Vasseleu on the oral camera, or in a very different way, Camilla Griggers on contemporary psychopharmacology, to address very real changes in practice specifically associated with the late twentieth century. Nonetheless, pace Haraway, the body of modernity lingers on and demands continuing attention. The second underlying moment of our belief in the material efficacy of a postmodernist perspective perhaps illustrates only too well that the body in question has an everyday flesh and blood physicality. Facing the onset of breast cancer, Eve Kosofsky Sedgwick alludes to the experience as 'an adventure in applied deconstruction' (1994: 12); a cognitive exercise that enables her to confront and survive the 'instability of the supposed oppositions that structure an experience of the "self"' (ibid.): safety and danger, hope and fear, past and future, thought and act, the natural and the technological. More recently Jackie Stacey (1997) has written extensively about her own experience of cancer using, among other strategies, Kristevan notions of the abject to forge a postconventional and resistant understanding of what is often a socially and medically devastating breakdown of corporeal normativity. These, and other undeveloped fragments, con-vince us that there is an exciting new area to be explored in which the distinctions between theory and practice, and between the ideational and the material can be reworked. We are not interested, in other words, in simply producing yet another feminist reflection on the body, nor yet in privileging the personal voice as a response to the 'victim' status so often assumed in the past. The deployment of the autobiographical voice is a deliberate strategy adopted in several essays in *Vital Signs*, but what it speaks to is not a nostalgia for the subject fully present to herself, but rather the possibility of mobilising a series of differentially embodied and multiple 'I-slots'. Indeed we have chosen to open the collection with Ailbhe Smyth's prose-poem 'Loving the Bones' which reminds us:

Continuous plurality, non-sequential simultaneity. There is no story of my body . . . (see p. 19)

What, then, are the particular features of postconventional/ postmodern modes of inquiry that seem to us to hold out the promise, not of abstract theory, playful or otherwise, but of a set of considerations that will make a substantive difference. The notion, already alluded to, of the bio/logical body as discursively constructed is perhaps the simplest and most immediately effective starting point. It tells us that corporeality can be/is always already other than the body of traditional biomedicine, that it is neither a container nor contained, but leaks and flows beyond the restraining definitions of the unreconstructed clinic. Lynda Birke's analysis of the heart is a case in point. Moreover, the notion of corporeality introduces a dynamic in which the relations of power and resistance are themselves fluctuating, and circulating, rather than vested in fixed and pre-determined positions. This dynamic is explored, for example, by Ros Diprose in relation to sexuality and the clinical encounter, where she focuses on not only the body of the patient but also the body of the clinician. Closely related is the implicit and explicit deconstruction of the endless binary differences and hierarchies which shape notions of what is proper and improper, normal and abnormal about the body, who has authority and who has not, what counts as the self and what as non-self. In a telling phrase, Sara Ahmed refers to the clinical body as 'the body that is being stitched up' (see p. 47), and it is precisely that sense of corporeal closure, and of the rigid categorisation of knowledge about being and the body, that deconstruction begins to crack open. Indeed it is in the very impossibility of securing normativities that we can account for the disciplinary function of conventional biomedical discourse and practice. But for all the strategies of mapping, policing and normalisation, the clinic cannot contain the body; there is always an inevitable excess. Even as they reconfigure the bio/logical body, the contributors to *Vital Signs* have reflected a slippage in attempts to hold firm the contours of the body as the site of discussion. And at the same time our initial plan as editors to gather a collection exclusively focused on biomedical discourse has leaked over into other discursive fields.

The blurring of the boundaries between what have hitherto been seen as distinct bodies of knowledge is a further characteristic feature of postmodernist methodologies. No one discipline can claim mastery, as has the discourse of medical science in the past in its attempts to speak the truth about the body. Indeed, contributors to this volume are deliberately drawn from a wide range of academic disciplines, encompassing variously the arts, social sciences and biological sciences. But it is not simply that biomedicine is irreducibly interwoven with other discourses – cultural, colonial, ethical, economic and so on – but that confidence in a coherent notion of truth itself has dispersed into a series of fragmented and conflicting claims. The Enlightenment hope of universalised historical progress, evident in the rationalist claims of science and medicine to displace superstition, must give way to specific, located knowledges that question not just the products of our theorising but the theories themselves. As Rajan argues: '"(t)heory" has become the contracted domain of the western 'sciences of knowledge' . . . 'whose limits are betrayed – rather than systematically explored – at the points where they break down as explanatory models' (1993: 8). Clearly, this does not mean that biomedicine is necessarily wrong in its theory and practice, but rather that there is no foundational truth of the body that biomedicine is uniquely placed to address. In 'Death of the Clinic', for example, Roma Chatterji, Sangeeta Chattoo and Veena Das address precisely those limits, as the points at which the regimes of western medicine meet with processes of aging in two markedly different societies. What matters from the perspective of postmodernism is that the shifting and multiple constructions of the body that come together at the temporary juncture of intersecting forces should be recognised in their differential specificity. Foucault has famously spoken of the task of '(exposing) a body totally imprinted by history and the process of history's destruction of the body' (1977: 148). The purpose of *Vital Signs* is to ask what are the substantive implications in and around the clinic of refusing the certainties of corporeal closure .

The aim is not to provide new solutions, or to replace the conventionally operative categories with, as it were, better, postconventional ones. On the contrary, it would be a serious misunderstanding of the project of postmodernism to merely replace one set of limiting binaries with another set: new/old, true/false, fixed/nomadic. Moreover, the 'methodology' of deconstruction which implicitly underlies the collection is not synonomous with destruction. As Spivak argues, '(t)he most serious critique in deconstruction is the critique of things that are extremely useful, things without which we cannot live' (1993: 4). Our focus rather is upon the effects, biomedical, cultural and political, of disrupting conventional categories, of uncovering their investments, and of making space for all those states of corporeal being that have been marginalised in the dominant discourse. In opening up the field to the flux and provisionality of multiple determinants, postconventional critiques in general allow the appeal to experience without essentialising it, a recognition of difference without reifying it, and the ability to act at strategic moments without the necessity for a totalising answer.

So what precisely is it that we mean when we offer this collection as providing 'feminist reconfigurations'? Are we claiming that

11

the articles all adopt an inherent, though self-evident, feminist line of argument in questioning modernist – and implicitly patriarchal – norms; that they deal with subjects that are recognisably of feminist concern, or of concern to women; that their authors are feminists; that they adopt a particular style of writing that challenges or disrupts phallogocentric conventions; that they are read by a self-proclaimed feminist audience? A quick scan through the contents will suggest that whilst these possibilities are consciously taken up in some of the contributions, there is no blueprint, no definitive answer to the question of what constitutes a feminist text.

As we suggested earlier, one highly relevant yet often overlooked consideration is the relationship between bodies and writing. If the body materialises text, it is not simply *any* body. All the authors in this collection have a sexually specific corporeality which embodies them as women, and which serves to constitute texts in particular ways that simultaneously conceal and reveal the operation of sexual difference. This is not to argue for a 'female' style of writing, a specific feminine sensibility that inevitably emerges in the text, nor to say that all women write feminist texts. Rather, it is that texts cannot escape being marked by the irreducible trace of the writer's sexually marked corporeality. We are not suggesting of course that the female body is a fixed form, nor even simply that we have no access to the body outside of discourse. It is rather that discourse materialises the body, is productive of the female body, and of the embodied subject as both writer and reader. Texts that work, albeit always provisionally, under the sign feminist – as all those contributing to this collection have chosen to do – mark and materialise the body in specific, uncertain and excessive ways that open up new lines of inquiry, exert inherently political effects, stimulate strategies of resistance, create new discursive spaces.

The conventional modernist understanding of the proper relationship between the writer, reader and text invests the first term alone with authority over meaning, and with intentionality. On this view, the author who writes 'as a feminist' writes from a clear identity, a self-presence that is implicitly opposed to non-feminists. From the postmodernist perspective, however, there are two problems with such a formulation. First, we must ask what 'truth' is at stake in naming oneself a feminist? It is not simply a question of what political or theoretical school of feminism one adheres to, or with whom else one claims identity or common cause. On the

12

contrary, what precisely is being claimed must remain always ulti-mately unclear, not because of any breakdown of communication, or failure of intellect, or lack of feminist conviction, but because meaning is ultimately undecidable, and identity necessarily unstable. Given that any identity, such as that of feminist – and by extension, woman – is defined as much by what it is not, as by what it is, it must constantly police its boundaries against difference. But the process of identification is never complete, and those same exclu-sions 'return to disrupt its claim to coherence' (Butler 1991: 15). Moreover, the unproblematised equation between identity and corporeal experience needs to be called into question. Within the field of feminist health studies in particular, women's bodily expe-riences are held to offer us 'the truth' of being a woman: they take identity as self-evident, and difference – including bodily difference – as natural. Scott suggests that the consequence of this is that 'the evidence of experience then becomes evidence for the fact of difference rather than a way of exploring how difference is established, how it operates, how and in what ways it constitutes subjects who see and act in the world' (1992: 25).

The second postmodernist insight is that reading a text is itself an act that works to constitute meaning. In other words, texts do not convey self-evident meaning, transmitted from the author via the pen (or computer keyboard) to the consciousness of the reader, but are sites of multidirectional construction. And whilst reading and writing are context-specific events, that context must remain indeterminate. Moreover, what Derrida terms the impossibility of 'empirical saturation' (1988: 92) – which stems, he suggests, in part from the nature of writing, the structure of language itself – results in an undecideable slippage of meaning. As such the notion of authorial intention is deeply problematised. In respect of the lack of closure of both meaning and identity, the question of feminism is, to some extent, in abeyance. For all that 'feminist' is a strategically/politically important position to occupy at particular moments in time – and we have no hesitation in subscribing to such a view – it conceals as much as it may be assumed to reveal. *Vital Signs* is a political text, but that should not be allowed to obscure its own more complex investments. As Liz Grosz argues, 'A text is feminist or patriarchal only provisionally, only momen-tarily, only in some but not all possible readings, and in some but not all of its possible effects' (1995: 24).

The present volume comprises a variety of textual forms which both further challenge the academic convention of knowledge transmission, and can tentatively lay claim to being disruptively feminist in conception. The chapters display many differing styles and presentational approaches, not simply theoretical and empirical pieces, but prose-poetry (Ailbhe Smyth), text and image collage (Sheba Chhachhi), or interwoven dialogue (Janet Price and Margrit Shildrick) – none of which is more essentially feminist in style than any of the others. They move in a wide variety of theoretical directions, drawing on and (re)appropriating not only writers who are recognised as feminist, but many whose work has been heavily criticised as anti-feminist; and they address both areas that have traditionally been seen as falling within a feminist remit – for example, foetal imagery (Lorna Weir) or hysteria (Lisa Diedrich) – and others whose relevance to a feminist political project might, at first glance, be seen as peripheral, as for example, Cathryn Vasseleu's piece on the mouth in dentistry. But all of them, in diverse ways and readings are reworking the relationships between feminism, biomedicine and the body. Each of those terms is called into question both to reveal some of what is at stake in our redrawing and disruption of foundational categorical boundaries, and to offer differing strategies for problematising the masculinist position of the self-present, fully self-aware author. However, this is not to deny that the authors' own investments and locations – of race, of sexuality, of age, of health or illness – leave their traces on the acts of reading and writing. For example the lesbian positioning of some authors offers a subtext that can serve to disrupt the neat binaries of sexual difference that underlie – albeit in markedly different ways – both medical and feminist thinking. At issue here is not whether any of us identify as lesbian authors but rather that the text, the author, and, indeed, the reader are implicated each with the other, the one always leaving an inevitable trace in/on the others, marking out subliminal spaces and leaking across boundaries, to offer new possibilities in embodied thought.

In the same way, the inclusion within the collection of pieces using presentational styles that do not fall within the traditional bounds of 'academic writing' is motivated not because we see them as attractive gimmicks, nor as adopting a 'feminist' writing style, but because we believe that the style of a piece has a serious influence on the ways in which it can be read. Differing modes of presentation offer new perspectives, demand that we look at issues from new directions, and offer new spaces for provisional feminist readings and ways of reappropriating apparently patriarchal texts.

And insofar as such pieces disrupt accepted conventions about the relationship between the body of the text and the body of the writer/reader, they highlight the notion of reading/writing as an embodied act.

Although *Vital Signs* does not state an overtly political agenda from the start, nonetheless, it takes as inherently political the effects that new paradigms of thought have upon material bodies. Moreover, we hold that the very critique, and construction, of theoretical forms is a political act, not a process of abstract contemplation to be set against practice. We would argue that the feminist engagement with postmodernism opens a field of critical practices that cannot be totalised, but makes possible a political intervention into both the discourse and applications of biomedicine and its related effects. Whilst our contributors occupy a variety of positions in relation to the postmodern, and are by no means all signed-up card-carrying members of a postmodern critical practice, the specifically feminist uptake of postconventional perspectives has served as an enabling device. Questions of the body, of biology, medical practice and materiality can be explored afresh without the perceived need to operate within pre-existing boundaries. The breakdown of binary modes of thinking is necessary to the displacement of the opposition between science and culture, to the notion of the body as discursively constituted and unstable, and to the understanding and critique of biomedical practice as *cultural* practice. But the ways in which contributors approach the bio/logical body lend themselves not to the political nihilism or unproblematised relativity of which much postmodernist writing is accused, but to a concern with the effects of theorising on the day-to-day lived experiences of embodiment – of health, illness, disability, aging, life and death.

Any attempts to hold the 'vital body' of the collection within the critical bounds of biomedical discourse must fail – the body is necessarily in excess of the discursive limits within which we had provisionally placed it. Similarly, our texts exceed and disrupt the limits of feminism itself. Whilst we would argue for the vital political importance of feminism, what we do not want, within the context of this collection, is to legislate for or against particular uses of the term, or to predetermine the political ends to which it should direct us. Rather, we aim to offer a new space in which readers/writers who have associated themselves – albeit provisionally – with the sign of 'feminist' can reconfigure the bio/logical body, and the cultural practices that are biomedicine, in ways that both

15

render visible and call into question the heteropatriarchal norms that disrupt and resist their operation, that destabilise their ongoing organisation. As such, the willingness to engage with contemporary theory demands a high degree of both risk and reflection. As Elizabeth Grosz puts it, a feminist text must

help, in whatever way, to facilitate the production of new and perhaps unknown, unthought discursive spaces – new styles, modes of analysis and argument, new genres and forms – that contest the limits and constraints currently at work in the regulation of textual production and reception (1995: 3).

We hope that *Vital Signs* will do no less.

NOTES

1. Notable exceptions are Diprose (1994), Epstein (1995), Shildrick (1997), and several essays in Komesaroff (1995). All of these, except Epstein, who takes a broadly postconventional cultural approach, are primarily concerned, however, with ethics. The only other obvious parallel is Fox (1993), who brings postmodernism to bear on health care, and acknowledges a relevant feminist input without developing it.
2. For a further critique of the place of bodies in the women's health and the disabled people's movements see Price J. (1996) 'The Marginal Politics of Our Bodies? Women's Health, the Disability Movement, and Power'.

REFERENCES

Boston Women's Health Book Collective (1976) *Our Bodies, Ourselves*, New York: Simon & Schuster.
Butler, Judith (1991) 'Imitation and Gender Insubordination' in Diana Fuss (ed.) *Inside/Out: Lesbian Theories, Gay Theories*, London: Routledge, pp. 13–31.
Butler, Judith (1993) *Bodies that Matter: On the Discursive Limits of 'Sex'*, London: Routledge.
Butler, Judith and Scott, Joan W. (eds) (1992) *Feminist Theorize the Political*, London: Routledge.
Derrida, Jacques (1988) *Limited Inc*, ed. G. Graff, Evanston, IL: Northwestern University Press.
Descartes, René (1979) *Meditations on the First Philosophy*, trans. Donald A. Cress, Indianapolis: Hackett Publishing.
Diprose, Rosalyn (1994) *The Bodies of Women. Ethics, Embodiment and Sexual Difference*, London: Routledge.
Epstein, Julia (1995) *Altered Conditions: Disease, Medicine and Storytelling*,

London: Routledge.

Foucault, Michel (1977) 'Nietzsche, genealogy, history' in D. Bouchard (ed.) *Language, Counter-Memory, Practice: Selected Essays and Interviews*, Ithaca, New York: Cornell University Press.

Fox, Nicolas (1993) *Postmodernism, Sociology and Health*, Buckingham: Open University Press.

Grosz, Elizabeth (1994) *Volatile Bodies: Towards a Corporeal Feminism*, Bloomington: Indiana University Press.

Grosz, Elizabeth (1995) *Space, Time and Perversion*, London: Routledge.

Hadd, Wendi (1991) 'A Womb with a View: Women as Mothers and the Discourse of the Body', *Berkeley Journal of Sociology* 36: 165–75.

Haraway, Donna (1991) 'A Cyborg Manifesto: Science, Technology and Socialist Feminism in the Late Twentieth Century' in *Simians, Cyborgs and Women: The Reinvention of Nature*, London: Free Association Books.

Komesaroff, Paul (ed.) (1995) *Troubled Bodies: Critical Perspectives on Postmodernism, Medical Ethics and the Body*, Melbourne: Melbourne University Press.

Potts, Tracey and Price, Janet (1995) 'Out of the Blood and Spirit of Our Lives: The Place of the Body in Academic Feminism' in Louise Morley and Val Walsh (eds) *Feminist Academics: Creative Agents for Change*, London: Taylor and Francis.

Price, Janet (1996) 'The Marginal Politics of Our Bodies? Women's Health, the Disability Movement, and Power' in Beth Humphries (ed.) *Critical Perspectives on Empowerment*, Birmingham: Venture Press.

Rajan, Rajeswari Sunder (1993) *Real and Imagined Women: Gender, Culture and Postcolonialism*, London: Routledge.

Scott, Joan (1992) '"Experience"' in Judith Butler and Joan Scott (eds) *Feminists Theorize the Political*, London & New York: Routledge.

Sedgwick, Eve Kosofsky (1994) *Tendencies*, London: Routledge.

Sherwin, Susan (1992) *No Longer Patient: Feminist Ethics and Health Care*, Philadelphia: Temple University Press.

Shildrick, Margrit (1997) *Leaky Bodies and Boundaries. Feminism, Postmodernism and (Bio)ethics*, London: Routledge.

Spivak, Gayatri Chakravorty (1993) *Outside in the Teaching Machine*, London: Routledge.

Stacey, Jackie (1997) *Teratologies: A Cultural Study of Cancer*, London: Routledge.

Walsh, Val (1995) 'Disability Feminism'. Draft of a conceptual entry in C. Kramarae and D. Spender (eds) *Women's Studies Encyclopaedia* (forthcoming).

Wicke, Jennifer and Ferguson, Margaret (1994) 'Introduction: Feminism and Postmodernism; or, The Way We Live Now' in M. Ferguson and J. Wicke (eds) *Feminism and Postmodernism*, Durham: Duke University Press.

Young, Iris Marion (1990) *Throwing Like a Girl and Other Essays in Feminist Philosophy and Social Theory*, Bloomington: Indiana University Press.

1

Loving the Bones
Medi(t)ating My Bodies

AILBHE SMYTH

> *To be rooted in the experience you have with your body and your mind*
> *– that is very difficult.*
> (Marina Abramovich)

> *To bring the two together, in unison – that may be impossible.*

I sift through the desultory notes from months of reading, stray phrases offering themselves for my consideration. I am a well-trained note-taker, precise and orderly. This time, there is no order, no nascent pattern, no argument beginning to emerge. No meaning I can lay my hands on, only warnings. I feel nauseous.

> *The numerous and heterogeneous nature of the practices associated with the making and marking of femininity. (Bordo) The State's microscopic surveillance of women's bodies. (Alexander and Mohanty) Every law has a hold on the body. (De Certeau) If there is any truth, it is the truth of the body. (Game) These models and metaphors inform not just the way we represent our bodies to ourselves, but how we live our bodies. (Diprose) The chaotic and incoherent experience of the body. (Anderson)*

ABSTRACTING

Dear Ones,

I'm sorry this abstract is so late, and really isn't an abstract at all anyway.

18

Loving the Bones: Medi(t)ating My Bodies

I cannot write an abstract of my body.

That doesn't mean I don't want to do the piece – I do. It terrifies me, while at the same time I know I really need to do it.

The terrible terrors my body holds in un/safe keeping.

Still, and not very usefully for you, at this stage I have only an inchoate sense of how it will turn out – a confusion of shapes, feelings, ideas. Maybe that *is* the way it will turn out. I've tried to say something briefly about that, but it's very vague. And I can't say how long it would be – certainly not 8000 words.

I cannot count my body.

I've been reading a lot of different things lately, including a piece about Orlan, who fascinates me – the metamorphoses. I saw some of her work last year. So only the goddess in her non-existence could know what might emerge from that – plus fifty years of bodilyness.

Love, Ailbhe

Abstract

'My body' is no more one or abstract than 'I'. So this will be a series of semi-discrete and immodest meditations on my bodilyness, beginning (if that moment can be located) with an experience of clinically diagnosed anorexia ('If you do not eat, you will die'), touching (if their materiality can be found) the sedimented layers of hatred, shame, confusion and sadness ('Don't bring your fat friend') which haunt me in memory, moving towards whatever lay beyond.

But these are not, in reality, discrete moments. The one bleeds into the other, and the other. Continuous plurality, non-sequential simultaneity. There is no story of my body, only the daily, momentary mediations between experience, senses, memory, desire, understanding – mediations between my bodies, and beyond. I am this body and that one and the other, the one before and the one after. There is no happy ending, only incorporations.

'Tell me one thing', said the eldest Princess to the Old Woman, when they had all applauded her story. The moon shone in an emerald sky, and all

19

the creatures drowsed and rustled. 'Tell me one thing. Was that you, ahead of me in the road, in such a hurry?'

'There is always an old woman ahead of you on a journey, and there is always an old woman behind you too, and they are not always the same, and may be fearful or kindly, dangerous or delightful, as the road shifts, and you speed along it. Certainly I was ahead of you, and behind you too, but not only I, and not only as I am now'. (A. S. Byatt)

So what shall I do with the fictions of my 'coherent', 'natural', woman's body, pathetic mockeries of its volatile truths, obstructing my vital arteries? What shall I do with all those illusions, lies, constructs and simulacra which have shaped my very core? How am I to shed their dead weight? How can I make peace with the relentlessly constant contradictions of my body, its insubstantial materiality, its provisional temporality? How am I to speed along in unison with myself, body and soul together? And what may be the point of the journey? Can I live with the dying of my body?

PREPARING

How to Eat an Apple

The core of the apple is not eaten and should be removed first. Quarter the cored apple precisely with a sharp knife, delicately peeling the skin from each segment, taking care to lick all traces of the blood from your fingers from its pale damp flesh. Cut each quarter in half, then pierce a halved and quartered segment with the prongs of a silver fork, and lift to the mouth. Sink the teeth slowly into the crisp fruit, gradually releasing the cool tart juice onto the warm pink tongue. Masticate and savour.

I choose a red apple from the large white bowl in my kitchen, rinse it under the cold tap and dry it carefully. The black-handled pure steel knife is best for fruit. It does the cleanest job. I never use a fruit-parer. I peel quickly to maintain momentum, seeing my mother peel potatoes in my mind's eye. I deftly turn apple and knife together, a perfect, smooth spiral flowing off the point of the knife.

I choose a silver-grey HB pencil, and insert one flat end inside the black sharpener. Pencil parers, we always called them here. I slowly turn the pencil under the small sharp blade and watch the wood-shavings fall on to my desk in a perfect, serrated spiral.

Vagina dentata. I can only make spirals if I concentrate and keep a steady hand. I stop turning, remove the pencil from the sharpener, and am satisfied with its point.

I lay them both on the table, neatly, although symmetry is not desired. The contrasts please me, conscious, chosen: of shape, colour, texture, function.

I sit down to write about my body. I twist in my chair, adjust the height, my lower back has seized up again. I take a headache tablet and a glass of cold filtered water. Turn the heat up a little higher. I force myself to sit again. My bones ache, my flesh hurts, my stomach turns over. The 'I' who is sitting here is not abstracted from her/my body, which dictates its own conditions of deployment. I am shivering now, because this is too hard to do. My joints swell, my eyes burn and develop small cysts if I spend too long at the computer. I must stretch my legs frequently – cartilage problems in my knees. My nose is blocked with the residue of a cold. I must stop thinking about my body, my physical reality, my concrete materiality. I must write over my dead body.

> *I have papered over my body for ever. Thick layer after layer of paper larded with words and more and more words. When you lay on the paper first, it is wet and glutinous, then it dries hard. Desiccation occurs over time. I must peel and pare carefully, precisely. I cannot bear to be stripped bare. See how the very words betray me?*

Skin deep Bone dry

The sickening anxiety I feel in the pit of my stomach – tightness, spasms – the retching and the diarrhoea. This time, I will not ignore them, will not pretend they are accident, coincidence, nothing to do with writing, performance, exposure, judgement.

I cannot write when there is someone here, only at (the dead of) night in my silent house, no voices, ears or eyes. I am my own surveillance. Yet when I am writing, I open all the doors and windows, open my house to the four winds, as if to expel demons and secrets, as if to welcome gentler spirits. Space for freedoms I am barely able to desire, in place of chattering fear. I am never sure of what blows in or away. I am giddy with the possibility of emptiness.

Marguerite Duras's *personnages* – always in vacant space, at the seashore, by the edge of the forest, in vague urban wastelands. She was filmed in her own house, but you hardly saw her, except in profile, outside. At least, that's how I remember it. *L'Amante anglaise*, Claire, murderess, turning her back on her house, on the heavy smell of meat stew, alone in her garden, crushing fresh, clean mint between her thin fingers, saying nothing.

I cannot bear excess.

> *Too fat, too big, too thin, too tall, too edgy, too fast, too cool, too vain, too little, too much, too close, too distant. Extreme. Extravagant. Over the top. Self-Portrait of the Superfluous Woman.*

> *Years ago, I cut off my long hair, hacking at it until my scalp was laid almost bare, and it lay in great swathes all around me. I lost three stone in a year, a year of my glorious, beautiful youth, a shadow of the self I loathed, OD'd four times, cut my wrists twice, the inside of my left elbow once, blood flowing freely everywhere. When I recovered (or so they told me) five years later, there was nothing inside, and I was still skin and bone. Self-Portrait of the Empty Woman.*

DESIRING

I

They want poems as fat as essays, she said, and visions as thick as theories.

I want loving as tender as a knife through butter, she said, living as sharp as the edge of the tongue,

> *Hold your tongue, bite your tongue, I'll cut out your tongue. Red tongue, pink centre.*

> *How to cook tongue.*
> Obtain a cleanly butchered tongue, and steep overnight in brine. Carefully trim the tongue, cutting off excess gristle and fat. Shape neatly into a round, and skewer firmly through the middle to retain the shape. Boil the tongue until it is soft but not falling apart. Remove from the pan and pack tightly into a small bowl or mould. Pour a little of the cooking liquid over the tongue, and put aside to cool. When the liquid has set to a jelly, gently turn out the tongue and slice thinly with a very sharp knife.

II

Is there room in our theories for tenderness? For the terrible poignancy of knowing that what is in front of her is what is behind you, that the two may meet in the exquisite heat of a pleasure which can transcend time, but never suspend history?

> *Your chronologies are out of synch. She talks, inconsequentially, of tampons and cramps, of a grey hair discovered over her left temple, plucked out, disbelieving, laughing. Your pubic hair is almost entirely white, your menses are over. 'Age is not relevant' she says, because indeed for her it is not. You smile and say, 'I'll make us some tea', because for you, in truth, it is.*

My body puts the fear of death in me, so I deny its vicissitudes, disguise its mortal stench, cheating and tricking it away by sleight of hand, cunning betrayals, artful resolution.

REMEMBERING

I

Oh my head is away with the band
entirely, she said
(hearing in memory her grandmother's voice)
having in mind generations of women before her
orchestrated by stiff proprieties
prim to all outward appearances

keeping their fingers to themselves in the dark
perfectly improper in their wild rills of desire
trumpets trombones cymbals tympani
rising vibrating pulsing
whipping up a creamy crescendo
the sax holding them
on a long note of reckless ecstasy
in exquisite unison with themselves

Oh my head is away with the band
indeed, she said,
for what do I know of generations of women before me
the passions beneath their silence
the pleasures beyond my remembering?

II

I dredge through the detritus of memory, unruly, careless of chronology. *I have the right to remember, the right to speak, the right to a past a present a future, to live on and beyond.* I wrote this once, and now I can no longer remember where it came from, or why, only that it was about a pain that comes from somewhere I will never fathom.

'I never touched my body,' my aunt said, 'we had to wear long vests in the bath – and we weren't allowed to wash beneath them.' I thought it was a mortal sin to look at my naked body. But I did, and never once confessed, and touched myself everywhere. For years I wondered what the bodies of the nuns who taught me were like under their habits, if they had breasts, if they shaved their heads, if they shaved their pubic hair, if they ever looked in a mirror. My breasts never grew very big. I was so proud of them, neat and barely tumescent question marks on my ungainly adolescent body. 'Where did she get those huge feet? They're grotesque.'

Don't stuff. Clean your plate. Wash your hands. Eat up now. That's good healthy food. Say your grace. Wipe your mouth. Where are your manners? Eat up now. Hold your knife properly. Have another slice, it's good for you. Don't grab, don't be greedy. Eat up now. My, you're a big girl.

My grandmother said I would wear out my skin with washing, that one bath a week should be enough for any girl. I wore dark navy knickers under my divided skirt for gym, sweaty and smelly. You had no gym or games or dancing or swimming during menstruation. Although that's not what we called it: 'my auntie', 'my friend', 'my monthly' – possessive, personal, never 'the curse'. I didn't know what to do with the sanitary towels in their brown paper parcel in the top drawer of the chest in my bedroom. My mother put them there, saying 'you'll need these soon', along with safety pins and a flesh-coloured elastic belt. I was always afraid the pins would prick my soft belly, drawing still more blood. The belt was pink, not like my white skin at all.

But Persephone ate of the pomegranate fruit in the kingdom of the gods, far below the earth. The grief of Demeter for the loss of her beloved daughter was so great, that the gods took pity on her, and permitted Persephone to spend six months of the year with her mother, the rest of her time being spent in the underworld.

LOVING

I

> 29/05/46, Dublin: To Ethna Mary and William Francis, a daughter, Ailbhe.

They cared for my body, fed, sheltered, clothed and washed it, caressed it, grew it tenderly, tucking it in beneath their wings, healed it when it hurt. They admired its firm rounded limbs, held it up high, walked it proudly into the world for all to see. When I fell off my bicycle and ripped my leg – the scar still livid forty years on – I saw them blench as the red blood of their first born spread across the pavement. A childhood drama. I knew then I was in debt to them and how they loved me, although we never talked about such things.

They said so little. They never said my body was mine, my bulwark against the world, my protection, never said my body was a pleasure, my pleasure, although the knowledge osmosed itself into my very entrails, so that when he reached out to touch me, I revolted, ran away, back to the safety of their nest. *Vagina intacta*. I didn't breathe a word. They never told me I was beautiful, and I wouldn't have believed them anyway.

My theories can never heal the world, or me. But nor could they. I retch with the pain of the knowledge – the casual everyday cruelty, the systematic brutality. I vomit up the anger of my incapacity, a visceral spasm which solves nothing at all. Yet they were never cruel or brutal – violence was never part of their world. What then is love? Will I ever find an answer, and even if I did, would I believe it?

> What does it profit a woman if her head is full of theories yet she knows nothing of love?

So I will go away to that familiar place in my head, cool white space, where no one speaks, where no danger lurks, where pain is soothed by illusory certainties originating out of harm's way, generated by fears just like mine. I will go to that rarefied place of abstraction where I can make sense of my desire and confine its intensity. I will go to that spectral place where I am never alone, yet totally untouched, where I will be with other wraiths, where for all our talk, history has no hold over our materiality.

Do not think about the pain. Do not think about the pleasure.

II

Sweetheart,
I have just spent 2 hours in my garden (yes, it *is* a garden, even though it looks like a yard) planting things and moving other things and sweeping and weeding and getting so dirty that everything I had on had to be thrown straight into the washing machine (by me) as soon as I stopped. That was tonight – it was still quite light at 10.15 – wonderful. How I love June evenings, it's such bliss to be outside and not be cold or shivery or anything. Mind you, I still, believe it or not, have this ridiculous sore throat and aches and pains, vitamins notwithstanding. But I have determined that I am in mind over matter mode and will carry on regardless. I am not to be defeated by this irritant, which is only my mere body, when all is said and done.

Sweetheart,
You say such kind and thoughtful things, it moves me very much. And you couldn't even begin to say them unless those layers of understanding were firmly there from your own experience and history, however differently framed. I don't mean to slide over the parts that are past – it's just that, ultimately and daily, you have to incorporate them and do the best with them you can unless you want to be a misery for the rest of your life. Which I certainly do not want. That's not courageous – it's simply being pragmatic. And in the end, I am more pragmatist than anything else. This doesn't mean there are not great *cicatrices* – 'narcissistic wounds' perhaps – the marks of abandonment, rejection, loss, all the griefs and pain of our living and our loving. But any woman worth her salt has those, hasn't she?

III

Elaine Feinstein's 'open heart poetry' – my body in love.

It is when I am in love (an echo of someone else's fiction), in the first fresh flush, that I am most intensely aware of my body. Yet I forget to eat – banal – and it grows slender, lighter than air. I run everywhere, expend quantities of energy, shed my loose flesh. The muscles tauten, my stomach hard as a board from the lusty exertions of sex. I anoint my skin with scented oil after my bath, like my lover – 'your skin is soft as velvet' – smoothing it over my hip bones, stretching to reach my back, my fingers meeting the rough brown mole under my right shoulder. I rub arnica, an old-fashioned remedy, on my elbows and nipples, pink and sore. I take pleasure in these necessary, sensuous rituals. I stand in front of the mirror and wonder that this blade-thin, sharp-angled body can feel so full and voluptuous. How does it feel to her? Can I ever truly know? Has she any idea how little I know, how precisely I feel as we touch?

IV

Cool, secure, I cruised the vast beautiful room
full of lilies, laughter, shining surfaces,
circling back now and then, a *voyeuse*,
catching the gleam of her eyes,
the edge of her smile, the whiff of desire
in glancing reflections,
a thick choker of green beads wound tightly
tantalising around her throat

'Yo, You!
with the arms of a go go goddess
reeling me in, *rapido*,
you smile like a child,
yeah,
when you do that thing with your hips'

Now I stand her before me
in the eye of the chaos
glistening glass beads scattered everywhere
to hold her still for an instant,
for my remembering

Chaos: source of primordial matter, ground of all being.

V

Nothing can be more exact than an image percieved by itself. (Gordimer)

Ah, Narcissus, beautiful boy, drowning in the image of his own beauty.

I have no certainty in any but the most simple sense, and even that may be – most surely is – a lure, a trap, a trick: 'To understand love, first you must love yourself'.

How could I love myself, my own flesh and blood, this sharp unbeautiful girl who couldn't hold her own tongue? I pared her down to the quick, excised, excoriated, exposing muscle, sinew, bone; erased her memories and stories; invented and performed her anew in ever-changing guises; scoured her clean of sentiment; left her lean and spare and empty.

I learned that all I am – heart, mind, body, soul – is both behind and beyond. I learned that this may or may not be enough for loving.

What slender fragile knowledge I have gleaned.

Who, I? Who knows?

> *– I walked across a rope bridge, a 200 foot drop below. I had to know the fear, not to know it any more – It's always about danger and knowledge – They said, having risked their souls in each others' hands for a whole night.*
>
> *The next morning, her body still aching and shimmering with love and fear, she sat in dead silence and started to write.*
>
> *I took my body to the top of a mountain, and the forest was bare as bones. When I love you with my body, will my soul be laid bare before you? And what will I do with your bones when you are gone?*

REFERENCES

Abramovich, Marina (1997) 'Fifty is just the beginning: Guy Hilton interviews Marina Abramovich', *Make 73*, December 1996–January 1997: 3–5.

Alexander, M. Jacqui and Mohanty, Chandra T. (1997) (eds) *Feminist Genealogies, Colonial Legacies, Democratic Futures*, London: Routledge, pp. xxiii.

Anderson, C. S. (1995) 'Volatile Bodies' in *Masculinities* 3, 2: 87–8.

Bordo, Susan (1993) *Unbearable Weight: Feminism, Western Culture and the Body*, Berkeley: University of California Press, pp. 166.

Byatt, A. S. (1995) 'The Story of the Eldest Princess' in *The Djinn in the Nightingale's Eye*, New York: Vintage, pp. 71–2.

De Certeau, Michel (1984) *The Practice of Everyday Life*, Berkeley: University of California Press, pp. 139.

Diprose, Rosalyn (1994) *The Bodies of Women: Ethics, Embodiment and Sexual Difference*, London: Routledge, pp. 129.

Game, Anne (1991) *Undoing the Social: Towards a Deconstructive Sociology*, Milton Keynes: Open University Press, pp. 192.

Gordimer, Nadine (1987) *A Sport of Nature*, London: Penguin, pp. 14.

2

Sexuality and the Clinical Encounter

ROSALYN DIPROSE

THE CLINICAL ENCOUNTER IS a curious event. Through it we open our body and our life, that which is most intimate, most private, to a virtual stranger. It involves an offering we would more usually reserve for a lover, a mother or a friend. And through this encounter, a corporeal itinerary which is specific to us, becomes generalised, subsumed under a medical discourse known better for its promotion of a universal objective body than for its sensitivity to different ways of being.¹ Given the intimate content of the event, it should not be surprising if the patient's sexuality becomes an issue in the encounter. And given the totalising tendencies of medical discourse, it should not be surprising that the occasion has arisen for critical examination of the relation between medical discourse and sexuality. AIDS, perhaps more than any other single health problem in recent times, has provided such an occasion, generating charges of latent prejudices within medical discourse against homosexuality in particular and calls for a more generous and sensitive approach to management of sexuality in the clinic.

Notwithstanding the wealth of critical analysis of the relation between medical discourse and sexuality, not just in the context of AIDS but from feminist and other perspectives, little attention has been given to the operation of sexuality in the clinical encounter itself. It is towards such an account that this paper is directed. Without abandoning insights into how medical science constitutes and normalises sexuality, I will suggest that there are features of the clinical encounter itself which makes the management of sexuality there uneasy at best. Understanding the encounter in terms of opening one's body to a stranger, whose own body seems exempt from scrutiny of the clinical gaze, may help to explain why better management of sexuality in the clinic is, at least under present circumstances, difficult if not impossible, despite the best intentions of those involved.

I take sexuality to mean the use (in the sense of both capacity and practice) of pleasure and pain.[2] Sexuality is not the social expression of a more original biological instinct. It is the way a person lives their pleasure and pain which presupposes a social existence. Sexuality is not contained within a singular body; it is lived through a body open to a world of the other. Yet, while open to a world, sexuality is not reducible to a single object (as categories such as paedophile and heterosexual would suggest); nor a single active or passive aim (as categories like femme and sadist would imply). While sexuality is indeterminate, outstripping a singular body with a definite aim and object, it is also inseparable from social discourses which would constitute and define it in those terms, as the work of Michel Foucault, among others, suggests.

Foucault's analysis of the deployment of sexuality, the elevation in the nineteenth century of the study of sex to a level of a science, points to the central role medical science plays in the constitution and normalisation of sexuality (Foucault 1980). In this, by now well-known, account he indicates how medicine, in concert with other circulating ideas about proper and improper bodies, is deeply implicated, not just in the division of bodies into the healthy and unhealthy, but simultaneously into the normal and the perverse. And we need not go past the discourses on AIDS to illustrate the way medical science and sexual politics can converge over bodies to siphon off the guilty from so-called innocent uses of pleasure and pain.[3] But it is important to note that such spectacular connections between sexuality and health do not exhaust the medical delimiting of uses of pleasure. Even my seemingly mundane practice of smoking has been transformed (through the intertwining of medical, legal and environmental discourses with the ever ready pointed finger of the passer by) from a relatively insignificant use of pleasure to an anti-social, immoral perversion. The work of medical discourse is pervasive, effecting not just who we exchange fluids with and how, but the course of other pleasures and pains inseparable from our manner of being.

While seemingly ubiquitous, it would be a mistake to view the relation between medical science and sexuality as some kind of conspiracy on the part of the few to control the bodies of the rest. The medical reduction and production of sexuality is often as unwitting as it is powerful and may proceed as much by neglect, say by the assumption that the paralysed body is devoid of pleasure, as it does by obsessive concern, say for my tar-soaked lungs. It would also be a mistake to view the recipient of medical attention as simply a passive body at the mercy of forces which would rearticulate its pleasures and pains in the interests of propriety. Foucault, through his analysis of the technology of confession, also points to our own complicity in constituting ourselves as the subjects of desire, in the face of medical discourse (Foucault 1980: 58–70). And this occurs, most obviously in the clinical encounter itself. After all, there seems a no more appropriate place for us to reflect on our uses of pleasure and connect these to the pains, leakages, spasms and paralyses which seem to overtake our body. In attempting to locate the origin of disease, asthma for example, can become, through our own words, a problem of sexual anxiety. Or, in unfolding our medical history we may link this broken leg to menopause and the sexuality and osteopathology that it now implies.

In this medical examination we are not simply confessing to an already constituted sexuality and unburdening ourselves of a truth which seems to infect us. Rather, as Foucault points out, we are constituting ourselves as subjects of sexuality in the presence of someone with the authority to make of us what she will:

[T]he agency of domination does not reside in the one who speaks [the patient] (for it is he who is constrained), but in the one who listens and says nothing [the clinician]; not in the one who knows and answers, but in the one who questions and is not supposed to know. And this discourse of truth finally takes effect, not in the one who receives it, but in the one from whom it is wrested (1980: 62).

The truth of our sexuality is not waiting for exposure in the clinic. Rather sexuality is constituted through confession, in the body of the spoken word.[4] The clinic, like the confessional in general, incites not just the desire to speak but desire itself. It is a place where pleasures and pains are articulated, formed and transformed; where a self is dissolved, dissembled and assembled. And the agent of production is not just the clinician (as some would have it), who, as the executor of medical discourse, examines and therefore objectifies and normalises the body. The agents of production are also the patients who would have their pleasures and pains represented, to their satisfaction, in the total picture of their medical life.

Since Foucault and others have pointed to medical science as a place where knowledge and sexual politics meets a body, it is no longer possible to simply assume that we encounter medical discourse (whether through television or in the clinic) with our sexuality entirely intact or that we leave it unscathed. In the meeting sexuality is constituted and normalised with certain uses of pleasure and pain ignored, condemned, transformed or abandoned.

This kind of analysis has been with us for around twenty years and has certainly left its mark. After at least two decades of feminist criticism of the medical normalisation of bodies,[5] of the way women's health is measured against a male standard, it is more likely that breast cancer, for example, will be treated as a serious infringement on a woman's use of pleasure. And there is some chance that the menopause will not be viewed simply as a failure of womanhood, as a lack of useable pleasure which could be rectified by anti-depressants. (Although, as some will be quick to point out, Hormone Replacement Therapy, which has superseded anti-depressants as the usual treatment for menopausal 'symptoms', does little to shift the old assumptions). Or, after at least one decade of criticism of the medical discourse on AIDS, particularly from the Gay community, there is perhaps a better chance that a person can live with AIDS rather than die with the 'stigmata of their guilt', to coin Simon Watney's phrase (1987: 78). In some respects twenty years of sustained and vigorous critique of the problematic assumptions of medical discourse has produced a generation of consumers and some practitioners attuned to, and critical of, the role medicine plays in the production and normalisation of sexuality.

Yet despite, and perhaps because of, this heightened awareness, there is much to suggest that we are far from dealing with sexuality in the clinic to the satisfaction of all concerned. For the patient, the management of sexuality in the clinic is at best clumsy with the effect that the clinical encounter is often disconcerting and sometimes alarming. From the patient's perspective, sexuality can become a problem in one of two ways. Either the clinical environment is sexualised by the clinician when there seems no need. Or the question of sexuality is elided or evaded when it would seem to matter.

I offer two examples of the first kind of problem.[6] In 1975 Jenny chooses a general practitioner at random to obtain a prescription for her asthma medication. The doctor, a pleasant enough man of about sixty, takes Jenny's blood pressure before returning to his position behind the desk. He then leans back in his chair and asks her three questions: does she masturbate, does she sleep with boys, does she sleep with girls. Jenny is so shocked, the best she can do is squeeze out a 'no' in reply to each question in turn. Satisfied with the answers and commenting that it is gratifying to see that a young woman can still be embarrassed in these times of loose morals, the doctor complies with Jenny's request and writes out a script.

We could dismiss this example as extreme, an isolated incident occurring at a time when liberties were taken which would no longer be tolerated. However, while unnecessary sexualisation of the clinical encounter may no longer be so crude, isolated cases of sexual assault aside, it is no less apparent, at least from the patient's perspective. It is 1995 and Claudia enters a clinic seeking a prescription for her asthma medication. She knows what she needs and this is all she wants. The doctor, a woman around Claudia's age and unfamiliar with her case, asks the usual two or three questions before happily meeting her request. But as she is writing the script, the doctor asks is there anything else Claudia would like. Even though Claudia replies 'no', several times, the doctor persists: did Claudia realise, for instance, that a simple course of hormone therapy could eliminate her problem of facial hair. Claudia is as mortified by this question in 1995 as Jenny was by those asked of her in 1975.

We could give this doctor the benefit of doubt by suggesting she is one of the new generation taught, at our request, to treat, not just the symptom, but the patient as a whole person. Perhaps in her world facial hair on a woman is a problem, a source of anxiety about sexuality and sexual difference. Not in Claudia' s world. She has lived with her hair forever; she likes it, as does her partner and friends; it is inseparable from her body open to a world, it is inseparable from her use of pleasure, yet no more relevant to this visit to the clinic than what she had for breakfast. While deeply disturbed at what to her is a challenge to her way of being, Claudia moderates her response, saying only that no, her facial hair is no longer a problem for her, except at times like this, and that the doctor should not assume otherwise, given that, if it was a problem, she would have already done something about it. Rather than conceding the point, the doctor escalates the stakes, suggesting that, while removal of the hair would normally be advisable, she would simply note in Claudia's records her objections to discussing the issue. Claudia leaves the clinic in despair, regretting her constraint in comparison to the doctor, wishing she had said what to her is obvious: that her own facial hair is no more aberrant than the doctor's severely sculptured eyebrows.

The second, and converse, way in which sexuality can become a problem in the clinic, from the patient's perspective, is in cases where the question of one's own use of pleasure is elided or evaded when it would seem to be the salient point. In 1980 Jael enters a clinic seeking a termination of her pregnancy. In order to satisfy the law it is necessary, first, to show that continuing the pregnancy would probably result in distress and hardship, and, second, to accept counselling on contraception to prevent a repeat occurrence. Jael can easily meet the first condition and does not need to accommodate the second. Her use of pleasure is such that her usual sexual partner is a woman and in parts of her usual world she would be called a lesbian. That she finds herself in this clinic of assumed heterosexuality is easily explained: one sexual encounter with an old and trusted male friend, of no lasting significance at least not to herself or the friend. But to tell the full story, and so properly prove the need for the termination, would result in as much distress and hardship to Jael's partner, her male friend and to herself as would continuing the pregnancy. Not only do the relevant facts not sit well with Jael's world, but they would be totally foreign to the social worker she faces. So rather than proving her case beyond doubt, she tells another story more in keeping with the expectations of the clinic and endures the advice about contraception with resignation. The individual is preserved through the art of dissimulation and she can only be trusted if, to use Nietzsche's words, she fulfils her 'duty to lie according to a fixed convention' (1979: 84).

It is likely that the itinerary of Jael's pleasure and pain would be just as transgressive of convention, both heterosexual and lesbian, now as it was in 1980 and that silence or evasion, both inside and outside the clinic, would be advisable. But while sexuality may exceed convention in this way, where convention is given reductively in terms of a regular object of desire, it is often not so easy to locate what convention might be, nor therefore to predict the potential to affront its agents. Hence, as the following incident suggests, the impulse to evade, elide or censor sexuality in the clinic is contingent and unpredictable as are the effects of this tendency towards self-regulation.

It is 1995. Simone has a problem with anal bleeding and is convinced she has bowel cancer. But heartened by the discovery, through conversations with friends, that cancer is the unlikely cause, she visits a doctor to have this conclusion confirmed. In the absence of a regular physician, Simone chooses a woman with a reputation among friends for a good 'bedside manner'. To assist the doctor, who has admitted to not having the equipment necessary for a proper anal examination, Simone begins to list factors she thinks relevant to the case: a prior history of pain from a hernia, although no bleeding; a brief period of constipation prior to the onset of bleeding; no anal penetration. Clearly disturbed at the mention of anal penetration, and before Simone had exhausted her list, the doctor jumps up from her chair, overrides Simone's speech, puts Simone on the table, rubber gloves on herself and performs a brief examination. While feeling slightly humiliated by the time they return to the desk, Simone does not blame the doctor for her obvious distaste for the procedure. But she is incensed when the doctor washes her hands, not once but three times, while reassuring her that she does not have cancer. And, given the nature of the problem, Simone thinks it strange that a doctor would find mention of anal penetration so disturbing and inappropriate when to her it seems so apt.

These stories of the problematic operation of sexuality in the clinic are not particularly spectacular, but are noteworthy for that reason. Whether sexuality is evoked unnecessarily or evaded, so common is dissimulation, misrecognition, confusion and discomfort that one suspects it is all part and parcel of the clinical encounter itself. But why might this be so? These stories do share features which are consistent with a Foucauldian analysis of the role of medical discourse in the production and normalisation of sexuality. It is clear, for example, that, in each case, the clinician is an agency of domination, a deputy of medical discourse and the conventions it may harbour. As the clinician has the authority to issue a prescription, the knowledge for reassurance and access to technical procedures, then patients must subject themselves to the questions and interpretations if they are to secure the help they need. And we may agree with Foucault that this game of truth over sexuality seems to take effect in the patient more so than in the clinician, who seems shielded from the medical gaze. Nonetheless there are indications that disturbing effects are not restricted to the patient and, even there, they are not exclusively in the mode of unification and transformation of pleasures. What Foucault's analysis cannot explain is the extent of dissimulation, agitation and friction at play in the clinical encounter, nor the way the effects are born, not just by the body of the patient, but at times by the clinician, e.g. Simone's doctor. On his account, the constitution of sexuality by medical discourse through the confessional is a much more harmonious and compliant affair than my examples would suggest. In other words, in the absence of a coherent account of resistance to normalisation by medical discourse there is little space for explaining the kinds of collisions which are apparent in the clinical encounter. Foucault does acknowledge resistance but without explaining its source, except with reference to what seems to be a pre-social use of pleasure which escapes normalising regimes.[7]

However, resorting to a realm of pure bodies and pleasures is not necessary to explain resistance to normalisation and, hence, the fractious way sexuality is played out in the clinic. There is another factor still to consider. In all this talk about the body of the patient, its docility as the object of the medical gaze and its stimulation through confession, we seem to have overlooked the body of the clinician. The clinical encounter is not just an encounter between a singular body (the patient) and medical discourse in the form of the ear and the pen of the clinician. The clinician may be an agent of medical discourse and therefore an agent of domination, as Foucault suggests, but he or she is also a body. And if sexuality is understood as the uses of pleasure and pain of a body open to a world, and, if the clinician is a body, then the clinician's sexuality is also at issue in the clinical encounter. The clinical encounter is an encounter between at least two bodies, two uses of pleasure and pain, two sexualities with different histories. How does the clinician's sexuality figure in the encounter? And how can the meeting of uses of pleasure and pain be better managed?

It does not pay to be coy in characterising this meeting of bodies: these bodies if they meet at all, meet through the touch of the medical examination even when the players stand apart. While everything about the architecture of the clinic (the physician's dwelling behind the desk, my exposure on the table, the location of the plaque on the wall above us) suggests that only one body examines the other, the examination is in fact contiguous and therefore ambiguous: bodies that touch are also touched. For every eye or hand on skin there is skin on hand or eye. Every body, including that of the clinician, while a subject for itself is also an object for others. For Merleau-Ponty, for example, the person could not be otherwise: I can only touch or see because I am touched and seen (1968: 133). I exist for myself in the hands of the other. So while the clinician transforms a de facto situation into medical significance, through examination of the patient, the itinerary of her own body conduct is open to the other, rendering the encounter indeterminate and ambiguous. For Merleau-Ponty, this ambiguity is the essence of existence, and, whatever transformations may occur in an encounter, can never be eliminated (1962: 169).

While not reducible to personal existence in general, sexuality has the same ambiguous structure. For Merleau-Ponty, like Foucault, sexuality is not a pure fact, not a bodily instinct hidden behind, and driving, existence, nor a conscious representation at its perimeter. But nor, as Foucault sometimes implies, are there bodies or pleasures exempt from passing through the other and the sociality that this involves. Of erotic perception Merleau-Ponty says: 'through one body it aims at another, and takes place in the world, not consciousness (1962: 157). And, he suggests, sexuality occupies such an important place in human life because sexual experience affords an 'opportunity, vouchsafed to all and always available' to acquaint oneself with the play of autonomy and dependence, with the ambiguity of body-intersubjectivity (Merleau-Ponty 1962: 167). Sexuality, then, differs from other modes of personal existence, not in structure, but in being an explicit indulgence in the pleasure and pain arising from the uncertainty of being caught in the other's body that you seek to capture and from the metamorphosis that this allows. And, because sexuality shares the ambiguous structure of personal existence, and is inseparable from the distinctive way a person patterns and gives meaning to their world, it is 'impossible to tell, in a given decision or action, the proportion of sexual to other motivations' (Merleau-Ponty 1962: 169). At the same time, it would not be inconsistent to suggest that whether an encounter could be considered sexual will depend on the extent that sexuality is an explicit theme and on the specific ways in which the bodies involved have lived their patterns of existence as sexual.

The clinical encounter, then, shares with both the sexual encounter and personal existence in general the same structure of an indeterminate, ambiguous relation to the world of the other. However, the clinical encounter differs from the sexual encounter in that sexual pleasure is not the dominant theme. As there is no agreement here to indulge in the pleasures and pains of body ambiguity then that ambiguity is less pre-eminent. Yet the clinical encounter stands out from expressly non-sexual conducts in so far as the itinerary of pleasures and pains of one body – at least – is explicitly opened to the other. And while the other's body, that of the clinician, may seem exempt from scrutiny it is, as I have suggested, implicitly open to the patient. I believe it is because the clinical encounter stands on the cusp between personal existence in general and the sexual experience that it is so often alarming. As I will go on to describe in more detail, it is the opening of your body to a stranger, whose own body, while apparently invisible, is no less in play, which makes the clinical encounter so often fractious and the play of sexuality there so open to mismanagement.

I am suggesting in the first place that understanding the clinical encounter in terms of an encounter between bodies requires abandoning the idea that human bodies are singular self-contained entities standing apart from one's agency and apart from others. When engaged in the world, the person, whether acting, observing, doing or knowing, is not a disembodied thinker. Rather the person is her body, its gestures, movements and habits, its uses of pleasure and pain. It is as a body-subject that the clinician and the patient orientate themselves, incorporate the surrounding field and engage in the situation.[8] The clinician performs the examination this way. She does not calculate the distance between her body, the stethoscope and the skin of the patient, and then consciously direct her movements. Rather, she projects her body, its gestures and spatial orientation onto the world and so makes the instrument and the other's body part of her body-space.

Perception of the other's body, then, is not the capacity to intellectualise its needs across the gulf that would seem to separate us. All perception, knowing and understanding is informed by non-conscious projection of a body. Or, as Merleau Ponty puts it:

Whether it is a question of another's body or my own, I have no means of knowing the human body other than that of living it, which means taking up on my own account the drama which is being played out in it, and losing myself in it (1962: 198).

On this understanding of an encounter between bodies, the clinician is a body open to a world of the other and immersed within it. And just as sexuality presupposes a social existence and is inseparable from it, being a body immersed in others is not fortuitous: it actualises one's social identity.[9] The capacity to use a stethoscope, for example, is a skill mimetically borrowed from another body. Similarly, Claudia's doctor's discomfort about facial hair is not an arbitrary conscious representation of uniform significance. It is an unease belonging to a body with a tradition of immersion in a world of other female bodies devoid of body hair. In short, the clinician brings to the present encounter, not just a medical model of a normal body, but a history of interlacing with other bodies, skills, gestures and uses of pleasure and pain, all pregnant with meaning, and all of which inform her body identity and hence her perception of the situation. And, in so far as the clinician is an agency of domination, her perception of the situation involves living that history through the body of the patient, imposing that history on the other's body and making it familiar, and hence similar to, her own.

While as a body-subject the clinician operates through the other's body with the absence of singularity that implies, she is maintained as a separate existence, however, by the feeling of a difference from the other. This difference emerges in the first instance because the clinician, while a body-subject with the power of projection, is also a non-thematic object for the patient. Through the touch of patients' skin, the look in their eye, through their gestures and speech, clinicians feel the difference in their own identity. In other words, the constitution of the body subject through the other, while based on possession of the other's body, also involves a sense of a difference between the two. This difference between bodies is irreducible, not because of an original or final individuality, but because of the ambiguity of co-existence as I have just described it.[10] And the difference is irreducible, not because one body has escaped the deployment of sexuality or the work of social discourse in general. Rather, it is because, added to this irreducible difference in the present is the condition that the drama played out in the body of the patient – while perhaps familiar to the clinician in some respects – is of a body with a different history.

This picture of the clinical encounter suggests two immediate points about sexuality under clinical management. First, in order to appreciate the needs of a different body, the clinician's body must have already lived through that experience or, at least, be open to it. It is unrealistic to expect that a particular clinician could be open to every possible body history and every experience of a particular patient, unless we assume the clinician is a God without a body at all. If she is not a God then her ability to know the other's

40

body is reduced in so far as her social history, and therefore uses of pleasure and pain, differs from that of the other. It should not be surprising, then, that, as patients, we so often encounter what seems like the shock of the new. We, like Jenny and Jael, manage this by dissimulation or, like Claudia, by refusal. This dissimulation is not a mask, deliberately worn to hide the truth of one's sexuality, but a refusal to open the indeterminate, any more than necessary, to the body of a stranger for her final possession. And/or we shop around, but not for a use of pleasure and pain which matches our own, for the style of a person's body is not open to objective analysis and no list of habits, skills or sexual preferences would give us a match, however similar to our own that list of attributes may appear to be The best we can so is find someone with whom we feel familiar. But, given that oscillation between dissimulation and familiarity, difference and indistinction, is already a feature of the ambiguity of existence, these contributions by the patient bring nothing new to the management of sexuality in the clinic. The problem could also be managed better by the medical profession by first of all granting that the clinician is a body. It is this body, including its uses of pleasure and pain, more so than that of the patient and as much as the body of medical discourse, which is generalised illegitimately in the medical examination.

Second, and somewhat paradoxically, while an understanding of the other implies immersion in her body, it is just as critical to maintain the difference. The indeterminate ambiguity of existence suggests this alterity and our ethics demands it. Too much familiarity on the part of clinicians or patients may transgress the indistinguishable line marking off their difference, threatening the security of the identities of both. The sexual encounter may be an opportunity for the exploration of the ambiguity of body-inter-subjectivity; the clinical encounter is not. Simone's doctor, for example, may have been threatened by the mention of anal penetration in a context where it seemed appropriate, not necessarily because it fell outside of her sexual experience, but perhaps because it did not. That is, the problem may have been that the patient inadvertently sexualised the very part of her body that the doctor sought to put at a distance. This is how we all deal with uncertainty in the face of body ambiguity: we build a partition between our body and the body of the other without any thought at all.

In the end, absolute resolution of the ambiguous relation between bodies is impossible, unless we assume that all bodies are the same. Hence, complete understanding of the patient's sexuality in a clinical setting is also impossible. A more generous and sensitive approach to sexuality in the clinic does not require resolution of this ambiguity, but recognition that the clinical encounter involves projection of bodies and an attendant clash and transfiguration of uses of pleasure and pain. Rather than attempting to better manage the patient's sexuality with the incorporation of them that this implies, perhaps a more constructive starting point would be acknowledgement of the clinician's sexuality and its constitutive role in the clinical encounter.

NOTES

An earlier version of this paper was presented at the 'Sexuality and Medicine' Conference (U. Melbourne, July 1995) and the 'Sexual Encounter/Clinical Encounter' Workshop (U. Warwick, November 1995) and was published in *Hysteric*, 2, 1996. I would like to thank Barbara Baird, Christine Battersby, Janet Price, Paul Komesaroff Philipa Rothfield, Margrit Shildrick and Nikki Sullivan for their comments on earlier drafts.

1. For critiques of the medical model of the body and discussion of the implications of these critiques for a medical ethics, see the various papers in *Troubled Bodies: Critical Perspectives on Postmodernism, Medical Ethics and the Body* (Komesaroff 1995).
2. The definition of sexuality I elaborate here might be broader than expected. A dictionary definition, for example, would confine itself to sex and/or sexual intercourse. But already such a definition locates and limits sexuality in a way which does not reflect the variety, richness and ambiguity of the pleasures which inhabit people's lives. (In fact the dictionary definition could be accused of the same reductionism levelled at medical discourse.) And such a definition presupposes an individualist ontology which is under attack in this chapter. The definition of sexuality I offer here is based on a different ontology, one which I think better captures the nature of both sexuality and the clinical encounter and one which I will justify in more detail later in the chapter. For the moment I am concerned with including, within a definition of sexuality, three terms: the pleasures of one's own body, the other and the social discourse within which these are embedded.
3. For discussions of this issue see, for example, Watney (1987) and Diprose and Vasseleu (1991).
4. Or, as Foucault puts it later in *The History of Sexuality, Volume I:*
   The notion of 'sex' made it possible to group together, in an arti-

ficial unity, anatomical elements, biological functions, conducts, sensations, and pleasures, and it enabled one to make use of this fictitious unity as a causal principle, an omnipresent meaning, a secret to be discovered everywhere . . . sex is the most speculative, most ideal, and most internal element in the deployment of sexuality organized by power in its grip on bodies and their materiality, their forces, their energies, sensations, and pleasures (Foucault 1980: 154–5).

5. For a number of such critiques see, for example, papers in *Body/ Politics: Women and the Discourses of Science* (Jacobus et al. 1990).

6. These two examples and the two I use to illustrate the second kind of problem are based on reports by friends of their experiences, although I have changed the names of those involved. While common, at least among people I know, these are the sorts of stories rarely documented in sociological or medical studies, presumably because the kind of discomfort their telling generates means they are usually reserved for private conversations between friends. I am therefore grateful that I am privy to these stories and have permission to use them here.

7. For example, following is one of the few references Foucault makes, in *The History of Sexuality, Volume I*, to the possibility of resistance:

It is the agency of sex that we must break away from, if we aim – through a tactical reversal of the various mechanisms of sexuality – to counter the grips of power with the claims of bodies, pleasures, and knowledges, in their multiplicity and their possibility of resistance. The rallying point for the counterattack against the deployment of sexuality ought not to be sex-desire, but bodies and pleasures (Foucault 1980: 157).

He does not explain how such bodies and pleasures, the 'rallying point' against normalisation, have escaped the all pervasive deployment of sexuality in the first place.

8. Merleau–Ponty describes this operation of body intentionality in *Phenomenology of Perception* (1962), Part One, Chapter 3.

9. For his account of how the body-subject is constituted through the other's body, through the incorporation and projection of conducts and their meaning, see Merleau-Ponty (1964). And for a more detailed reading of this aspect of Merleau-Ponty's work than I have the space to provide here, see Diprose (1994, Ch. 6, and in particular pp. 118–24).

10. Merleau-Ponty describes this ambiguous structure of simultaneous blurring of, and disjunction between, bodies as follows: 'There is thus a system (my visual body [as it appears to others], my introceptive body [as I live it], the other (as I perceive her) which establishes itself in the child, never so completely as in the animal but imperfectly, with gaps' (1964: 135).

REFERENCES

Diprose, Rosalyn (1994) *The Bodies of Women: Ethics, Embodiment and Sexual Difference*, London: Routledge.

Diprose, Rosalyn and Vasseleu, Cathryn (1991) 'Animation-AIDS in Science/Fiction' in A. Cholodenko (ed.), *The Illusion of Life*, Sydney: Power Publications.

Foucault, Michel (1980) *The History of Sexuality, Volume I: An Introduction*, trans. R. Hurley, New York: Vintage Books.

Komesaroff, Paul (ed.) (1995) *Troubled Bodies: Critical Perspectives on Post-modernism, Medical Ethics and the Body*, Melbourne: Melbourne University Press.

Jacobus, M., Fox Keller, E. and Shuttleworth, S. (eds) (1990) *Body/Politics: Women and the Discourses of Science*, New York and London: Routledge.

Merleau-Ponty, Maurice (1962) *Phenomenology of Perception*, trans. Colin Smith, London: Routledge and Kegan Paul.

Merleau-Ponty, Maurice (1964) 'The Child's Relations with Others' in *The Primacy of Perception*, trans. and ed. James M. Edie, Evanston: Northwestern University Press.

Merleau-Ponty, Maurice (1968) *The Visible and the Invisible*, trans. Alphonso Lingis, Evanston: Northwestern University Press.

Nietzsche, Friedrich (1979) 'On Truth and Lies in a Nonmoral Sense' in *Philosophy and Truth: Selections from Nietzsche's Notebooks of the Early 1870's*, trans. and ed. D. Breazeale, New Jersey: Humanities Press.

Watney, Simon (1987) 'The Spectacle of AIDS', *October* 43: 71–86.

3

Animated Borders:
Skin, Colour and Tanning

SARA AHMED

THEORISING EMBODIMENT IN a way which recognises the constitutive nature of racial as well as sexual difference has become
increasingly important to feminism. Bodies are not only the mark
of a difference which is excluded from the identity of the rational
subject, but are always already marked by differences. However,
despite many appeals to the differentiated body, I think there
has been less substantive analysis of how 'bodies' are determined
through the violent collision of regimes of difference. In this paper
I analyse how bodies come to be 'lived out' and marked by differences by focusing on 'skin' as the unstable *border* between the body
and its others,which comes to be fetishised (in the sense that it is
seen to 'reflect' the truth of the subject's identity and well-being).
My argument is elaborated by considering how biomedical readings of the skin as a marker of health construct 'the tan' in relation
to racial colour. This construction of skin and skin colour (surface)
as reflecting health and well-being (depth) does not hold bodies in
place, but constitutes the animation of the borders that appear to
separate one body from an-other.

1. FEMINISM AND THE RACIAL BODY

Bodies have become the subject of much appeal within feminism.
On the one hand, the body seems appealing as a site on which to
wage war against the rationalism which pervades western philosophy. On the other hand, the body is appealed to, as a sign of the

materiality of being-in-the-world: an appeal which situates the feminist critique of Cartesianism and ideality in general (that the subject gains its identity and distinction from the exclusion of the material, that is, divisible realm of bodily experience). But there has been a third appeal. This is an appeal to re-situate the body, not only as material, but also as marked by social division and antagonism. However, this appeal to the body as already determined and as differentiated in terms of gender and sexuality, and also race and class, does not always involve in practice an analysis of the particularity of bodies or of subjectivity in general. I admit that it is too easy simply to point out that appeals to difference do not always involve an analysis of difference (those moments where, often in brackets, a theorist will add – and also, race, class, disability and so on). But the appeal to the differentiated body as a rhetorical ploy which does not operate beyond that level has structural implications for the bodies that are discussed and re-inscribed in feminist discourse. For example, in Elizabeth Grosz's *Volatile Bodies*, there is little mention of the racialised nature of the multiple and differentiated bodies she dedicates her text to, except in the following quote:

The more or less permanent etching of even the civilised body by discursive systems is perhaps easier to read if the civilized body is decontextualised, stripped of clothing and adornment, behaviourally displayed in its nakedness. The naked European/American/African/Asian/Australian body (and clearly even within these categories there is enormous cultural variation) is still marked by its disciplinary history, by it habitual practices of movement, by the corporeal commitments it has undertaken in day-to-day life. It is in no sense a natural body, for it is as culturally, racially, sexually, possibly even as class distinctive, as it would be if it were clothed (Grosz 1995: 142).

Here, Grosz is including race as a signifier of cultural difference ('European/American/African/Asian/Australian') in order to illustrate her point that there is no natural or indeed real body, that the body is always clothed or inscribed within particular cultural formations. Race becomes a means by which Grosz illustrates a philosophical shift in thinking about bodies. It appears then (and also *disappears*) as a figure for the differentiated body. It becomes a means to signify what the body is, or I should say, what it becomes. In this sense, 'race' is made present only through an act of negation: it is included as a vehicle for the re-presentation of a philosophy of the body rather than as a constitutive and positive term of analysis. This metaphoric reliance on race to signify the

differentiated body has quite clear theoretical and political implications. It means that a philosophy of the differentiated body – of
difference – does not necessarily involve, in practice, a recognition
of the violent collision between regimes of diffcrence. As such, a philosophy of difference *can* involve a univcrsalism; a speaking from the
place of (for example) the white subject, who re-incorporates difference as a sign of its own fractured and multiple coming into being.
This abstraction of race as a figure of difference is a danger that my
own argument will necessarily flirt with. Too often calls for an analysis of the impact of regimes of difference on material (or materi-
alizable) bodily experience proceed through the rendering of 'the
racial body' as a figure for a difference which is *missed out* or elided.
This is argued in 'Woman Skin Deep' where Sara Suleri discusses,

the methodological blurring that dictates much of the discourse on
identity formation in the colouring of feminist discourse. To privilege
the racial body in the absence of historical context is indeed to generate
an idiom that tends to waver with impressionistic haste between the
abstractions of postcoloniality and the anecdotal literalism of what it
means to articulate an 'identity' for women writers of colour (Suleri
1993: 249).

The project becomes then: how to theorise the collision between
regimes of difference without rendering 'the racial body' a sign for
the (missing) historicity in discourses of the body and the subject?
As I hope will become clear, such a project requires that we begin
to think through the skin as a surface upon which differences col-
lide (a war fuelled through the outer limits of our bodies).

2. THE SKIN TIIAT SEEPS

Within biomedical discourses, 'the skin' is policed as the boundary
which determines the ontological difference between one body and
an-other. The skin becomes a means by which beings are constituted
as separate and distinct. Indeed, the skin must be contained – as a
container, it must be contained. It must not seep beyond itself until
it ceases to be itself. Its seeping must only be a breakage that is to
be closed: its breakage demands closure as the closure of the
clinic. Here, the clinical body is a body that is being stitched up.
The stitches close the wound or cut in the subject imperfectly,
leaving the scar as the trace of the bodily trauma. The scar
demands and negates the integrity of the body: its form is a
rem(a)inder of the failure of such integrity, yet keeps in place the
desire for integrity as the measure of well-Being. Indeed, a good

scar is one that is barely visible: it is one that does not look like a scar at all and that allows the fantasy of being whole. The skin weeps through its scars as we wait for the healing: 'the cover(ing) over of the surface gap' (Anderson 1952: 31). We must not scratch or pick, despite the itching. The patient's treatment is only thinkable, then, through the necessity of closing the skin (the cut in being, the surface gap): closing it to the danger and risk of the contaminated other. We march through, each *in our skins*. This is the fantasy of the clinical relation between two subjects who know their place.

Within the clinical encounter, the skin is always seen and read. The skin measures the truth of the subject in terms of its health or well-being. It is the doctor who sees and reads, demanding to tell the difference. In *An Introduction to the Symptoms and Signs of Surgical Disease*, the medical student is advised: 'You must be constantly *alert* from the moment you first see the patient, and employ your eyes, ears, nose and hands in a systematic fashion to collect the information from which you can make your diagnosis' (Browse 1991: 1). *In Hutchison's Clinical Methods*, doctors are provided with a methodology which involves both rules on how to look, what to look for, and how to interpret or read what is seen on the skin. The privileging of the skin as a measure of health is predicated on a conception of 'nakedness': 'For the examination of the skin and its appendages, the patient should be stripped as completely as circumstances permit and should be examined by daylight' (Bomford, Mason and Swash 1980: 48). Here, 'stripping' reveals the skin to the gaze (enlightenment) of the medical practitioner. The skin-surface reveals, then, the truth of the subject's well-being which must be mediated by touch (the physical examination) and then narrated through the doctor's history-taking (history-making). The differential diagnosis – whereby bodily symptoms are traced to a range of more and less likely causes – hence involves the combination of gazing, touching, reading and narrating which begins with the surface/skin and penetrates the interior. Outside to inside: the skin is here the text which authorises medicine as a hermeneutics. Hence, in *The Introduction to Clinical Examination*, the methodology for physical examination suggests a sequence of examinations, each of which 'should be *initiated* by the inspection of the skin' (Munro and Ford 1989: 104; emphasis added). The skin is here the point of 'first contact' on a voyage of discovery. The gaze of the other is hence always alert to the skin in the clinic. The skin shows and tells about otherwise hidden depths: in the clinical encounter, the skin has already been seen and has already spoken (in a language that is impenetrable to the one who is, so to speak, inside the skin).

Within biological discourses, the skin is afforded a kind of agency as a police force. Take Anthony Smith's *The Body*, which represents itself as 'popular science': indeed, it dedicates itself to making bio/logical science accessible to the mainstream reading public. This book has a chapter dedicated to 'the skin'. It begins:

The only unprotected tissue which has the living body on one side and the outside world on the other is the skin. Taken as a whole it is the body's largest organ; it is enormously versatile; it keeps out foreign agents; it keeps in body fluids (Smith 1978: 482).

Here, 'the skin' marks and polices the difference between inside and outside. It is a boundary which guarantees a separation. Like the body-politic, its task is to ward off the danger of the foreigner, to keep out the other, to protect the self from the unruliness of others. Its task is not simply one of policing the outside. Its task is also, at one and the same time, to keep in: to prevent the inside from becoming outside and to prevent the self from becoming other. The skin, then, is the body's own private police force. As an agent which polices, the skin is also an organ. It is constituted as a discernible object which belongs to the body as an aspect of the body's wholeness and oneness with and for itself. The body-with-organs is here the body which manages itself and works at being itself.

The biological construction of 'the skin' as keeping the body firmly in place is reinforced by psychological models of the skin. In Ashley Montagu's *Touching: The Human Significance of the Skin*, for example, the skin is positioned as a 'tactile organ', a 'cloak', a 'screen' and a 'mirror'. In the first construction, the emphasis is on how the skin is central to 'the growth and development of the organism' (Montagu 1986: ix). In the second, the skin is positioned as a container, a physical cloak that 'covers us all over' (Montagu 1986: 4). In the third construction, the skin projects 'the gamut of life', as 'on a screen' (Montagu 1986: 6). And in the final construction, 'the skin is the mirror of the organism's functioning; its colour texture, moistness, dryness, colour and everyone of it aspects, reflect our state of being, psychological as well as physiological' (Montagu 1986: 12–13). These various constructions of the skin position skin as a telos (determining the 'development' of the subject), as constituting the limits and boundaries of the subject, and as a record or *reflection* of the subject's experiences through which we can establish the 'truth' of the subject's well-Being. The skin, here, enables us to measure the 'truth' and 'health' of the subject precisely insofar as it forms a barrier between the subject and what is beyond or outside it. But it is the gaze of the other that installs that 'truth' in the form a judgement (of what is on the screen). The subject's relation to the skin – as a form of self-possession – is here mediated and split by the demands of others.

And so, of course, as the always already seen by the gaze of the other, we must work at our skin if it is to reflect our well-being. The agency of the skin (its role as police force) is displaced on to the self: we must police our skin so it can police our bodies. The skin here belongs to the self and we must take care of it, if we are to care for ourselves. In the pamphlet produced by Boots Chemists in Britain, 'Skin Conditions: Symptoms, causes and treatments' we are reminded of our obligation to care for our skins:

Your skin is the largest organ in your body, and one of the most hard working. It protects you from the elements, helps control the amount of moisture in your body, excretes waste products, regulates body temperature, yet it is so sensitive that it can detect the gentlest touch. Strong, supple and remarkably elastic, it's certainly worth looking after.

Our duty to our skin is here a moral duty to a friend who loves us. The skin works hard to look after us – it even expels what is undesirable from within us (waste). Without the skin we would disappear in abjection, we would die amidst our waste. The testament to the extra-ordinary work done by the skin is also a call for action. What must we do to ensure the skin is doing its job? We are given some tips 'that will help you to keep your skin trouble free'. Here, the guarantee posed by the skin is not assumed. The potential *failure* of the skin to do its job is constituted as a demand. The agency of the skin is here the subject of a negation: the skin can only police if we police – it may not perform its duty, unless we are dutiful to it.

The demand to care for the skin which keeps us in place does not fall equally on subjects. To assume this is to reinstall 'the skin' as a mark of difference, rather than marked by difference. In advertisements for cosmetics, the folds of the skin are often depicted through the folds of the woman's body: its softness is her softness as she stands beneath the shower or in front of the mirror, folding soap or cream on to her skin. Her body metonymically conveys the forms of skin itself: the shape of her body evoking the dimensions of the skin, touching itself. Indeed, the call to manage and care for the skin so it can fold back into ourselves – reflect our true selves – falls particularly on women. The woman's skin must be protected from the dangers of being if she is to maintain the value of her femininity. Her skin must be supple, it must have this shape, wrinkles must not hide its form. Here, the gaze of the other fixes the woman's skin as a commodifiable sign of her body-value. The discourse which fetishes 'the skin' as a marker of well-being does so through metonymy; through figuring the boundaries of the woman's body as its boundaries. Such figuration both *reveals* and *conceals* the difference that is marked on the skin.

The contradictory concern with the skin as a workforce and police force, and the skin as in need of 'being worked on' and 'policed' interrupts this gendered discourse on healthy skins. The danger of disease, aging, sunburn and varying ailments points to the gap between the skin and (her) well-Being. That gap constitutes the seeping of the skin beyond the border through which it is designated as 'my skin', even as the dis-orders of the skin become read as dis-orders of the self (the skin as mirror). The dis-ordering of the skin is at once its rupturing, its refusal to contain 'the self' and to 'protect' the self from foreign agents. The 'skin' as the organ(ic) means through which medical discourse polices the boundaries of the body, undoes itself in a fragmentation of bodily parts in which self and other are no longer opposed. The danger of mingling is the constitutive possibility for 'doing' and 'policing' as such.

The undoing of biomedical constructions invites a different writing of the skin. The skin, here, is irreducible to a surface or a screen. The skin is not simply a mirror upon which images of others are traced. The skin has folds. It has more than one dimension. The skin is tactile. It can be touched. In the work of Irigaray the touchability of the skin, and the way the skin 'envelops' different subjects, makes it crucial to an analysis of love, sexuality and desire (Irigaray 1993). Sue Cataldi's concern with skin as an 'ambiguous, shifting border' centres on the question of how our skin 'paradox-ically protects us from others and exposes us to them. How we touch and how we are touched affects us' (Cataldi 1993: 145). The skin forms the relation between subjects as the locus of desire and pleasure. The skin is also vulnerable. It can be broken; it can be hurt and damaged. The skin, then, is a border which feels (an animated border). It is a border which purifies and expels. The skin remembers: it transforms itself in the passing of time (for example, it changes colour, it gets tanned and fades; it re-forms itself). It is the site of desire, repulsion and the amorous passage into being with others. It frames the necessity of love (getting inside the skin of the other) and its impossibility (the alterity of the other). The skin, rather than keeping the subject in place (and the other out of place), represents the constitutive possibility of a seeping between one and an-other. Insofar as it is all these things, the skin is a site of social crisis and instability, of the difficulty (if not impossibility) of being-in-the-world and of the constant slippage between the phantasy of being (I am inside my skin) and the fear of not being. The skin deconstructs the opposition between being and not being, *as the impossible boundary between different forms that appear living.*

3. COLOURFUL SKINS

Chromotism – the reduction of race to skin colour (Spivak 1986: 235) – involves a form of fetishism in which 'skin colour' becomes an object that tells us the truth of the subject's racial origin. Hence, within the clinic, diagnosis does not simply read the skin, but reads the skin's colour or its pigmentation. *Hutchison's Clinical Methods* begins, 'first notice the colour of the skin' (Bomford, Mason and Swash 1980: 48). Skin colour is that which must be seen and valued before any clinical judgement can be made. The rules and regulations here assume a white skin and look for signs of colour on that skin as markers of disease and ailment (redness, purpleness, blueness, yellowness, and so on). The doctor's duty is to assign each colour a meaning: the surface/skin/colour reflects some truth within the body (for example, redness might signify overheating, extreme exertion, sunburn, some fevers or some exanthemata and skin disease). The doctor reads the colours of the body: a reading which traces the symptom to a likely cause. As such, the act of diagnosis of symptoms must assume the category of the 'normal skin' (Bomford, Mason and Swash 1980: 48). The search for ailments or diseases is a search for pigmentation which is not normal to a white skin, hence equating the healthy or normal body with the 'unmarked' white body. As a result, there is no mention of how to read the black skin: the black skin is present only as a sign of a colour which deviates from the normality of the white body.

Indeed, *Lecture Notes on Clinical Medicine* suggests that the two

possible causes of 'increased' skin pigmentation, other than particular skin diseases, are sun tanning and 'racial' (Rubenstein and
Wayne 1991: 354). Here, sun tanning stands for white (the acquisition of colour) and race stands for not-white (already coloured).
Race has a cause/effect relation to pigmentation: race causes colour
which is then read as a sign of race. The clinical encounter with
skin colour is here organised around the desire to distinguish what
colour is caused by race and what is not. The colour is assumed to
reflect the real of the subject's (well)being. In this way, diagnosis
hovers on the question of pigmentation as a sign or indicator of
the subject's truth, either in terms of health (skin conditions) or
being (racial).

In biological discourses, 'colour' or 'pigmentation' indicate
different categories of being in relation to health: that is, the two
diagnostic modes collapse into each other such that race – here
conflated with a deviation from the normalised category of 'whiteness' – becomes a skin condition (pathological). This is clear in
anatomical text books. In Le Gros Clark's *The Tissues of the Body: An
Introduction to the Study of Anatomy* there is an acknowledgement
that most skin contains pigmentation: 'Even in the white races of
mankind most regions of the skin contain a brown pigment' (Le
Gros Clark 1958: 292). What follows is an explanation not simply
of pigmentation as such, but *how it comes to be acquired*. Le Gros
Clark considers, for example, what happens when unpigmented
skin is transplanted on to pigmented skin. He writes:

Unpigmented skin transplanted into a pigmented area appears to be
invaded and eventually replaced by the pigmented epidermis . . . the
melanogenetic dendritic cells of the pigmented epidermis at the
margin of the graft establish contact with the non-melanogenetic cells
of the unpigmented skin (perhaps by forming direct syncytial connex-
ions with them) and 'infect' them permanently with melanogenetic
properties. The curious manner in which pigmentation thus spreads
has been described in detail by Billingham and Medavar, and has
been compared by them with the mechanism of the virus infection
(Le Gros Clark 1958: 293).

Here, the descriptive language of biological discourse attempts to
account for the 'phenomena' of grafting skins with different pigmentation. But that descriptive language is also evaluative. The
affect of the mutation in pigmentation is defined as an 'infection',
immediately equating dark pigmentation with disease: a disease
from which light skin must be protected. Blackness spreads over

the surface. It is a contagion which we have a moral duty to contain. The moral and racial aspect of this biological discussion of the skin as tissue eventually feeds into an evolutionary narrative: 'Indirect evidence makes it certain that pigmentation of the skin is a primitive tract in mankind, and it may be inferred that this character was lost to a greater degree or lesser degree independently by different races during the course of their evolution' (Le Gros Clarke 1958: 295). Here, dark pigmentation is (almost) assigned to the pre-history of the white races – an assignment that implicitly evokes a narrative whereby whiteness constitutes a relative *overcoming* of, and relative immunity towards, infection. To this extent, colour is read as a sign of being (different racial beings) through a discourse on the healthiness of certain beings over others.

The biological narrative on pigmentation evokes a model of the skin as an indicator of both the different levels of evolution of racial beings, and of *infectability* and pathology. In John Barker's text *Race*, which provides such a biological reading of racial difference, the concern to categorise through skin colour hovers on the question of a distinction between real colour and colour that is acquired through the state of being-in-the-world (or under-the-sun). He writes: 'the skin of Negrids darkens long before any ray of light has touched it' (Barker 1974: 152). He goes on to quote from Thomas Browne: 'not onely their legitimate and timely births, but their abortions are also duskier, before they have felt the scortch and fervour of the sun' (Barker 1974: 152). Here, Blackness' is located as prior to the state of being-in-the-world. The temporality of this narrative is important. Blackness is prior to existence itself – prior to the very constitution of any meaningful subjectivity. This temporality evokes death. The dark aborted foetuses become a figure of the prior-ness of Blackness precisely insofar as they evoke Blackness as death; as the impossibility of entering the world as fully human. The future of death is *already* marked on the skin of the aborted foetuses. As a result, their abortion cannot be seen as tragic (their death is not an end of life). The brutality of this image is for me unforgettable. The future of their death is already their past. Here, the 'dusky' abortions are celebrated as a sign or confirmation of a difference that is pre-ontological or pre-subjectal. It is a difference that is absolute and that is not troubled by the changes of skin colour that are a result of being-in-the-world. This distinction between natural or pre-subjectal colour and unnatural or post-subjectal colour will be taken up later in my analysis of sun tanning.

The pathologising of Blackness through its assignment as a

death before entry into the world (the Black person enters only as subhuman) relies on 'Blackness' as prior to acts of signification. However, this reliance on the both the beforeness and transparency of Black skin is open to confusion and displacement. Black skin, rather than guaranteeing the meaning of racial origin as an indictor of degrees of (in)humanness, is subject to instability. The problematic of 'skin colour' and the potential for colour to destabilise as well as secure racial identifications is central to John Howard Griffin's *Black Like Me*, an autobiographical account of a white man who receives medical help to alter the colour of his skin so that he can 'discover' the truth of Being/Black. Here, the clinical encounter enters the text through providing the means for a self-transformation: medicine becomes a *technique* for investigating the link between skin colour and being. John Griffin wants to know about the truth of being-Black and it is dermatologists who provide him with the means for changing his skin colour (through oral medication and exposure to ultraviolet rays). But the clinic does not simply enter the text as the site in which Griffin's body is transformed. The narrative itself, in its construction of skin colour as the measure of a subject's truth, repeats the biological construction of the racial body as tied to the surface of the skin.

It is quite clear that the story about the truth of the Negro involves a fetishising of skin colour. By altering his skin, the narrator becomes a Negro: 'How else except by becoming a Negro could a white man hope to learn the truth?' (Griffin 1970: 9). Here, the becoming-Black of the skin is reducible to the assumption of a true and proper Negro identity. He asks himself, will they realise I am the same man, 'or will they treat me as some nameless Negro'? The reply is, 'As soon as they see you, you'll be a Negro' (Griffin 1970: 12). Here, one becomes a Negro in the event of being seen as Black, in being found and fixed in the horrified gaze (or 'hate stare') of others. The narrator looks in the mirror:

In the flood of light against white tile, the face and shoulders of a stranger – a fierce, bald, very dark Negro – glared at me from the glass. He in no way resembled me.
The transformation was total and shocking. I had expected to see myself disguised, but this was something else. I was imprisoned in the flesh of an utter stranger, an unsympathetic one with whom I felt no kinship. All traces of the John Griffin I had been were wiped from existence. Even the senses underwent a change so profound it filled me with distress. I looked into the mirror and saw reflected nothing of the white John Griffin's past. No, the reflections led back to Africa,

back to the shanty and the ghetto, back to the fruitless struggles against the mark of blackness. Suddenly, almost with no mental preparation, no advance hint, it became clear and it permeated my whole being. My inclination was to fight against it. I had gone too far. I knew now that there is no such thing as a disguised white man, when the black won't rub off. The black man is wholly a Negro, regardless of what he once may have been. I was a newly created Negro who must go out that door and live in a world unfamiliar to me (Griffin 1970: 19).

Here, the transformation of skin colour from white to Black becomes causally linked to a total personal and collective transformation. Skin in this way is seen to hold the 'truth' of the subject's identity (like a 'kernel') as well as functioning as the scene of the subject's memory and history (with a Black skin there is no *trace* of his previous identity). The essentialising image of his Black skin leading to Africa creates an absolute link between skin colour and racial origin. His transformation into a stranger (where he 'passes' as Black in the mirror) produces the naked face of a Black man; a face that immediately gets coded as fierce and glaring, as monstrous and bestial. In passing as Black in his own mirror image, the vision of the Black face is overdetermined by the 'knowledges' available of Blackness central to the violence of colonialism (it is a 'fierce' face). The Black skin creates the face and re-creates the subject. It is not simply a disguise; the mask becomes the skin which is his 'real'. And yet, at the same time, despite the fixity of Blackness, through a technology of the body, one can become Black. Blackness, as something one possesses (that leads in an unmediated way) to Africa, can also be something which one is yet-to-become. But as soon as one becomes Black one *is* Black. The white man who becomes Black takes on the fact of Blackness and loses his 'white interiority'. The Black man's fate is forever sealed in the fact of his Blackness. But if the white man's Black mask can become the skin, cannot the Black skin become a white mask (see Fanon 1972)?

In this story, which is a story of the transformation from white to Black, we have a split attention to the truth of racial identity as contained by the facticity of skin colour (fetishism as a mode of operation for racism), and to skin colour as constituting the instability of the subject and the potential for transformation (fetishism as determining the loss of its own object). The narrator's Blackness is a mask that becomes his skin and determines his destiny. But the distinction between the narrator's Blackness which is temporary (a mask which *becomes* skin) and the Black man's Blackness (skin

56

which *is* skin) refuses to stay in place. If skin is the subject's fate and facticity, then skin itself is predicated on the possibility of a mask or a disguise. The skin, then, is both the locus of the subject and that unstable space in which the subject can become an-other; the skin is both already coloured and open to transformation. That openness threatens the absolute distinctions between white and Black which inform the colonial notions of racial purity. It also threatens the temporal narrative which is installed through biomedical discourses whereby Blackness is located as before signification itself: as the impossible mutuality of before and after, 'pigmentation' resists being assigned to the subject's pre-history.

4. TANNING BODIES

So far I have considered the demand within biomedical discourses to separate 'skin colour' which is a marker of race (pre-subjectal) and 'skin colour' which is acquired through being-in-the-world. One way of thinking through the latter is, of course, to consider 'tanning'. However, in this section I am concerned with 'tanning' as the *intentional act of transforming the colour of one's skin*. In other words, I want to think more about the implications of tanning as a *cultural practice* and less of tanning as the effect of being-in-the-world. My analysis will raise how the instability of 'skin' and 'colour' relates to the collision between regimes of difference on the forming and de-forming of bodies.

Tanned colour has a complex and ambiguous relation to the marking of status and health. In the first instance, one can consider how 'tanning' became a sign or outward display of healthy bodies in the early twentieth century. In an article in the *British Medical Journal* from 1915 the 'healing powers of sunlight' are celebrated:

To return from a holiday with a well-tanned skin, whether it be from the sea side or mountain tops, has always been regarded as the outward and visible sign of sound health. Sunlight in each case, together with wind, has been the agency by which such hygienic perfection has been brought about (cited in Carter 1996: 12).

Here the medical concern with 'tanned skin' as an indicator of health relies on assumptions about how such tans are acquired. The 'tan' is not simply about 'colour' derived from *any sun*. Rather, tanning refers to the leisure time of tourism: the tan's relation to healthiness is here precisely determinate on its equation with 'the holiday'. The medical construction of tanned skin as a display of health here renders health a commodifiable object: the healthy skin is wealthy skin: it is skin whose colour marks the exchange value implicated in tourism. The perfectibility of 'tanned skin' remains bound up with notions of hygiene. Tanned colour is clean colour and is hence immediately distinguished from the infecta-bility of being-Black. Here, the techniques for tanning the body provide the means for cleanliness ('hygienic perfection'): the tanned surface-skin denotes the moral hygiene of the white soul (underneath).

In contemporary medical literature, 'tanned skin' is no longer seen as an indicator of health but has become a measure of the threat of disease. Here, the tan is linked to the danger of cancer. In Australia, the medical research on skin cancer has affected cultural practices and perceptions of tanning. What we have here, though, is not so much a social refusal to equate tanning and healthy-looking bodies, but the development of a model of 'safe tanning' (with the catchy jingle I remember well from my youth: 'Slip, Slop, Slap – slip on a shirt, slop on sun screen and slap on a hat') The skin can acquire colour but it must do so through tech-niques which limit exposure at certain times and places. The safer tan guarantees the continued acceptability of bronzed bodies as markers of health. Healthy bodies are determined though rituals which assume the vulnerability of white skin and its need for protection. In this sense, the skin becomes subject to management and policing; the boundaries of healthy bodies are not given but are constituted through self-surveillance and care. Here, 'tanned colour' becomes a marker of 'health' through the care of 'the skin'. In this sense, the meaning of 'the tan' is constituted through the rituals which police the boundaries of white bodies.

However, the meanings of 'tanned skin' are not always assured. The relation between 'racial colour' and 'tanned colour' is open to confusion and displacement whereby that latter is not guaranteed in the form of the linear narrative: '*being* white and *becoming* brown'. Take the following example. This event occurred when I was fourteen years old, walking around the streets of Adelaide. I was stopped and addressed by two policemen in a car. They called me over, asked me what I was doing (I said I was walking). The policeman closest to me asked me if I was Aboriginal. I was indig-nant, replying 'no'. The other policeman interrupted, gave me a wink, and said 'It's a sun tan, isn't it?' I smiled, but did not say yes or no.[1]

It seems to me now that the policemen addressed me, in the

first instance, as Aboriginal (from colour). This identification *read* me as a subject, *by rendering me a suspect*, as a danger to the Law (of property), a potential robber. Their question demanded to know the extent of my threat by demanding to know whether my racial origin was Aboriginal. In this sense, Aboriginality becomes figured as the most threatening or disruptive presence. As the outsider inside, the Aboriginal becomes the contagion that threatens the moral health of the imaginary white community (or, the neighbourhood: an imaginary white community which is constructed most violently in the Australian soap opera *Neighbours*).

However, a shift occurs which forces a dis-identification from my identity as suspect. Not an Aboriginal (but perhaps only sun tanned). My denial of being Aboriginal and my failure to name or declare my race (which of course was unnoticed or invisible to them) implicated me in their structure of address, by rendering Aboriginality something to be disavowed. The gesture of smiling can here be figured as a collusion, a desire in some sense to be figured as white, as respectable, as somebody who has a legitimate right to walk in these leafy suburbs. My disavowal thus suggests an implicit desire for 'whiteness'. That desire creates an imaginary (and impossible) conception of a purified, ideal and healthy self, as well as a coherent social order (to which I could 'fit in'), by assigning certain values to 'whiteness'. Such an assignment entails a disavowal and repudiation of the other, of 'Blackness', or Aboriginality.

The structure of identification which involved the exchange of a wink and the quip about being sun tanned caused me the most discomfort. Although inspired by my dis-identification as Aboriginal (which was implicated in the assigning of certain values to Aboriginality, as something to be disavowed) and my refusal to identify my race, this quip both made light of their mistake (their hailing of the wrong person, their error of reading) while positioning me as woman, a recipient of a wink (and of a gaze), and as someone who sun bathes, who tans her body. The entrance of the body into the exchange, shifted me from being suspect to object, from being a threat to property, to property itself. While defining the body in terms of leisure, where colour is a sign of a 'higher' class, the quip shifted my attention from the social relation of policeman to suspect, to the sexual relation of man to woman. The colour of my body was evoked as an adornment rather than a stain, as 'a paying attention to the body'. Here, colour is literally a detachable signifier, a 'mask' that can be put on and taken off, inessential

59

to the subject, and hence acceptable. By rendering colour a mask rather than essential, the exchange rendered my body something to be valued, adorned, protected. Colour becomes inscribed as a detachable signifier, positioned me as essentially white, as truly and properly white underneath the luxury of a brown veil. Inscribed as a white woman, I was the legitimate object of the policeman's protective gaze. Here, colour is a mask that guarantees the well-being of the white self and white community. It is a sign of the acceptably cultivated body: a body whose outer limits are recon-figured (white to brown) as a sign or even confirmation of its racial and moral hygiene.

The shift in racial identifications which positioned me as Abori-ginal (read *Black skin*) to sun tanned (read *white skin* which has become brown) cannot be isolated from the gendering of the sub-ject positions. In my account of the event, I discussed the police-man's address as positioning me as an Aboriginal and as a suspect. However, the explicit racial confrontation does not suspend the gendered nature of my position. The original address was surely an address not simply to an Aboriginal, but to an Aboriginal woman. As theorists such as Jan Pettman in *Living in the Margins* have argued, the Aboriginal woman is always already sexualised in white Australian colonial narratives (Pettman 1992: 27). So if the original address (are you an Aboriginal?) positioned my colour as a stain, as a sign of a natural criminality determined by the fact of my skin, then how does this criminalisation of colour link with the sexuali-sation of the address? What I want to argue is that the two positions determined by the policeman's address (the Black woman and the white woman) involve contradictory constructions – in the form of 'colourings' – of femininity. In the former, the Black woman is defined in terms of the physicality of her skin, as a stain which confirms her oversexed being, her threat to the proper social and sexual order of the domesticated suburb. In contrast, the sun-tanned white woman's sexuality is directed towards cultivating her body for the proper attention of the policemen's protective gaze. These two constructions of colour have different relations to moral health: a coloured (stained) being is a sign of a disease which threatens the racial and moral purity of the (sun-tanned) white woman. Henceforth, the white woman requires policing from the dis-ease of the Aboriginal woman (she polices her body, the policeman polices her).

This kind of approach to the collision between racial and sexual identifications in the culture of sun tanning is implicit to Judith

Williamson's article 'Woman is an Island: Femininity and Coloni-zation'. Here, she discusses some advertisements for sun-tanning products which involve the promise or lure of an exotic or foreign place, often unspecified, and best expressed in terms of the trope of the desert island. The exotic other can be inhabited and visited by the white female consumer. In the act of travel one can acquire the 'colour' of that exotic place: the white subject can become brown or rather 'bronzed'. Williamson writes: 'Of course, when the caption offers its product "to all skin types for a safe, dark and natural tan", it doesn't really mean a "natural tan". If one were nat-urally dark, of course, one would be black' (Williamson 1986: 117). Here a natural tan is the sign of racial otherness (of blackness) which is simply *there*. A tan can be acquired and it is the effort to produce a tan, its *cultivated* nature, that is the rem(a)inder of the white subject's (the white woman's) difference and the value of her *skin* whose lack of natural darkness enables her to tan in the first place. On her skin, 'nature' is reinvented. She 'takes on' the signi-fier of darkness, an act or event which represents the conversion of darkness from a dirt or disease to an adornment. The link between the bronzed body and the erotic also suggest that the white woman can flirt with 'Blackness' as a signifier of sex *without becoming Black*. By taking on 'darkness' through tanning, the white woman can domesticate the hyper-sexuality of the Black skin, making 'Black-ness' a mask that is both desirable and safe (in the sense that it is temporary). Within this schema, the Black woman is placed on the side of the oversexualised. She cannot transform her skin; she is reduced to the fact of her Blackness which constitutes the threat of a stain that cannot be washed off, or that does not fade with time. Her racial body is simply a sign of moral ill-health (a being which lacks well-Being).

Increasingly central to this link between tanning and white fem-inine skin is the division between natural and fake tans, no longer understood as the division between Blackness or 'race' and the tanned body. For now we can get creams which can make us appear to be tanned (or we can pay to use sun beds). The division between the fake and authentic tan creates a double mask; that is, a mask that appears like the mask of the tan (the adorned body). We have the endless deferral of Blackness as a sign of otherness (Blackness as depth). The play with colours on the *surface* of the white female body is distinguished from real colour which is a question of a skin which is not transformable; skin that is already Black and con-stitutes the 'depth' of Blackness as racial difference. The bronzed body (the white body which is beautified) becomes possible because the skin is pliable; it is open to be remade and transformed through the ritual of the sun tan. The Black skin is not pliable. It is a surface which simply contains or reflects a Black depth.

Indeed, in Kenneth Dutton's analysis of male body builders in *The Perfectible Body*, he considers the fake tan as a stage make-up, as a production of the skin as a bronzed and glossy surface which separates being from looking: 'the skin need not *be* tanned, but it must *look* tanned' (Dutton 1995: 312). Here the perfectibility of the tanned white body resides in the over-production of skin as *a surface which is detached from Being*. In some sense, it is the detach-ability of the skin-surface which constitutes the white being: that is, the very movements of the animated surface demonstrates the pliability of white subjectivity. Dutton's work is interesting as it examines a form of masculine self-presentation which is ordered around the male body being *on display*. Here the (fake) tanned body signifies the working body – the 'polished skin' is a means of 'looking hard' (Dutton 1995: 315). In typical constructions of the white female (fake) tanned body, the body is at leisure: passively waiting to be touched by the sun (bed). The detachment of her being and her look is here embedded in the passive attainment of a colour whose eroticism does not mark or stain her being.

In contrast, in this discourse around (fake) tanning, the Black skin lacks animation: the skin is the soul – being and looking can-not be separated. The reduction of being to looking organises Black subjectivity around 'the skin' as the marking of both the inner and outer body. If 'colour' becomes linked with the 'exotic woman' as argued by Williamson, then the containment of the Black woman within her skin is ordered around a model of her sexuality as *a stain on her Being*. In other words, the Black woman's skin-surface reflects a sexualised interior which constitutes the risk of disease or even death. But is that containment fully secured? Is her skin always already assigned a place?

Returning to the auto-biographical incident, the shift in the police questioning from 'Are you an Aboriginal?' to 'It's a sun tan, isn't it?' involved a shift from the position of the Black woman (the diseased or contaminated other) to the white woman (whose purity is under threat). But this shift in identifications enabled me as a subject to renegotiate and resist my positioning. By not naming my race (and hence 'passing' for white), the relation of address involved the destabilisation of racial signifiers and my own eventual resis-tance to the policeman's gaze. Skin and colour do not function here as a guarantee for determining who does and does not have the right to walk in the leafy suburbs. The automatic system of racial identifications is in this way always open to confusion. The opposition between real colour and fake colour, which is re-figured in the opposition between depth and surface, is unstable. It is my contention that the transformability of the skin (including Black skin), which appears so naked, so 'obvious' and 'visible' within the clinical encounter as the measure of the truth of the subject's well-Being, constantly *threatens* the colonial encounter that demands the total exclusion of Blackness from the realm of the proper subject and the proper suburb. Is she Black? Or is she tanned? I would reply now: I am Black and I am tanned. Being both, I question your construction of either.

Indeed, being both, I question the distinction between being (Black) – which is constituted as prior to being-in-the-world – and becoming (Black). The crisis posed by this event is a crisis precisely of 'Being' and its relationship to 'the skin': a crisis that returns to the clinic as its moment of undoing. Colour, as an indicator of Being, is not transparent: it is not naked to the colonising gaze of the doctor or policeman. One is not already Black before the act of reading that Blackness as a stain on Being: not only is Blackness not the always-has-been (the dead past), but it is also not the always-will-be (the dead future). This crisis announces itself also as a crisis of reading that transforms encounters within and beyond the clinic: how can we see or tell the difference now or then? How can the difference be re-told through taking the history of the patient or suspect? The gap between seeing and being is performed in the very *necessity* of the question that demands a policing of one from another. The necessity of the question conveys that it is always *possible* that the difference cannot be told. The skin, rather than providing the site in which the difference of one being from another is assured in a discourse of well-Being, is the site of an uncertainty which animates the social encounter.

AND THEN . . .

In this chapter, my concern with animating the skin – that is, with the instability of the borders of embodied subjects – involves a rewriting of the clinical encounter from a feminist and post-colonial perspective. Here, there is an attention not only to how the patient/subject is held in place by the narratives and looks which are legitimated within the clinic, but also a concern with how such narratives and looks cannot keep the subject in place. The subject's skin seeps beyond the border. The skin's lack of transparency is a crisis of (medical) hermeneutics: how can we really tell the difference between beings, as the difference between the healthiness of beings, through seeing the colour of their skins? This crisis of telling, which assumes that there is some-thing which is yet to be told, forces a recognition of the differences that mark skins/bodies. Here, as a mark of the difference of difference, the Black woman figures the danger not only of disease and contamination, but of a diseased sexuality which threatens the moral purity of sun-tanning white women. But as a figure, the Black woman is an impossibility: can we see her within her skin? Is she there or not there? Is that colour a stain on her being or a cultivated mask which confirms her moral and sexual purity underneath? Am I her or not her? Am I to be policed from her or as her? Here, a recognition of the impossibility of the surface/depth model of the racial and gendered subject, within and beyond the clinic, is a movement towards a politics which accounts for violence and fixation, without assuming either work to hold us fully in place. The impossibility of skin and colour holding us in place here is also a demand for a different writing of embodiment. The writing isn't a forming of a new body. It is a de-formation which is at once a transformation of the conditions from which it is possible to speak and live.

NOTES

1. I have written extensively about this event which includes other aspects I cannot mention here. For a fuller account please see Ahmed (1996). For a consideration of this event in relation to autobiography see Ahmed (1997).

REFERENCES

Ahmed, S. (1996) 'Identification, Gender and Racial Difference: Moving Beyond a Psychoanalytical Account of Subjectivity' in Sharma, R. (ed.) *Representations of Gender, Democracy and Identity Politics in Relation to South Asia*, Delhi: Indian Book Centre.

Ahmed, S. (1997) '"It's just a sun tan isn't it?": Auto-biography as an Identificatory Practice', in Mirza, H. (ed.), *Black British Feminism*, London: Routledge.

Anderson, W. A. D. (1952) *Synopsis of Pathology*, London: Henry Kimpton.

Barker, John R. (1974) *Race*, London: Oxford University Press.

Bomford, Richard, Mason, Stuart and Swash, Michael (1980) *Hutchison's Clinical Methods*, London: Bailliere Tindall.

Browse, Norman L. (1991) *An Introduction to the Symptoms and Signs of Surgical Disease*, London: Edward Arnold.

Carter, Simon (1996) 'Becoming Brown: A Short History of the Sun Tan'. Unpublished paper.

Cataldi, Sue L. (1993) *Emotion, Depth and the Flesh: A Study of Sensitive Space*, New York: State University of New York Press.

Dutton, Kenneth R. (1995) *The Perfectible Body: The Western Ideal of Physical Development*, London: Cassell.

Fanon, F. (1972) *Black Skin, White Masks*, London: Paladin.

Griffin, J. H. (1970) *Black Like Me*, London: Panther Modern Society.

Grosz, E. (1994) *Volatile Bodies: Towards a Corporeal Feminism*, NSW: Allen and Unwin.

Irigaray, Luce (1993) *An Ethics of Sexual Difference*, Ithaca: Cornell University Press.

Le Gros Clark, W. E. (1958) *The Tissues of the Body: An Introduction to the Study of Anatomy*, Oxford: Oxford University Press.

Montagu, Ashley (1986) *Touching: The Human Significance of the Skin*, New York: Perennial Library.

Munro, Michael and Ford, John (1989) *Introduction to Clinical Examination*, Edinburgh: Churchill Livingstone.

Pettman, J. (1992) *Living in the Margins: Racism, Feminism and Sexism in Australia*, NSW: Allen and Unwin.

Rubenstein, David and Wayne, David (1991) *Lecture Notes on Clinical Medicine*, Oxford: Blackwell Scientific Publications.

Smith, Anthony (1978) *The Body*, Harmondsworth: Penguin Books.

Spivak, G. C. (1986) 'Imperialism and Sexual Difference', *Oxford Literary Review* 2: 225–40.

Suleri, S. (1993) 'Woman Skin Deep: Feminism and the Postcolonial Condition' in P. Williams and L. Christian (eds) *Colonial Discourse and Post-Colonial Theory*, New York: Harvester Wheatsheaf.

Williamson, J. (1986) 'Woman is an Island: Femininity and Colonization' in T. Modleski (ed.) *Studies in Entertainment: Critical Approaches to Mass Culture*, Bloomington and Indianapolis: Indiana University Press.

4

The Mouth and the Clinical Gaze

CATHRYN VASSELEU

IF YOU GO TO A DENTIST these days, the first thing that might be put in your mouth is not a mirror but a tiny video-camera. Having given yourself up to a chair in whose arms you are gently laid prone, and after voluntarily opening wide, you will be able to view what the dentist is seeing and doing in your mouth. It will be there larger than life on a computer screen in front of you, augmented by any imaginable collage of split-screens displaying X-rays, diagrams, charts and other images that can be manipulated digitally.

This experience comes to you by way of a pencil-shaped camera that fits easily inside the mouth and is connected to a computer screen. The arrangement, which is called an intraoral camera, has many possible clinical applications. These include live-action viewing inside the mouth by both patients and clinicians, as well as the storage of selected images for future screenings. It also allows the viewing of other material along with or in place of the live action. Furthermore, these live-action images can be transmitted to computer screens in multiple locations anywhere. Within the profession the intraoral camera is currently regarded as an expensive novelty rather than a clinical necessity, but its applications are growing exponentially. About 10 per cent of private operators in the United States are currently using variations of the system to promote and organise their practices, and hospitals and universities around the world are acquiring it as a desirable adjunct to teaching and research.

When you think of dentistry, a theatre intimately concerned with the visualisation of the body may not be the first association that springs to mind. The performance of dentistry has immediate

66

associations with pain and fear which are more intimately embedded in the familiar fabric of everyday life than the performance of surgery in any operating theatre. The incorporation of computerised intraoral imaging systems into the performance of dentistry reiterates the extent to which the practice has emerged at the intersection of *both* powers of visualisation and powers of pain and fear. In one piece of promotional literature which features an enactment of the camera's use, a quotation from the fictional dentist depicted in the scene exemplifies this nexus: 'If patients don't feel pain they *can't really see* the need for treatment. A picture from my [intraoral camera] is almost as compelling as a tooth ache.'[1] Pain and visualisation are depicted here as having a common motivational value.

It is arguable that the capitalisation on this value in the visualisation of an intimate space also heralds a change in the clinical gaze and its relation to the mouth as an orifice or portal of the body. According to Foucault in his well-known analysis of nineteenth-century medical perception, the clinical gaze emerges as a practice which sees itself as visualising an invisible which the organic depth of the living individual had hitherto kept hidden from the gaze of the morbid anatomist. The clinical gaze replaces the anatomist's knife with an incisive and eroding language which penetrates the body and delivers up its imperceptible secrets 'live', through inscription rather than a mortal penetration of the body. By an exhaustive spatialisation, in the surfacing of that which is occurring in the layered depths, the individual tissues of the body are ultimately spread out before the eyes, ears and touch of the clinical gaze. The body is no longer perceived as a blind dark orifice but as a folded fabric which has the transparency of a veil (Foucault 1975: 165–72).

The body within the clinical gaze is enveloped in a 'see-through' discursive skin. It is perceived indirectly in the surfacing of its depths. The interior brought to common light by the clinical gaze is a view of a passive, compliant, readable body, ultimately offering up its singular disorder as a patently clear, skin-deep truth. This is a gaze projected on to the body of a corpse, a view which effaces any difference between the indeterminate interiority of a body with orifices, and the penetrability of an inscribable body-surface. It is a manner of spatialising the body which is perpetuated today in sophisticated electronic medical imaging systems, where ultrasound, X-ray computer tomography (CT) and magnetic resonance imaging (MRI) scanners deliver to view in three dimensions an otherwise inaccessible domain inside-out, point by point in multiple animat-able slices. The activity of neurons, the velocity of blood flow, the concentration of chemicals, the contents of cavities, and the arrangement of anatomical structures can all be elicited from any viewpoint, with tissues that can be gratuitously sectioned or peeled away to reveal whatever is desired.[2]

The spatialisation of the body in the rendering of a visible invisible is not entirely adequate to an account of the gaze in the practice of dentistry, where emphasis not only falls on the surfacing but also on the maintenance of an oral space in the visualisation of the mouth's interior. This is not simply an act of surveillance, or as Foucault describes it, an order produced through the investment of bodies in depths under the surfaces of images (Foucault 1977: 217). It is also, as I will be arguing, the mobilisation of a body-image whose ordering differs from the depth/projection of clinical perception.

In a sociological study of modern dentistry, Sarah Nettleton (1992) traces changes in the object of dentistry from the mouth with teeth, which was a nineteenth-century discovery. With the realisation in the early twentieth century that pain had a psychological as well as a physiological dimension, the focus of dentistry shifted to the elimination of pain, which it singled out as the greatest obstacle to its successful operation. The object of dentistry was extended to a mind that was linked to the mouth, with the attendant complication of the oral cavity into a site of eroticism and aggressivity. The mouth with teeth became an orifice whose functioning was in the grips of a psyche whose dimensions needed to be mastered.

A further transformation in the object of dentistry occurred with its idealisation of anaesthetised pain or the concept of painless dentistry. As an ultimately manageable and quantifiable phenomenon, pain was relocated from a psycho-physiological space to a space which transcended any individual body. The conceptualisation of pain resided not only with the feeling patient but also with the sensitivity and attentiveness of the dentist to the pain of others. With this division of pain-perception the object of dentistry became an intersubjective or social space which surrounded and transcended the mouth and the patient (Nettleton 1992: 64–77).

From this brief sketch of Nettleton's analysis a movement can be drawn of the shifting construction of orality within dentistry from a passive accessible cavity, to a perverse but trainable opening or orifice, to a site of negotiation or space in common. Nettleton's own conclusion is that in its ideal form the dental regime serves as a dream if not a tangible exemplar of disciplinary power (Nettleton 1992: 106). Her conceptualisation is based on the dental profession's self-appointed policing role in relation to the care of the mouth, through the monitoring of populations and the fashioning and training of individual bodies. It is in this respect that dentistry's response to disease differs to that of general medicine. In Foucault's terms, as a disciplinary regime dentistry is aligned on the side of public health and plague control (seen in its commitment to preventive education, personal hygiene, water fluoridation and epidemiological studies). While medicine has focused on the three-dimensional space of the body, dentistry and public health have focused on a socio-environmental space which traverses the body, although the division is far from absolute (Nettleton 1992: 117).

The point at which I part company with Nettleton's account is the characterisation of the object of dentistry as 'an object that has been constituted by a disembodied *gaze*' (1992: 106). Nettleton argues in line with Foucault that the sovereign clinical gaze has an efficacy which is freed from the distortions of pain or pleasure. In the ideal system the mouth itself would not be touched, it would simply be monitored (1992: 64). The thing which is valued in this encounter is a mouth parading its conformity to a formalised orality under a gaze attuned to the slightest signs of oral delinquency. My difference rests with the suggestion that in the opening of the mouth and its secrets to the world in the disciplinary encounter, it is incorporated into the social space of a *disembodied* gaze that traverses and transcends the body.

The way I will pursue this issue is by addressing the visibility of the gaze, both in the performance of dentistry and in the way that dentistry sees itself. The ultimate goal of modern-day dentistry is to practise by non-intervention. This goal represents a shift from the ideal of prosthetic replacement of a loss, in which dentistry came to see its activity unfavourably as a scar. Along with the notion that 'the prematurely edentulous [would] carry a painful scar which may never be healed', the body marred by toothlessness came to represent the antithesis of dentistry's ideal (Harris 1947: 600). In the production of an individual who is capable of the surveillance and care of her or his own mouth, dentistry sees its task as being an alteration of the embodied subject's relation to itself, not by external assault but as an intentionally constituted delineation. This individuation is not a process we undertake by ourselves, nor is the subject entirely active or passive in the configuration. The body of the dental subject is never merely an object – its *compliance* is the object. I would argue that dentistry sees itself as invisibly supplementing the mouth, or as an intervention which desires to erase all traces of itself from the mouth.

Nettleton identifies two fundamentally different forms of social organisation of the gaze in dentistry, which are consistent with Foucault's differentiation between public spectacle and surveillance as regimes of power (Nettleton 1992: 18–23). I will take some licence in describing these. The first form is the spectacle of the toothdrawer or barber-surgeon working before a group which gathers around to watch. In the eyes of all, the mouth whose contents are on display is a component in a corporeal system which must eliminate its refuse. The operation being performed on the hapless participant is a public display of skill that is illustrative of the exploitability of such theatrical events in the demonstration of seventeenth-century political power. The second form of organisation is the dental surgery. Gone from this scene are spectators, itinerant theatre, rot to be expelled, and displays of bodily assault. Even the mouth is present only by implication. Its contents are something that together the patient and dentist keep between themselves. People will not stand and watch, but will one by one, sit in a chair and render their mouths up to the dentist's gaze. What the dentist sees is paramount here, and ideally what the dentist sees is not a body-orifice but precise structures, through mirrors and X-rays and probings and chartings.

The introduction of the intraoral camera into the practice of dentistry marks another shift in the organisation of its gaze, to a communicative space. This space is organised around the projection of a digitised image of a mirror's point of view from inside the mouth. If the new arrangement has any connection with earlier forms of spectacle and surveillance it is not in any evolutionary sense but as an after-image. Any clear distinction between spectacle and surveillance is lost in the screening of its performance, which can be to an audience in the room or to others anywhere. Dentistry has turned its performance inside out, and in directing it to the gaze of the patient, transformed her or him into a spectator. Not only are the insides of a patient's mouth being screened. Both patient and dentist are open to each other. At the same time the patient's mouth is the scene. Instead of an interior opened to the gaze of the dentist it acts as a background to the performance.

There is something paradoxical about a profession that is deliberately exploiting a non-interventionalist gaze to make a spectacle of itself. As the quotation from the advertisement mentioned earlier suggests, an unforseen consequence of the profession's disassociation of itself from pain has been that a different incentive is required to elicit participation in treatment. As an indefinable yet compelling reduction of the body and its powers to an immobilised state, pain has a power to motivate involuntarily. Pain traverses the interiority and exteriority of psychical and physical embodiment. Like pleasure, it can be characterised as an ambiguously mental and physically locatable experience (Levinas 1990: 61). Pain has an actuality despite the fact that pain itself has no establishable referent.

For the purposes of re-establishing an incentive for treatment which is unrelated to pain, the intraoral camera is being used for its expressive rather than incisive powers, or as a tool of seduction. Another advertising slogan states: 'In the best of relationships few words are needed.'[3] As its brand name, *Insight*, suggests, the image it gives is hard to define. The image has been recruited in the place of pain as a means of reincorporation through intimate blind connection and involuntary response. It is being used for the communication of a need, not for the illumination of an object.

In the shift of the object of dentistry from a psycho-social space to an image created for the gaze of the spectator, screen and mouth are *deliberately presented* as extensions of each other. With the task of a non-interventionalist gaze now focused on displaying its objective, its act of presentation includes an inadvertent performance. I have borrowed this term, again with some licence, from art historian Norman Bryson (1983: 163–71). An *advertent* performance is one which is projected for the gaze of a patient or to an audience. The performance is also partly *inadvertent*, or directed towards the space of the working dentist, as might be observed by a dental assistant or another performer on a stage. The space of this presentation exists in another space from that of the image on the screen. It has moved to the body which is performing the presentation. Instead of intersecting with patients' own view of their mouth, this is a view from the 'wrong side'. The space of the screen contains traces of the body operating in the mouth which are below the threshold of intelligibility or recognition.

On the one hand, the alteration of the mouth in its screening and digitisation mobilises the dynamic space of body-image. Merleau-Ponty observes that the recognition of the specular body is as much the recognition of oneself as an object that is seen by others as it is a recognition of oneself (1968: 130–55).[4] Furthermore, he notes that, insofar as it is seen by others, the assumption of a specular body is far from fixed. Instead, it remains a fascination which persists throughout life (1964: 136–39). The mouth on the screen is not immediately recognised, and certainly not as recognisably one's own. It is ambiguously incorporated in being objectified.

At the same time the image on the screen appears to come from nowhere. It is strange to its owner, and it is also not the dentist's view, who sees the mouth from the outside, back to front in a mirror. The image appears as a given, as a product, not a production in which a patient or a dentist has played any part. Somewhere in the choreography, or the transfer of the performance between bodies and in their changing of place, the mouth has been altered. Pleasures and pain have been forgotten, saliva dried up, lips parted with, organs disembodied, extraneous fingertips and tools added, tongues tied down, structures shifted, enlarged and multiplied, tangible connections severed, and aims fixed.

It is easy to miss the production taking place in the self-erasing non-interventionalist gaze, and swallow the ideal of a mouldable, changeable body that is being implied and sold in the presentation. It is more difficult to see that recognition of the body is always in movement and that alteration refers to a body that is constantly shifting beyond interpretation. Instead of having a plasticity in its determination, the body is an indetermination. The series of elective plastic surgery operations devised and undertaken in a fully conscious state by the multi-media artist Orlan helps to make this point more clear.[5] In the progressive changes to Orlan's face, modelled according to a chosen facial characteristic of each of the Renaissance muses, the calculation of the body's propriety is interfered with in an elaborately staged performance that takes place in an operating theatre and is recorded, watched by an audience, and in one instance (the seventh operation, in 1994) transmitted in real time to screens located in New York and Tokyo.

Orlan's performance-art has been addressed from techno-scientific and psychoanalytic perspectives (Armstrong 1995: 53–63; Adams 1996: 141–59), and also in art-historical analyses that address her work as self-portraiture (Moos 1996: 67–73). Orlan's 'self' production is a portraiture that does not have an end in mind such as the enhancement of beauty or restoration of normality (as elective plastic surgery often does), but produces a face that physically alters in conformity with a changing composite image composed of features chosen from paintings of the Mona Lisa, Diana, Psyche, Europa and Venus. I am using Orlan's performances for the purpose of illustration here, as instances that reiterate the difference between the idea of the body as a site of physical transformation and the mobilisation of a dynamic body-image that takes place, for example, in conjunction with the intraoral camera.

At issue for Orlan is the physical assumption of a pre-conceived image and simultaneous failure to become identifiable as it, where that assumption is made in an act of conformity and is also a transformative act. She says of her changing identity: 'The flesh is deceiving . . . it is unnecessary, because the being and the appearance do not co-incide, and this possession is a cause of misunderstanding in all human relations. I have the flesh of an angel, but I am a jackal; the flesh of of a crocodile, but I am a pup . . . the flesh of a woman, but I am a man. I never have the flesh of who I am. There is no exception to the rule because I am never who I am.'[6] While on reflection Orlan's motivation cannot be pinned down, being conscious and articulate during the surgery is an important and disturbing aspect of her performances, which both reproduce and raise anew for inspection the view that intentionality (to act towards, or 'in order to') is the action of a guiding consciousness. The fact that commentators are provoked to question her motivation in electing to undergo such radical surgery without therapeutic or aesthetic benefit is thus precisely the desired effect.[7]

In the screening of surgical transformations whose details and determination are ostensibly the feat of a disembodied clinical gaze, Orlan's work is an act designed to produce an experience along the lines that Felix Guattari describes as follows: 'Performance art delivers the instant to the vertigo of the emergence of Universes that are simultaneously strange and familiar. It has the advantage of drawing out the full implications of this extraction of intensive, a-temporal, a-spatial, a-signifying dimensions from the semiotic net of quotidianity. It shoves our noses up against the genesis of being and forms' (1995: 90). Equally frustrating in Orlan's 'in-your-face' theatre is that the genesis of being and forms is not a conceivable thing. While as viewers we may gape or recoil in horror at the graphic detail of the procedures and the encrypting of the material remains, it is the production of a body over which Orlan and we have no individual control, and of which we have no individual perception, that incorporates us in the performance. The point that I want to emphasise is that an alteration occurs that is different from the physical changes that are seen. Each alteration by surgical intervention involves the body, not just as a physical object – as a bloody pulp under the surgeon's knife or globs of fat embedded in inscribed artefacts of the event that Orlan calls *Reliquaries* – but as the incarnation of a shifting corpus of medical, aesthetic, erotic and social conventions in which we recognise and experience our own and others' bodies as things of propriety and value.

Returning on this point to the non-interventionalist gaze, the alteration of the mouth is a shifting of the corpus of dental conventions which are isomorphic with an imaginary body that it values, and which together comprise the morphology of its ideal object. Its body is neither real nor illusionary, but is interwoven in a constant movement between differentiation and recognition. In the brushing of teeth, in the periodic examinations, in the giving up of sugary foods, one's mouth is being mobilised and brought involuntarily into line with a body that is not entirely one's own. The body of the dentist is the one that is appealed to in television commercials, as an ideal to be achieved with the same toothbrush that four out of five dentists recommend.

Rather than replacing the anatomist's knife with an incisive and eroding language which penetrates the body and delivers up its imperceptible secrets 'live', the non-interventionalist gaze introduces an alien system of determination in the functioning of its parts in such a way that an aim is produced, and that aim is to maintain the system. The implications of plague control in plaque control, fluoridation and regular attendance, along with the implication of disarmed defences in supine dentistry and nitrous oxide sedation, adhere to a social formation which constructs the mouth as a vulnerable focal point of pollution. Small wonder then that today the dentist's body is seen as a source of contagion, not only as a link in the transmission of HIV–AIDS, but in films such as *The Dentist*, which depicts aliens who can only reproduce when placed in the drilled teeth of unsuspecting Earthlings.[8]

While the oral cavity is a space in which patient and dentist are in a system of communication with each other, alteration of the mouth occurs without it even having to be touched. Within the determinations of the clinical gaze, the orifice, whose only motivation is a compulsion to test that each suck, lick, taste, kiss and chew elicits pleasure, comes to acquire the propriety and purposiveness of jaws that are governed by a will. The rationale of controlling the mouth is to safeguard the teeth, which are privileged over all other parts of the body. As the mouth's adherence to a corpus of dental

74

conventions passes from a matter of unconscious identification to an accordance with a law, ethical conduct becomes a dentist's question (Nietzsche 1968: 25). The subordination of the mouth is vital to the alignment of teeth in a body-politic whose integrity, as Nietzsche observes, is maintained by a moral conscience which is transposable between the proper mouth and laws which bite. This correlation is not a summation but a point where the mouth slips away, undone in an averting of the truth or, in Nietzsche's terminology, becoming female (Derrida 1979: 87). The mouth's conformity with certain values – compliance, competence, submission, cleanliness, attractiveness, diligence – is what makes it recognisably part of the body-politic.

Beside the tongue and between the lips and separated rows of teeth, the non-interventionalist gaze is a view aligned with a dental system of the mouth. Along with the shift from orality to morality, the loss of teeth is associated with a degenerate, scarred and impotent body, and incisiveness becomes the index of its integrity. As a source of foment, the mouth and the privileging of orality are associated with pleasures which are dysfunctional, indecisive, perverse, unruly and undermining. Despite all efforts, any fixation of the libidinal currency of orality is always incomplete. The fixation is lost in the traces of the mouth's morphology. In the non-interventionalist gaze, the body does not have the transparency associated with the readable, 'see through' skin of clinical perception. Included with the image is an attitude towards it that is alien to the viewer's perspective. It appears as a stranger, not as an image of one's own mouth. Identifying as the originator of the orifice that has been brought into view is not the effect. The mouth that is communicated in its on-screen performance is shot with ineradicable aversions and presents instead a task of incorporation that is constantly and never done.

NOTES

1. Promotional literature for *AcuCam*™ intraoral camera system, supplied by New Image Industries Pty. Ltd, Sydney.
2. See Mitchell (1992: 14–15, Figs 2.2 and 2.3) for the presentation of a sketch by Leonardo da Vinci of a dissection through the skull and an MRI image of the cranial cavity as examples of 'seeing beneath the skin'.
3. *Insight Intraoral Camera System*, Regional Pty Ltd, Sydney, as advertised in the *Australian Dental Association News Bulletin* 214: 16–17, 1995.

4. Merleau-Ponty's account of the commonality of perception is based on the transitivity of an anonymously given intercorporeality in which he distinguishes the lived body or 'flesh' from the physical body. He argues that the lived body is produced within an elaborate system of correspondences and borrowings that collectively make up a perceptual field. Flesh refers to the body, whose existence must be assumed contingently as the condition for the expression of a point of view. By way of contrast, the physical body is an object of biology, which treats 'the body' as a thematisable object, moving towards an already abstract meaning. (See Vasseleu 1998: 28.)

5. For a fuller description of Orlan's performances see for example Kelly Coyne (1995) and Jane Goodall (1997).

6. Orlan, as quoted by Coyne (1995: 334) from an article by Cynthia Robins in 'An Artist's Changing Face', *San Francisco Examiner*, 4 February, 1994.

7. Jane Goodall comments: 'it is not the effect of the experiment – the evolving look of Orlan – that generates the strongest reactions, but rather the unreadable motivation for her work. Why is she doing this? . . . Motivation in medical experiment is not obscure or complex in comparable ways. "What for?" is not usually a problematic question for a medical scientist, but Orlan problematises it is heavily that it threatens to explode back on those who ask it' (Goodall 1997: 10).

8. *The Dentist*, producer: Mark Borde; director: Tobe Hooper, *Variety* May 15–21, 1995.

REFERENCES

Adams, Parveen (1996) *The Emptiness of the Flesh: Psychoanalysis and Sexual Difference*, London: Routledge.

Armstrong, Rachel (1995) 'Post-Human Evolution' *Artiface* 2: 53–63.

Bryson, Norman (1983) *Vision and Painting: The Logic of the Gaze*, New Haven: Yale University Press.

Coyne, Kelly (1995) 'On Orlan: Interview with Penine Hart', *Felix: A Journal of Media Arts and Communication* 2, 1: 218–27, 330–35.

Derrida, Jacques (1979) *Spurs: Nietzsche's Styles*, trans. Barbara Harlow, Chicago: University of Chicago Press.

Foucault, Michel (1975) *The Birth of the Clinic: An Archaeology of Medical Perception*, trans. A. M. Sheridan, New York: Random House.

Foucault, Michel (1977) *Discipline and Punish: The Birth of the Prison*, trans. Alan Sheridan, Harmondsworth: Penguin Books.

Goodall, Jane (1997) 'Whose Body: Ethics and Experiment in Art', *Artlink* 17, 2: 8–14.

Guattari, Félix (1995) *Chaosmosis: An Ethico-aesthetic Paradigm*, trans. Paul Bains and Julian Pefanis, Sydney: Power Publications.

Harris, R (1947) 'Pain – Its Significance in Dental Practice', *Australian Dental Journal* 19, 11: 595–606.

Levinas, Emmanuel (1990) 'Sensibility', trans. Michel B. Smith, in Galen A. Johnson and Michel B. Smith (eds) *Ontology and Alterity in Merleau-Ponty*, Evanston: Northwestern University Press.

Merleau-Ponty, Maurice (1964) James M. Edie (ed.) *The Primacy of Perception and Other Essays*, Evanston: Northwestern University Press.

Merleau-Ponty, Maurice (1968) *The Visible and the Invisible*, trans. Alphonso Lingis, Evanston: Northwestern University Press.

Mitchell, William J. (1992) *The Reconfigured Eye: Visual Truth in the Post-photographic Era*, Cambridge, Massachusetts: The MIT Press.

Moos, David (1996) 'Memories of Being: Orlan's Theatre of the Self', *Art & Text* 54: 67–73.

Nettleton, Sarah (1992) *Power, Pain and Dentistry*, Buckingham and Philadelphia: Open University Press.

Nietzsche, Friedrich (1968) *Twilight of the Idols/The Anti-Christ*, trans. R. J. Hollingdale: Harmondsworth: Penguin Books.

Vasseleu, Cathryn (1998) *Textures of Light: Vision and Touch in Irigaray, Levinas and Merleau-Ponty* London and New York: Routledge.

5

Pregnancy Ultrasound in Maternal Discourse

LORNA WEIR

INTRODUCTION

ONE AXIS OF POSTSTRUCTURALIST inquiry has been a research problematic concerning the relations between social semiosis and social practice. This problematic has been aimed at social science practices that treat social semiosis as a representation of the real, adding nothing to how the social was put together – a dream of the social without language (Weir 1993). The counterclaim, shared across a wide range of analytical positions in the social sciences from ethnomethodology to systemic functional grammar to genealogical studies, is that language and other forms of semiosis are constitutive of the social rather than a repetition of it. With respect to the human body in particular, poststructuralist work – and notably that of Foucault – maintains that signs are part of how bodies are formed, not optional additions made to corporeality composed in the first instance physically or anatomically, and only secondarily incorporated into systems of representation. Recent feminist work (Duden 1993; Haraway 1997; Kirby 1991; Grosz 1994) has questioned the binary of the real and the representational in interpretations of the human body, with particularly telling impact upon analyses of the effects of contemporary biomedical practices on pregnancy.

In her foetal imagery study Rosalind Petchesky (1987) suggested a distinction between 'public' and 'personal' uses of foetal ultrasound. It is with the latter that I am concerned here, concentrating on women as users of the images given them in routine foetal ultrasonography rather than as readers of mass-media images.[1] Previous studies have focused on meanings given to visual and verbal representations of the foetus in mass media and social movements (Berlant 1994; Condit 1990; Franklin 1991; Ginsburg 1989; Taylor 1992). Feminist commentaries have documented the ways in which foetal imagery has been mobilised as a component of political claims, pervasively constructing prenatal bodies as independent persons, agents, and individuals (Dawson 1991; Franklin 1993; Hartouni 1992; Petchesky 1987; Stabile 1992); a process these texts have understood as a cultural removal of the foetus from the context of pregnancy. The present study explores another domain: the meanings given pregnancy ultrasound in pregnant women's and maternal discursive practices. This work parallels Rayna Rapp's studies (Rapp 1994) of the ways in which women hear genetic counselling information and differentially act on it. Following the work of the photographic theorist Mary Price (1994), the text studies meanings given to images in the context of their uses in social relations. The research project provides an account of social contexts into which women placed sonograms, the key social relations affected and the inscriptive practices of women with respect to ultrasound images, including what/whom they are taken to represent.

The project sketches a set of practices transformative of the imagined body of what has been called historically the 'expected child.' It is also a study of the social attachments made to foetal outside health care, and the ways in which women use foetal ultrasound to change previous meanings of 'baby'. Marilyn Strathern's concept of domain provides a concept for thinking foetal ultrasound as meanings that are both contextually determined and socially mobile. She defines domain as 'the manner in which sets of practices and expertise offer relatively discrete or self-contained ways of contextualizing experience' (Strathern 1993: 145). Interactive, domains constantly borrow from each other, decontextualising and recontextualising items; these are subject to the 'domaining effects' of the particular domain in which they are located. Domains connect and disconnect, but Strathern notes there is no master domain into which they all resolve (Strathern 1993: 134). An example of a domain would be kinship, which, is 'governed by its own conventions and internal structure inviting ramifications' (Strathern 1993: 136). The foetal sonogram does not, therefore, represent a unitary body, but rather one that varies according to the domaining effects of the context in which it is located, signifying quite differently when subject to the domaining effects of kinship than it does within diagnostic medicine.

The research project reported herein is informed by questions about pregnancy, biomedicine and women's bodies: classic questions in the sociology of women's health. Nonetheless, its poststructuralist stance distinguishes it from the central research trajectory in the sociology of health and illness towards policy-relevant health-care reform. The growth of evidence-based medicine and health services research has resulted in new knowledge functions for social science, creating opportunities for the sociology of health and illness to act as a quasi-independent voice in health-care research. The reorganisation of knowledges governing health, such as the growing importance of epidemiology, additionally present a pool of research funds for the social sciences, driving inquiry. With certain important exceptions, the sociology of health and illness has always had an applied cast. This instrumentalisation of social-scientific knowledge comes at the price, however, of restricting research questions and theory to those consonant with biomedical and cultural understandings of the human body as outside history and semiosis.

In contrast, poststructuralist work is not easy to instrumentalise in these ways, given its contestative reading of the human body as material-semiotic and its foregrounding of a critical vocabulary related to discourse practices. This chapter offers no advice on health-care reform and is removed from policy matters, but is nonetheless about fundamental changes taking place in the culture of pregnancy and thus may have diagnostic value for feminist politics.

METHODIC PROCEDURES AND LOCUS OF RESEARCH

From October 1996 to July 1997 I interviewed 51 pregnant women and mothers who had been given foetal sonograms in the course of ultrasound examinations.

Interview participants were recruited through personal and professional networks. Contacts through personal networks (N=17) were two and three times removed from me, none known prior to the interview. Four participants were recruited through a community health centre in rural, Northern Ontario, 8 through two midwifery practices in Southern Ontario and 22 through a midwifery practice in Northern Ontario. Women were contacted and asked if they remembered having been given foetal ultrasound during a current or past pregnancy; if they remembered this having happened, an interview was requested. The place of interview was chosen at the participant's convenience, with 28 occurring in participants' homes, 10 by telephone, 9 at a midwifery clinic, 3 at their places of paid work, and 1 in a restaurant. The interviews, which were semi-structured and lasted between 25 and 45 minutes, were all done by the author. Participant ages at the time of interview ranged from 20 to 49 years.

One aim of the project is descriptive: to document an area that has not previously been investigated. The study asked what women do with the foetal sonograms given them in ultrasound clinics: to whom are they shown; what are the social contexts of viewing; to what extent is the sharing of the sonogram an occasion of speech, and on what topics; where are the sonograms placed during and after the pregnancy, what are the sonograms taken to represent? These questions provide an account of how foetal sonograms circulate and investigate their activity in forming relational ties. The inquiries about the places sonograms are kept and the kinds of discussion they precipitate were intended to provide an account of how they were being read as representations, both what kind of signifying practice they were classed as being, and what they signified. The report also draws on observational research done in two Northern Ontario prenatal ultrasound clinics, one a private clinic providing diagnostic services and the second a non-teaching, general hospital.[2]

Pregnant Canadian women in prenatal care receive on average three to four ultrasound examinations. Prenatal ultrasound examinations are funded through the public health-care system, and thus access is available to all Canadian citizens and landed immigrants, a fact that carries the consequence that access is not class-stratified, although North–South regional distinctions do exist, the North being sparsely populated over large land areas with consequent problems in health service delivery. Prior to June 1997, the sonogram prints were given free of charge to women, but a Ministry of Health guideline issued at that date required patients pay a fee for the sonograms, the standard amount being $5.00 (Can),[3] although the fee had been unevenly implemented at the time the research was being concluded.

Sonograms are not given to pregnant women at the conclusion of every prenatal scan. Women known to be seeking an abortion are not supplied with a sonogram print. The practice of supplying sonograms for personal use is commonly associated with routine scans where the expectation is that the pregnancy will be carried to term and where there are no problematic findings. Physicians and technicians print copies for personal use when an image recognisable as a human body can be figured. When ultrasound exams are performed at an early gestational age, women are often not given a sonogram, since the image cannot picture limbs or a head due to both technical limitations of ultrasound and to the appearance of the foetus at mid-first trimester. When a scan has been ordered for specific indications, that is, where the procedure is not routine, or where there has been a 'positive' finding – ie an indication of foetal disorder – health-care providers frequently elect not to give women copies, although, in cases where the results are negative and will be welcomed by the patient, sonograms are supplied.[4] Due to the number of scans pregnant women undergo, they are likely to be given a sonogram print at one of the scans, and some women have collections of sonograms from several exams.

The health-care providers in the two clinics in which I did research, and the Northern midwifery practice which referred potential interview participants to me, expressed ambivalence about the medical aspects of prenatal ultrasound (Weir 1998). Personnel at ultrasound clinics mentioned that the section of the scan in which they explained the image on the screen was time consuming and they were sometimes placed in difficult positions when positive findings occurred during routine testing. Clinic personnel made a distinction between 'medical' and 'non-medical' aspects of the procedure, sometimes calling these 'entertainment' ultrasounds (a standard phrase in ultrasonography – see The American Registry of Diagnostic Medical Ultrasonographers 1994), and mentioned problems related to patients' demands for high-quality videotapes. The spectacle of entertainment ultrasound had limited appeal for health-care personnel. These reports are consonant with the results of one study that reported American women stating that, in cases of healthy pregnancies, half the importance of ultrasound for them was non-medical: knowing foetal sex and having a picture prior to birth (Berwick and Weinstein 1985). In an unproblematised way, ultrasonography operates through the formation of desire in women, not through coercion of the reluctant. Nonetheless, placed in the wider context of a project to govern pregnancy liberally, that is, according to women's freedom, ultrasound has the character of 'government at a distance': networks of agents that are socially, temporally and spatially dispersed, and that rely upon each other 'because they have come to construe their problems in allied ways and their fate as in some way bound up with one another' (Miller and Rose 1990: 10). The meanings of pregnancy ultrasound to health-care providers and to pregnant women are not identical (Weir 1998), but women in the study reported herein have come to regard ultrasound as a way of achieving their ends, some of which are about governing the self in conformity with the goal of health, and others of which – such as a desire to see 'my baby' – exceed health government.

FOETAL SONOGRAM AS SIGN OF 'MY BABY' DURING PREGNANCY

Given that pregnancy in the Canadian context has been incorporated within health government, pregnancy ultrasound might well be expected to be productive of new forms of knowledge. As Foucault aptly remarked, truth regimes – forms of discourse that attach statements about truth to relations of power – constitute 'new objects of knowledge and accumulate new bodies of information' (1980: 51). Nevertheless, Daker and Bobrow's (1995) review of the medical and social science literatures on diagnostic ultrasound noted that women's reactions to ultrasonography had not received much attention. In addition to the feminist literature focused on state, social movement and mass-media discourse, there is a small social science literature on pregnant women's attitudes towards prenatal ultrasonography (Berwick and Weinstein 1986; Hyde 1986; Tymstra et al. 1991), and an earlier literature on ultrasound as a facilitator of maternal–foetal 'bonding' (Fletcher and Evans 1983; Kemp and Page 1987; Reading 1982). The research reported herein links with the findings of previous studies (Hyde 1986) that report women who have undergone foetal ultrasound experience a confirmation of the reality of the 'baby' prior to foetal movement. Milne and Rich's exploratory study exceeded the bounds of the 'bonding' literature to which it was a contribution in showing that pregnant women viewing foetal sonograms formed personalised mental images of 'their babies in utero' (Milne and Rich 1981:34), which were elaborated in fantasy: what Milne and Rich termed a 'gestalt' of cognition, emotion and touch sense.

There is a general incitement to read foetal sonograms as baby pictures; the research literature and clinical practice facilitate that incitement rather than standing outside it. Mitchell and Georges's (1997) recent comparative study of Canadian and Greek diagnostic ultrasound clinics contains documentation of the interactions among clinic personnel, patients and their supporters during Canadian prenatal scans, demonstrating how clinic personnel read foetal imagery as 'baby pictures' and speak to patients in these terms. The Mitchell and Georges's study is part of a broader research problematic in contemporary anthropology that is investigating scientific knowledge and social relations, with a subset of studies exploring the ways in which Euroamerican kinship patterns are being changed in interaction with late twentieth-century biomedicine (Conklin and Morgan 1996; Edwards et al. 1993; Franklin 1997; Morgan 1989; Strathern 1992b). Sarah Franklin (1993) has argued that the embryo was positioned as a kinship member during British parliamentary debates on the Human Fertilisation and Embryology Act. Lynn Morgan (1989 and 1996) has argued that, in the United States, the historical conflation of 'biological' and social birth is currently being taken apart, with social birth increasingly socially placed before labour in childbirth. The present study pursues this problematic in its concern with the domaining effects of kinship on foetal sonograms.

When the interview participants spoke of what the foetal sonograms and clinical imagery represented, each woman referred to it at some point as a baby, and not an abstract baby found in anatomy text books, but rather '*my* baby', or, less frequently, 'child', 'little person', 'human being', 'human body'. They spoke of the sonogram and the images on the clinic monitor as 'proof, 'evidence', 'verification', a 'reality check', not that they were pregnant, but that, 'This is like a human body inside you' (D. G., 29 November 1996). The interview participants reported being excited by the sonogram images, enjoying the detail of the visuals in the clinic or by themselves later:

B. H.: Well, I guess, there is a bit of a sense of awe, you know, because you, you know, when you're carrying this baby around inside you, it's sort of abstract, it, you know, you know, your belly gets bigger and you know that there's a baby moving around inside, you're not sure where the arms or legs or anything is, or what it looks like, or you, what form it's taking, or anything. You can feel it kicking, but, you know, but this is the first time you actually see, like a body and with arms and legs and bones and. You know. So it sort of makes it more real, more like a person, and helps you sort of visualise more what the outcome of your pregnancy is going to be, that it's actually a person, you know. (3 July 1997)

LW: Why did you want the picture so much?
DM: I don't know. It's a symbol of something, you know. You can see it; they label it: the head, the hand, the heart. You can see it in there, and when it's in your stomach, you know, I couldn't even feel him in there, and sometimes it felt like I wasn't even pregnant. (24 November 1996)

D. G.: I think it means that our pregnancy is actually more real, like its actually not just a bunch of bumps and kicks I'm getting in my stomach. There is something that is an actual human being inside. (29 November 1996)

The reality of the pregnancy is being confirmed for these women by a scopic economy in which reality takes a specific visual form filled with the recognisable features of human bodies: heads and noses, fingers and spines.

The foetal sonograms taken home for personal use meet with varying degrees of interest partially dependent on how satisfactory an image of a human body can be rendered from their shadows. Sonograms taken early in the first trimester may be experienced as a rather uninteresting 'blob' as one woman referred to a sonogram of a 7-week embryo, or, in the case of a woman with a history of miscarriages who was examined at 7.5 weeks gestation, a joyful, much-wanted 'little shrimp'. Interview participants tended to engage less with foetal sonograms taken later in pregnancy, when the limitations of the technique make imaging the foetal body as a whole more difficult, resulting rather in close-ups to specific parts of the body:

M.G.: I understood what the picture looked like. I saw a human being, you know. But I had more than one [scan] too, but after we got further on I couldn't read it at all. So then I wasn't really that interested in it. (8 October 1996)

Another woman discarded a foetal sonogram at 32 weeks' gestation because, 'It wasn't discernible as a baby' (P. H., 23 April 1997).

Foetal sonograms were used by the interview participants to form a complex visual image of their bodily interiors during pregnancy. The image had the visual characteristics of a baby in this culture, with a body, head, limbs, hands, feet, and some internal organs and bone structure. Configuring the sonogram as the sign of a human, specifically baby's, body inserts the reading into a particular set of cultural equivalences, analysed by Marilyn Strathern: 'Culturally speaking, we can see the person when the person appears as an individual, and we can see an individual when we see a body ' (Strathern 1992a: 50). In the passages quoted above, the interview participants, all of whom had made decisions to accept the pregnancy and not seek an abortion,[5] read body-person-individual as a set of synonyms. However, the moment of interpreting the sonogram as a human body is also the moment of its transformation into 'my baby'; the image becomes a point for initiating relational ties, as I will later outline.

Several women with more than one child reported foetal sonograms enabled them to focus on the fact that a new family member would shortly be arriving in their hectic lives. They configure the sonogram as representing a baby in a sequence of existing children:

C.S.: I don't feel like oh-oh the baby's on its way, my whole life is going to change again. I'm going back to diapers and bottles you know. So when I see the pictures, like, mm-hmm: you know, this is going to be small, this is not going to get up and make toast in the morning for itself ready for school like my eleven-year-old does. So that kind of reality check sets in when I see it. (26 June 1997)

C.C.: It made us focus a little more on the fact that we're having another one, you know. Yeah. It was just nice. (6 June 1997)

Foetal sonograms were not read by the participants as a generic representation of a foetus at a particular stage of development, but rather as representing a specific baby, 'my baby'. The particular baby is recognised as going through developmental stages in utero, but these embryological processes are subordinated to an interpretation of the sonogram as a portrait of a specific 'little person', after the convention of personal photography. In this regard, one interview participant reported that, after she had shown one of her first sonograms to a colleague who pronounced it to look like all ultrasounds, she showed it only among family members because, 'To me, it would probably not look like all ultrasounds; it was my baby, you know' (L. S., 17 June 1997). The ultrasound examination is conceptualised as an opportunity to 'see the baby' for the first time, as a woman recalling being pregnant with her second baby remembered: 'I looked, really looked forward to it. I couldn't wait for the eighteenth week to come, to go in and see this baby, you know. To me it was like seeing the baby' (P. L., 17 October 1996).

Personal and clinic viewings of foetal sonograms introduce a new image and new interpretive schema into pregnancy. The sonograms do not displace any prior local, maternal uses of images related to what was once called the expected child. Depictions of foetal development based on anatomical specimens have long been located in morphological embryology (Duden 1993; Jordanova 1989; Newman 1996), but this was not taken up as a photographic or visual practice by pregnant women. The signified of the foetal sonogram is neither the foetus of morphological embryology nor the earlier tiny adult of the Soranian tradition of foetal illustration used from the thirteenth to late seventeenth centuries (Newman 1996). Nor is the signified a toddler or six-month-old baby found in pregnant women's dream imagery (Gilman 1968). The viewing conventions of the interview participants read foetal sonograms as individuated, personalised portraits of 'my baby'. Indeed, far from providing a visual reading open to interpretation, the image becomes a fixed reality.

The relation between women's self-perceptions of their bodies during pregnancy and their constructions of what the foetal sonograms signified showed considerable variation. Contrast, for instance, the following two passages, the first by a woman who was not pregnant at the time of the interview, but had kept foetal sonograms of two children, and the second pregnant with her first child:

K.O.: I don't know who they are yet. So to me these pictures aren't as important to me, say, as the pictures I have of them now. I look at these pictures and I say, well, that's to be Anna, and that's to be Kyle, but I had no idea that was them at the time. I think it's more astonishing not so much as a picture, but the fact that you made this, and this is part of you, and this is living inside you, and this is to be your child, rather than the fact of you carrying around the picture and you saying, 'Oh! This is the eyes, and this . . .' – you know. I think it's just the meaning of the whole thing that's important to me, anyways, than the picture. I wouldn't carry around the picture and say this is my son or daughter. I'd just say this is part of me, isn't this amazing. (2 December 1996)

LW: What did you think about, or how did you feel [looking at the foetal sonogram at the bedside table]?
A.F.: Amazed. Overwhelmed.
LW: By?
AF: The fact that it's a picture of what's inside me, that this is my baby, this is my baby's spine, my baby has hands, little face. That's actually inside me. Very overwhelming. Excited.
LW: Is it also a picture of something that's happening to you?
AF: No. No. Just my baby. (7 June 1997)

These two passages pose the subject of foetal sonograms in different ways. The first passage constructs a part–whole relation between the foetal body and the pregnant woman's own body: 'This is part of me.' The woman understands her body as agentic, the sonograms as a representation of her agency. The second text treats the foetal sonogram as a representation of an entity paradoxically inside her, but not part of her. In the first text, the speaker understands the sonograms as representing the precursors of her children: 'That's to be Anna, that's to be Kyle'. Viewing the sonograms in her baby's albums while speaking, she makes a distinction between their social birth as named persons and their in-utero representations, which are not yet her children.

Under conditions where foetal sex may be known during pregnancy through ultrasonography and/or amniocentesis, the social possibility is created for prospective parents to confer proper names prior to birth, thus reversing the cultural practice of waiting until after birth. When the expected child is given a proper name prior to birth, the foetal sonogram is employed as a representation of a named baby. This practice lends support to an argument that 'expected children' are being incorporated as kin members in association with ultrasound scans in pregnancy. Nonetheless, the interviews show that conferring personal names prior to birth as a result of diagnostic knowledge is, at least at this point, still a minority practice. Moreover, the emerging patterns are complex, with personal names given, but not used, and in some cases, simply not given, until after childbirth. Many women reported refusing the information about foetal sex when it was offered;[6] others wished to have the information, but the technician was unable to determine foetal sex. In one case, the pregnant woman did not want to know the foetal sex, but, with her consent, her partner was told; he adopted the strategy of alternating 'he' and 'she' when referring to the expected child.[7]

Of the 51 interview participants, 8 were told foetal sex prior to birth as a result of diagnostic testing. They acted on the information in very different ways, with six naming the expected child prior to birth. One woman, believing the information insufficiently reliable, neither conferred a proper name nor used gender-differentiated personal deictics (he or she; her or him, and so on). Lastly, one participant waited until after her labour before conferring a personal name, but modified her speech practices to conform to the diagnosed foetal sex. And of the six women who named their children before childbirth, only 3 referred to the expected child by personal name, the remaining 3 reserving its use until after birth. One woman, as a practising Jew, observed the religious prohibition against naming, obtaining clothes or preparing a place for the expected child until after birth. Thus, while for all participants the foetal sonogram was a representation of 'my baby', it was only a minority of the participants that used foetal sonograms as a representation of a baby with a personal name.

The interview participants show an intense interest in foetal sonograms, bearing out Barbara Duden's remark that, 'Women of my generation look at their insides with medical optics that create scientific facts' (Duden 1993: 81). Perhaps more precisely, interview participants viewed their insides through the lens of kin relations, rather than the lens of medicine, and saw 'my baby'. Long prior to the development of foetal ultrasound pregnant women had complex fantasies about the appearance, temperament and communicativeness of the foetus in utero (Gélis 1991; Stainton 1985; Wilson 1992). They did not, however, possess clinical representations that they took to be portraits of 'my baby' in utero.

FOETAL SONOGRAM AS A SIGN
OF THE FOETUS

Under particular conditions, interview participants sometimes read the foetal sonogram as a representation of a foetus rather than a baby. I deal here with foetal sonograms as representations of 'the foetus' so as to avoid colluding with an understanding of prenatal ultrasound as a bearer of reassurance, security and happiness, leaving unmentioned the anxiety and fear which attach to the foetus. As Robert Castel (1991) and Abby Lippman (1991) have emphasised, security and fear are alternate registers, integrally connected in the contemporary government of pregnancy.

The interview participants would refer to the foetus in several contexts, particularly those involving fears for the health of their babies, whether in cases of 'false positives' from screening tests or foetal demise. In four cases of false positives from maternal serum screening, women used 'foetus' in the transcripts to refer to the period between the screening test results and the amniocentesis report, referring to 'baby' before and after that period. This pattern is consistent with the findings of Barbara Katz Rothman (1986), who has argued that 'foetus' is a 'language of abortion' used during the weeks awaiting the results of amniocentesis, a time when having a 'baby' is no longer assured, an interval Rothman called 'the tentative pregnancy'. Interview participants also attached 'foetus' to the sonograms in cases of actual or potential miscarriage and maternal illness.

The sample also contained examples of women who under these same conditions of false positives, maternal illness and potential miscarriage, did not use 'foetus' during the interview and reported not using it at any point during pregnancy. Under virtually identical diagnostic knowledge pregnant women may attach very different meanings to foetal sonograms, which may come to signify 'baby' or 'foetus'.

In situations where the health of the expected child was potentially or actually in jeopardy, the women treated the foetal sonograms in quite distinctive ways, sometimes, either by themselves or with the partners/parents, looking at the image with great intensity to find evidence that would confirm or disconfirm the test results or diagnosis. Women also responded by distancing themselves from the image, with three women losing or throwing out their sonograms, and another leaving it under a placemat, still there eighteen months after childbirth – a reversal of cultural practices that treat foetal sonograms as precious objects to be preserved. For these women, the sonogram became a representation of potential loss: 'All we really got was a really clear picture of what perhaps we were going to lose. Which was pretty startling' (L. R.: 17 June 1997). One woman and her partner continued to look at the sonogram after the birth of a son with Down's Syndrome, a condition that had not been diagnosed prenatally:

J. T.: Yeah, we probably re-examined things to look for any signs, you know. And I suppose that at one level emotionally, you know, you think back to a time of innocence, of not knowing that there's a problem. (18 June 1997)

The interview participants reported calling the foetal sonogram 'the foetus' when describing it in terms of stages of embryological development, citing books or health-care providers as the source of this term. 'Foetus' operates as an abstract, biomedical term contrastive with 'baby':

M. W.: A foetus could be anybody's fetus, it's not my baby. (10 June 1997)

M.W.: I think it would be when I was being more descriptive about what's happening, in an objective way, about the development of the foetus or whatever . . . If I was referring to the picture, I would, I would start out, 'my baby' and then I would talk about 'the foetus' – if I was explaining the picture to people, I would refer to it as a 'foetus' in a broader sense of what they were looking at. (15 June 1997)

A distinction is thus made by interview participants between the abstraction and generality of the foetus, in contrast to the relationality and particularity of the baby. What they seem to indicate are differential regimes of knowledge: on the one hand that of biomedical science which has the force of 'objective' social authority, and on the other, the 'personal' experience of motherhood.

FOETAL SONOGRAM AS SIGN OF A FAMILY MEMBER

It is a culturally established practice to share personal photographs with people unacquainted with those represented in the pictures – a kind of introduction in the absence of the represented person. The showing of foetal sonograms to friends and relatives is part of this practice, although with a medical intertext as a personal photograph and the image of an entity not yet born. The interview participants put the foetal sonograms into discourse as attachment practices. Foetal sonograms are used during pregnancy to form relational ties with the expected child before birth, mainly, though by no means exclusively, among core kin members. With the exception of seven women who reported showing the sonograms to strangers, the majority of the sonograms were shown to family members.

The first people to see the images were those in the ultrasound examining room with the pregnant woman. Of the 51 women participants, 40 reported being accompanied by their partners for at least one scan. Less frequently, women stated they had been joined by daughters (5), sisters (4), mothers-in-law (3), sons (3), friends (3), grandmothers (2), and fathers-in-law (1). Because women frequently had their scans during worktime, many returned to their places of paid employment afterwards, and often elected to share the sonograms with their co-workers. Twenty-three women reported they did this, and 17 said their husbands had done so at their own work sites. The photos were shown to friends in the workplace and to those pregnant or having young children. Participants remembered sharing the sonograms with a restricted range of kin members, most commonly with maternal mother (33), maternal father (24), sister (20), husband's father (19), husband's sisters and husband's mother (10). This pattern was repeated among the 8 participants

91

who had photocopies or facsimiles of the sonograms; the copies
were sent to their own or their partner's parents, brothers and sisters
living at a distance. One woman refused to let her husband programme the sonogram to run as a screen saver on his computer:
'It's more of a personal thing and I didn't want it just sitting in my
computer' (K. A., 22 April 1997).

In several cases, the sonogram functioned as a way of announc-
ing the pregnancy for the first time; this was possible only where
ultrasound imagery is a culturally acceptable/available knowledge.
Thus, a Lugbara-speaking participant, whose kin remained in
Ghana, reported neither sharing nor mentioning the foetal sonogram since, first, it 'would make no sense' given the absence of
prenatal ultrasound in her region of Ghana and, second, Lugbara
women do not talk about being pregnant. This contrasted with
what she felt was a general incitement in Canada for pregnant
women to constantly speak about their pregnancies.

The showing of foetal sonograms was part of an incorporative
kin practice: introducing family members to a new kin member.
Asked why they chose to show the sonogram to family members,
women responded:

E. R: I think it was really normal that I showed it to them, because,
well, I felt like I was showing them this little person who was going to
be part of our family soon. (24 November 1996)

S. H.: And we said, 'We have a surprise for you! [to father-in-law]. And
we showed him the picture. And he didn't know, so we just kind of
used it as a, 'Surprise! You're having another grandchild!' thing. (26
April 1997)

S. J.: And it's that whole awakening of there's a baby in there – Oh my
god! – tell all these people in my family, you know. Like you know, but
you don't know, and then sort of show them the picture and it makes
it all real for everybody I think. But it was a private thing for me, like
I said, I feel like the people I showed it to was select, and it wasn't
something I would show to someone on a bus, you know, like if you
were carrying photos of your children. (17 June 1997)

D. M.: I rushed to Mom to show her. It's her first grandchild too. It
was just becoming more and more real.

The passages indicates that the showing of the picture operates as
a means of establishing a relational tie between 'the baby' and what
is or will be her or his grandparents. The participants sometimes
place the tie in the future, and other times locate it in the present.

The practice of showing the sonogram is meant to incorporate 'the baby' as a family member, part of core kin, with the timing of the entry into group membership varying: either before or after birth.

Sharing foetal sonograms occasions conventional topics of conversation: orientation to reading the picture as a baby's body together with speculations about 'family resemblances' and sex. It also provides a kind of prompt for 'baby talk', a range of discussion topics dealing with feelings and preparations for a new baby. Interview participants transfer the interpretive schema they learned in the clinic to other kin members, explaining the markings on the sonogram as parts of a human body – the leg, the head, nose, eyes, hand and so forth. (These are often computer labelled on the sonogram by the clinic technician.) The viewers are thus enabled to share in an authoritative discourse on how to view the sonogram as an image of a human body, moreover, the body of a kin member. After the viewers have learned the skill of reading the image as human, the interview participants reported speculation about family resemblances and foetal sex – a common but not universal practice among the interview participants and the sonogram viewers.

In the face of the authoritative and productive power of both biomedical and maternal discourse in fixing the social reality of the image, there were nevertheless, signs of variation. Many of the interview participants had ironic, even jaundiced, views about showing the sonograms to other viewers, a perspective that contrasted with the sentimentalised readings of other participants. Three participants were reluctant to share the images since, as one stated, 'I sort of thought of them as, like being forced to sit through someone else's vacation slides' (J. T., 18 June 1997). Another saw the sonograms as an opportunity to wrest attention from those whose sonograms she had already seen: .

C. W.: Hey, they're first baby pictures. We get to get our own back – everybody else has had kids. We've looked at a million pictures. (25 June 1997)

Several participants referred to the image as skeletal or looking like an 'alien'. The woman quoted immediately above had become sufficiently at ease with foetal sonograms that the imagery held no terrors:

LW: What did you show them?

C. W.: Oh, just pointing out body parts mostly: 'Oh look! There's a back.' 'Mmm, nice Darth Vader shot! I got a cross-cut of a skull or something – it looks really exciting.' (25 June 1997)

Some women were quite dismissive of remarks about family resemblances as 'silly remarks . . . Because there's not very much you can say, because you cannot see very much' (L. L., 9 June 1997). Equally, those shown the foetal sonograms entertained themselves and their listeners with clearly counterfactual statements about sex and family resemblances, a send-up of conventional conversational topics.

The foetal sonograms were located in the range of places typical of personal photographs: refrigerator doors,[8] wallets, daily agendas, journals, lockets, purses, drawers and countertops, where they might remain easily accessible throughout pregnancy. One woman placed a sonogram among the images in her Buddhist shrine at home, using it for meditation. The final locus of the sonograms was in the baby or family album. Of the 51 interview participants, 44 stated that they either had placed or were going to place the sonograms in photo albums. Foetal sonograms have entered the realm of family photography, incorporated as baby pictures. Within baby albums the placement of sonograms clearly varies a great deal, although due to logistic constraints, I was only able to view 17 albums, and thus the following comments are more diagnostic than systematic.

Baby albums differ among each other in format, with some containing clear instructions about where to place a foetal sonogram, others not specifying any place, and yet others being keepsake albums that assign places for cards, hospital identification bracelets, hair samples and other memorabilia. One baby album has a heading on the inside cover that reads 'My First Photo', with a heading two pages later, 'I Was Born;' the distinction indicating that the first picture is expected to occur before birth. Other albums are directive: 'Place sonogram here' (*A Star Is Born* 1995: unpaginated). Where no place for a sonogram existed in a photo album that had a constrained format with printed headings and subtitles, several informants fixed the sonogram to the inside front cover. Others preferred albums in which they could make their own decisions about the selection and sequencing of images and other memorabilia. The resulting image sequences evidenced considerable variation, with some women choosing the foetal sonograms as the initial image, others locating the sonogram(s) on the same page as images of pregnancy, and some affixing the sonogram(s) to the same page as the first picture of mother holding her child, and two rejecting the inclusion of sonograms altogether. Including or excluding foetal sonograms from photograph albums, placing the sonogram in a metonymic series of pictured events that signify its relation to pregnancy and the maternal body, visualising the time and point of entry of a new member into a kin unit: these are all local, variable practices worked out in prosaic decisions about family albums.

When interview participants who had given birth spoke of the sonograms in the baby or family albums, they constructed them retrospectively as images of named persons with whom they had the relation of mother. These were images of 'Emily' and 'Paul' – daughters and sons. Whereas up to about ten years ago, the threshold of entry into the baby or family album occurred at or after birth, these images shift the threshold to a point before birth. The foetal sonogram, reconfigured as a family photograph, becomes the sign of a named kin member. Because baby albums configure the baby in a sequence of developmental stages, both the time of the baby and the social identity of the baby have been reconfigured in baby albums to begin before birth. Moreover, the coding of the foetal sonogram as baby picture adds a new image to the standard repertoire of images found in personal photography.

The placing of foetal sonograms among family photographs subjects the medical image to the domaining effects of kinship. Here the effect is one that Strathern calls 'substitution', where an entity from one domain is linked to another domain such that, 'a different order of knowledge is introduced' (Strathern 1992a: 73) into the recipient domain. The foetal sonogram introduces culturally new, individualised in-utero images to the kin domain, which then are subjected to the reading strategies appropriate to kin representations: portraits of a kin member circulated among kin networks and placed in the standard loci of familial representations. The process of incorporating foetal sonograms into family photography changes the conventions of representing babies: kin representations are changed by the transmogrification of the medical image, and the medical image is changed by being made subject to the domaining effects of kinship. Neither is stable, but always in a process of (re)construction.

CONCLUSION

The empirical research presented here about the personal uses of foetal sonograms has shown that pregnant women and mothers located the images in the kin domain. The sonograms thus became subject to the domaining effects of kinship, where they were interpreted as representations of 'my baby': individualised bodies one generation descendant from the maternal body. In contrast, when considered under the aspect of positive diagnostic or screening results or interpreted in light of embryological development, 'my/ the baby' became 'the foetus', an entity that does not enter into kin relations in the discourse practices of my informants. By incorporating foetal sonograms as representations of kin members, the interview participants changed the conventions of representing new kin members from after birth to before birth. The sonograms were used to form relational ties with core kin and incorporated into the repertoire of family photography.

This study has examined foetal sonograms within women's discourse practices and the sonogram as a sign given to variant meanings and bodies. The text has described cultural changes in the representations of babies and the earliest stages of becoming a kin member. Such an analysis of images and kinship, babies and representation falls outside the usual parameters of health-systems research. It is, however, in poststructuralist terms, a quite conventional way of framing research questions and results, which rejects the distinction between semiosis and practice. More specifically the process by which foetal sonograms are put into circulation is illustrative of the way in which discursive mechanisms may simultaneously, as Foucault put it, 'produce knowledge, multiply discourse, induce pleasure, and generate power' (1979: 73).

While the project may have potential instrumental uses, there are limitations to an applied sociology of health and illness tied directly to state and health system relevances. Many of the fundamental changes relating to contemporary pregnancy, indeed to organic bodies, fall outside that frame. In order to undertake the present study, it was necessary to take a critical distance from a number of culturally specific interpretations of the human body as the signifier of an individuality that exists prior to relationships (Strathern 1992a: 65), for this would simply reproduce the participants' knowledge rather than understand it. Pragmatists, feminist and non-feminist, who wish to shape health policy and provision often find such problematisations annoying, assuming that the constructive thing to do is simply to take the autonomous, individual body as given prior to signification, and to get on with the practical business of counting these discrete units and doing right by them. This discrediting attitude to the study of discourse practices breaks down as an explanatory strategy, however, at those points when the rules for how bodies signify, indeed how to recognise a human body, are subject to social change. Such is the case with procreation, pregnancy and childbirth today.

The line of investigation in this chapter has focused on the ways in which kin represent themselves to each other, in changing conceptions of family as a kin unit, in new ways of visualising babies. These are sociologically interesting questions. Moreover, given the use of foetal sonograms in political struggles related to the government of pregnancy, the topic of how women signify foetal sonograms is of particular feminist interest. The negotiated effects of quickly changing biomedical truth regimes on the gendered body suggest that the analysis of discursive practices must not be sidelined. In materialist-feminist terms, the results of the descriptive study reported here may constitute difficult knowledge, but ignorance makes for political vulnerability at a time of rapid change in the culture of pregnancy.

Acknowledgements

An earlier version of this paper was given to the Department of Sociology and Women's Studies at Lancaster University, England. Many thanks to Sarah Franklin, Maureen McNeil and Bev Skeggs for their critical comments. I am grateful to Holliday Tyson for her editorial suggestions and to Megan Butcher for her immense labours in transcribing interview tapes.

NOTES

1. On the distinction, both theoretical and methodological, between studying photography through looking at uses rather than readings, see the photographic theorist Mary Price 1994.
2. Research involving clinic and maternal distinctions in the social classification of foetus and baby is forthcoming (Weir 1998).
3. In some Ontario clinics videotapes of the scans were also available to patients one to two weeks after the examination had occurred. The custom in this case has been to charge a fee for the tapes, varying from $10.00 to $15.00 (Can).
4. In cases where unanticipated findings of a serious nature occurred during routine scans, technicians are placed in a difficult position since they are not legally permitted to share the information with the patient. Other routine diagnostic procedures may result in positive findings known to the technician or physician, but not the patient;

however, the interaction with the patient is particularly acute in foetal ultrasound because it is the only diagnostic procedure that has a standardised explanatory component, where personal supporters accompanying the patient expect to be invited into the examining room, and where diagnostic images are routinely given to patients. Breaking with these conventions is then a violation of the patient's expectations, and difficult for patients, their supporters and health-care providers to handle.

5. It is clinic practice to withhold foetal sonograms from women seeking abortions or those having miscarriages.
6. Certain Ontario clinics have policies against revealing foetal sex except when it is medically relevant. Others volunteer the information or provide it on request.
7. Her partner confirmed this information. Both the interview participant and her partner wished that he be present at the interview, with the understanding that he was not being asked questions.
8. In North America refrigerators are about 6 feet tall, with a considerable portion at the top being at eye level for most people. The top half of the refrigerator has come to be used as a locus for shopping lists, postcards, recycling pickup days and photographs – assorted friendly debris.

REFERENCES

The American Registry of Diagnostic Medical Ultrasonographers (1994) 'Board Developments Position Statement on Entertainment Fetal Videotaping', in *Registry Report* 12 (3): 1.

Berlant, Lauren (1994) 'America, 'Fat', the Fetus' *Boundary* 2 (21): 145–95.

Berwick, D. M. and Weinstein, M. C. (1985) 'What Do patients Value? Willingness to Pay for Ultrasound in Normal Pregnancy', *Medical Care* 23: 881–93.

Castel, Robert (1991) 'From Dangerousness to Risk' in Graham Burchell, Colin Gordon and Peter Miller (eds) *The Foucault Effect*, Chicago: University of Chicago Press, 281–98.

Condit, Celeste Michelle (1990) *Decoding Abortion Rhetoric*, Urbana and Chicago: University of Illinois Press.

Conklin, Beth A. and Morgan, Lynn M. (1996) 'Babies, Bodies and the Production of Personhood in North American and Native Amazonian Society', *Ethos* 24(4): 657–69.

Daker, Michael and Bobrow, Martin (1995) 'Ultrasound in Pregnancy' in Murray Enkin, Marc Keirse, Mary Renfrew (eds) *Effective Care in Pregnancy and Childbirth*, Oxford: Oxford University Press.

Dawson, Brettel (1991) 'A Feminist Response to "Unborn Child Abuse:

Contemplating a Legal Solution"', *Canadian Journal of Family Law* 9: 157–76.

Duden, Barbara (1993) *Disembodying Women: Perspectives on Pregnancy and the Unborn*, Cambridge, Mass: Harvard UP.

Edwards, Jeanette, Franklin, Sarah, Hirsch, Eric, Price, Frances and Strathern, Marilyn (1993) *Technologies of Procreation*, Manchester: Manchester University Press.

Fletcher, John C. and Evans, Mark I. (1983) 'Maternal Bonding in Early Fetal Ultrasound Examinations', *The New England Journal Of Medicine* 13 February 13: 392–3.

Foucault, Michel (1979) *History of Sexuality, Vol. 1*, London: Penguin.

Foucault, Michel (1980) *Power/Knowledge*, ed. Colin Gordon, London: Harvester Wheatsheaf.

Franklin, Sarah (1991) 'Fetal Fascinations: New Dimensions to the Medical-Scientific Construction of Fetal Personhood' in S. Franklin, C. Lury and J. Stacey (eds), *Off-Centre: Feminism and Cultural Studies*, London: HarperCollins, pp. 190–206.

Franklin, Sarah (1993) 'Making Representations: Parliamentary Debate of the Human Fertilisation and Embryology Bill' in Jeanette Edwards, Sarah Franklin, Eric Hirsch, Frances Price and Marilyn Strathern, *Technologies of Procreation*, Manchester: Manchester University Press; pp. 96–131.

Franklin, Sarah (1997) *Embodied Progress: A Cultural Account of Assisted Conception*, London: Routledge.

Gélis, Jacques (1991) *History of Childbirth: Fertility, Pregnancy and Birth in Early Modern Europe*, Cambridge: Polity.

Gilman, R (1968) 'The Dreams of Pregnancy: Women and Maternal Adaptation' *American Journal of Orthopsychiatry* 38: 688–92.

Ginsburg, Faye (1989) *Contested Lives: The Abortion Debate in an American Community*, Berkeley: University of California Press.

Grosz, Elizabeth (1994) *Volatile Bodies: Towards a Corporeal Feminism*, Bloomington: Indiana University Press.

Haraway, Donna (1997) *Modest_Witness@Second_Millenium.FemaleMan© _Meets_OncoMouse™: Feminism and Technoscience*, New York: Routledge.

Hartouni, Valerie (1992) 'Fetal Exposures: Abortion Politics and the Optics of Allusion', *Camera Obscura* 29: 130–9.

Hyde, Beverley (1986) 'An Interview Study of Pregnant Women's Attitudes to Ultrasound Scanning', *Social Science and Medicine* 22 (5): 587–92.

Jordanova, Ludmilla (1989) *Sexual Visions: Images of Gender in Science and Medicine Between the Eighteenth and Twentieth Centuries*, Madison, Wisconsin: University of Wisconsin Press.

Kemp, Virginia and Page, Cecilia (1987) 'Maternal Prenatal Attachment in Normal and High-Risk Pregnancies', *Journal of Obstetrics, Gynecology and Neonatology in Nursing* May/June: 179–83.

Kirby, Vicki (1991) 'Corporeal Habits: Addressing Essentialism Differ-ently', *Hypatia* 6 (3): 4–24.

Lippman, Abby (1991) 'Prenatal Genetic Testing and Screening: Con-structing Needs and Reinforcing Inequities', *Am. J. of Law and Medicine* 28 (1 and 2): 15–50.

Miller, Peter and Rose, Nikolas (1990) 'Governing Economic Life', *Economy and Society* 19 (1): 1–31.

Milne, Lynne S. and Rich, Olive J. (1981) 'Cognitive and Affective Aspects of the Response of Pregnant Women to Sonography', *Maternal-Child Nursing Journal* 10: 15–39.

Mitchell, Lisa and Georges, Eugenia (1997) '"Baby's First Picture": The Cyborg Fetus of Ultrasound', *Feminist Studies* 23 (2): 373–401.

Morgan, Lynn (1996) 'Fetal Relationality in Feminist Philosophy: An Anthropological Critique', *Hypatia* 11 (3): 47–70.

Morgan, Lynn (1989) 'When Does Life Begin? A Cross-Cultural Perspec-tive on the Personhood of Fetuses and Young Children' in Edd Doerr and James N. Prescott (eds), *Abortion Rights and Fetal 'Personhood'*, Long Beach, Cal: Certline Press for Americans for Religious Liberty. 2nd edn: 89–107.

Newman, Karen (1996) *Fetal Positions*, Stanford University Press.

Petchesky, Rosalind (1987) 'Foetal Images: The Power of Visual Culture in the Politics of Reproduction' in Michele Stanworth (ed.) *Reproductive Technologies: Gender, Motherhood and Medicine*, Cambridge: Polity, pp. 57–80.

Price, Mary (1994) *The Photograph: A Strange, Confined Space*, Stanford University Press: Stanford CA.

Rapp, Rayna (1994) 'The Power of 'Positive' Diagnosis: Medical and Mater-nal Discourses on Amniocentesis' in Donna Bassin, Margaret Honey and Meryle Mahrer Kaplan (eds), *Representations of Motherhood*, New Haven: Yale University Press, pp. 204–19.

Reading, Anthony (1982) 'Health Beliefs and Health Care Behaviour in Pregnancy', *Psychological Medicine* 12: 379–83.

Rothman, Barbara Katz (1986) *The Tentative Pregnancy: Prenatal Diagnosis and the Future of Motherhood*, New York: Viking.

Stabile, Carol A. (1992) 'Shooting the Mother: Fetal Photography and the Politics of Disappearance', *Camera Obscura* 28: 119–205.

Stainton, M. Colleen (1985) 'The Fetus: A Growing Member of the Family', *Family Relations* 34: 321–6.

A Star Is Born: An Album to Record the Events of the Birth and Early Experience of Baby (1995) Norwalk, CT: C. R. Gibson Company.

Strathern, Marilyn (1992a) *After Nature: English Kinship in the Late Twen-tieth Century*, Cambridge: Cambridge University Press.

Strathern, Marilyn (1992b) *Reproducing the Future: Anthropology, Kinship and the New Reproductive Technologies*, New York: Routledge.

Strathern, Marilyn (1993) 'Regulation, Substitution and Possibility' in

Jeanette Edwards, Sarah Franklin, Eric Hirsch, Francis Price and Marilyn Strathern, *Technologies of Procreation*, Manchester: Manchester University Press, pp. 132–61.

Taylor, Janelle (1992) 'The Public Fetus and the Family Car' in *Public Culture* 4 (2): 67–80.

Tymstra, T. J., C. Bejema, J. R. Beekhurst and A. Mantingh (1991) 'Women's Opinions on the Offer and Use of Prenatal Diagnosis' *Prenatal Diagnosis* II: 893–8.

Weir, Lorna (1993) 'Wanderings of the Linguistic Turn in Anglophone Historical Writing', *Journal of Historical Sociology* 6 (2): 227–45.

Weir, Lorna (1998) 'Ideology and Intertexts: Fetal Sonograms in Clinical and Maternal Discourse', *Economy and Society*. 27 (2 and 3): 249–58.

Wilson, Philip K. (1992) '"Out of Sight, Out of Mind": The Daniel Turner–James Blondel Dispute over the Power of Maternal Imagination', *Annals of Science* 49: 63–85.

6

Raktpushp (Blood Flower)

SHEBA CHHACHHI

WITH INTRODUCTION BY
SHEBA CHHACHHI AND JANET PRICE

THIS CHAPTER OFFERS A MOSAIC, a series of image-text associations which map the multilayered polyvalent way in which contemporary Indian women look at their own bodies. It is an investigation of the overlapping, often contradictory codes which constitute body and self for postcolonial Indian women.

Differences in naming, whether of disease, body part or process, emerge as important signifiers of the imposition of a mechanistic (western, allopathic) view of the body over existent, indigenous systemic or energic perceptions of the body. Menstruation is described as 'the blossoming of the red flower' in many vernacular traditions; referred to as 'period' or 'monthly' by doctors/health workers; named 'being down' or 'having one's chum' by English-medium-educated adolescents. These differences are not merely of nomination but are indicative of the multiple discourses that speak to the contemporary experience of menstruation and, thus, are a vital factor in determining the actual efficacy of health education and health care.

The state and health institutions based on a western medical model operate on a notion of a pan-Indian female body. In contrast, postcolonial female subject/bodies must be differentiated by, amongst others, class, education, rural/urban situation, and ethnic and religious affiliations.[1] Critical reformulation by feminists and alternative health groups initially focused on shifting attention from population control to women's health and, later, to the specificity of local needs. These latter initiatives are relatively small experiments whose ideas have been appropriated by state and health institutions in the drive towards social marketing. Within this context, considerable attention has been paid to the transition from what are characterised as 'traditional' attitudes to modern methods to what is held to be a wholly modernist view. The emphasis has been and remains on making this transition smoother, more complete – and thus on achieving greater user acceptance/compliance.

Any attempt to engage with women's health in India needs to problematise such notions as 'traditional' and 'modern', and to develop a critical understanding of the constructions of women's bodies and health as they are produced through the reiteration of both authorised texts (oral, written and visual) and subaltern knowledges. Such an engagement must, of necessity, incorporate an examination of the simultaneous co-existence of many layers of bodily meaning, thus revealing the instability of the supposed pre-existent categories, ancient and modern.[2] These layers may exist in an articulated, conscious manner or in subliminal form, interweaving each with the others and assuming relative primacy in differing contexts. They offer us multiple meanings, permeable sites and temporal interplay.

Whilst the texts are drawn from across the centuries, they are all extant, part of current knowledge and usage in India. They speak to the immanence of the past in the present, to the history of discourses that not only precedes but conditions their use. The events of history and of the here-and-now are not construed as happening to, or being instigated by, subjects always already present to themselves. Rather the postcolonial female subject is simultaneously agent, object and effect of the reworking of these texts within contemporary Indian society. The specificity of the texts is apparent not in re-presenting the originary convictions of a tradition, but in reading the traces that permeate the following passages of word and image. The 'I' of the linking subjective voice in the text is a fictionalised self, drawn from my own (Sheba Chhahhi's) memories and experiences, as well of those of women I know, have talked to and worked with, and of stories that I have heard. This 'I' changes, becoming sometimes a rural woman in Bengal, sometimes a college girl in New Delhi – not representations, but articulations of particular experiences.

The intention of the layered configuration of the text that follows is to create the possibility for perceptual shifts in the way in which we think the postcolonial female subject/body in India today. The work is a series of juxtapositions, derived from an original that was formulated in 3-D for showing in a gallery space. This shift in structure from 3-D to 2-D has produced a tension within the work. A book format seems to demand of the material a narrative, a set of obvious connections (organised here roughly around the lifecycle), whilst in the 3-dimensional installation, the viewer is the narrative – she constructs her own version of the story in response to the juxtapositions as she walks through and round the layers. She creates her own map of the/her body and the act of reading is itself embodied in her movements. In engaging with this piece, laid out on the page, the reader is faced by multiple, yet physically more constrained, possibilities. The challenge remains to focus on the geography of body space rather than on the linearity of time.

NOTES

1. Although this work looks primarily at the experience of the Hindu woman and employs Hindu texts, there are nevertheless overlaps with the experiences of women of other communities, particularly in relation to colonial and western medical discourses.
2. The texts are not dated as they appear in the text, for it becomes too easy to locate a particular attitude as ancient, another as modern. Texts are drawn from sources ranging from the Vedic era (1500 BC) to the present, but it should be noted that Indian language texts are often difficult to 'date' as they are constantly evolving. For instance, the *Mahabharat* took over 1000 years to reach a 'settled' version around 400 AD, was transmitted orally for many hundreds of years before being written down, is told in different versions in different parts of the country, and has recently been retold, with considerable changes, in the form of a television serial.

PushpFlowerSvayumbhuKusumSelfbornflowerBesiSittinga
touchableDoorBaithnaSittingfarPeriodsSamurtaBecomingma
tureKhapuspaMysflowermenstrualbloodofavirginCennirA
SonitaAkindofwaterintheformoffeelingBeingDownRajasPass
onRajasvalaMenstruatingpassionatewomanRasFluidemotion
fromwhichRajasrisesfromwhichtheembryoisMahavariThegrea
tcycleMahinaMonthlyperiodMasikDharmMonthlylawTheCurse
PushpFlowerSvayambhuKusumSelfbornflowerChetiBesi
sehaiUntouchableDoorBaithnaSittingfarPeriodsSamurtaBec
ermenstrualbloodofavirginCennirAuspiciousredwaterRakt
achandanaRedsandalwoodSonitaAkindofwaterintheformoff
passionatewomanRasFluidemotionfromwhichRajasrisesfrom
edMahavariThegreatcycleMahinaMonthlyperiodMasikDhar
MonthlylawTheCurseKhapuspaMysticflowermenstrualbloodof
RaktachandaRedsandalwoodSonitaAkindofwaterintheform
valamenstruatingpassionaRaktachandanaRedsandalwoodSoni
formoffeelingUntouchableDoorBaithnaSittingfarPeriods
KhapuspaMysticflowermenstrualbloodofavirginCennirAuspi
iousredwaterachandanaRedsandalwoodSonitaAkindofwater
ntheformoffeelingBeingDownsvalaMenstruatingpassionate
womanRasFluidemotionfromwhichRajasrisesfromwhichthe
isformedMahavariThegreatcycleMahinaMonthlyperiodMasik
CursePushpFlowerSvayambhuKusumSelfbornflowerChetiBesi
PushpFlowerSvayumbhuKusumSelfbornflowerBesiSittinga

Raktpushp *(Blood Flower)*

SHEBA CHHACHHI
Photos from *Notes to the Body*
by Sheba Chhachhi and Sonia Jabbar

Pushp: Flower **Svayambhu Kusum**: Self-born flower **Chums**
Cheti Besi: Sitting apart **Chine se hai**: Untouchable
Door Baithna: Sitting far **Samurta**: Becoming mature
Khapuspa: Mystic flower, menstrual blood of a virgin **Periods**
Cennir: Auspicious red water **Raktachandana**: Red sandalwood
Sonita: A kind of water in the form of feeling **Being Down**
Rajas: Passion **Rajasvala**: Menstruating/passionate woman
Ras: Fluid/emotion from which *Rajas* rises, from which the embryo is
formed **Mahavari**: The great cycle **Mahina**: Monthly period
Masik Dharm: Monthly law **The Curse**

Multiple names.
Each name a body. Each body a text.
Overlapping, often contradictory codes.
Patriarchal Hindu, Agrarian magical, British colonial, Western medical.
Simultaneously co-existent, permeable, polyvalent.
The voices of brahmins and doctors, law makers and tantriks,
anthropologists and worshippers.
Voices which proscribe, prescribe, conceal, bind, reveal, celebrate.
I negotiate these multiple namings, becoming the body-self, described by
one and then the other.
Tensions, ellisions, fusion, separation

107

When a woman has her menses she should abandon all her works. She will have to remain in a secluded place with shame so that she may not be seen by anyone, wearing only one piece of cloth and giving up bathing and the use of ornaments. She will have to remain as a destitute without exchange of any word with others and any movement of eyes, hands and legs, eating only once at night in an earthen pot. She will have to lie on the ground without being excited and having passed three nights in this way she will be pure on the fourth day after the rise of the sun when she will bathe and wash her clothes.

Vyasa Samhita

All the women came. They rubbed my body with turmeric and took me to the river to bathe.
They made me put three dots of the blood on the wall and draw a line at the end. This will make it stop in three days they said.
New cloth, bangles. They fed me raisins, sesamee, ghee, almonds. Patted my cheek, smiled conspiratorially and called me Gauri, Laxmi, Mangala.

'Now', my mother said, 'you must not
laugh loudly
climb trees
wear short skirts
leave your hair open
go out alone stand in the doorway
speak to boys or men.'

The mere presence of a woman with such a stain is noxious.
What she looks at the Gods will not take in sacrifice.
It is forbidden to speak to her.
If she wilfully touches a Brahmin man, she shall be flogged with a whip.

Manu, *Vishnu Puran.*

PERSONAL PROBLEMS OF MAIDENS

Maidenhood is a special time of life when maidens experience rapid physical and emotional changes. These changes are particularly linked to sex. Indian society, by refusing to allow young girls to learn about sex keeps maidens ignorant of a

necessary reality. Detailed information on physical problems such as monthly law, monthly discharge, pain in genitals, sex-related diseases, hygiene, hormonal problems, masturbation. All kinds of sex problems of maidens in simple direct language. The best book on sex education for maidens.
Viswa Sulabh Sahitya, Delhi Book Company.

Advertisement in *Femina* (women's magazine, Hindi edition)

'Don't', she said, 'enter
the temple
the kitchen
the puja room
or let a man see you.'

For the coming of this event is for the Indian girl a source of pride and rejoicing, like the sprouting of the moustache on the youth . . . the girl on the Ganges from her earliest years knows all about everything, and with her the coming of puberty excites a lively interest, and is even hailed with much rejoicing. That most delightful thing in the world – the maiden blossoming in sweet ignorance, and the half-painful, half-joyful emotional billowing of her soul, wrapped in holy and pure dream secrets – this indeed, the Hindoo does not know.

J. J. Meyer, *Sexual Life in Ancient India*

'Don't touch,' she said
'Anybody.
Anything holy – altar, icon, scripture,
clean utensils,
washed clothes,
pickles – for they will turn mouldy
fruit – for it will rot
flowers – for they will die'

a flower has burst open in the sacred grove
three coloured – dark, radiant, clear.

this flower blooms only after twelve years
sheds its petals every month.

do you wish to hear its story?
i can speak of it only to a true connoisseur, a knower of essence.

for on the fruit the tongue loses itself
in the flower intoxication hides

drink the honey-wine of this forest
this is the way to your own divinity.

the guru said this flower bloomed on a formless branch
its story is secret.
once you know it,
nothing will contain your amazement.

Radheyshyam Baul, *Baul* song, Dehattatva Tradition

... with the growth of hair in the pubes a girl is enjoyed by the moon,
with the flow of menstrual blood by the gandharvas (sensual spirits)
and then by Agni (God of fire) and only then by her husband.

Paraskara Grihasutra, Samvarta Samhita

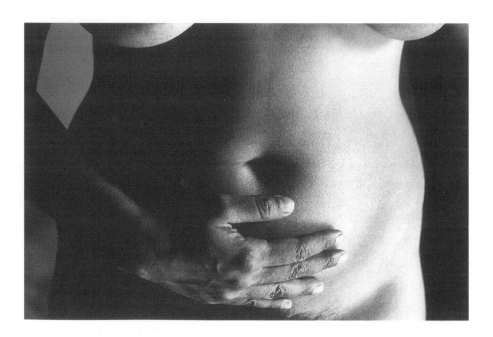

Raktpushp (Blood Flower)

Red mark on my forehead
Red filled in the furrow of parted hair

The Bengali orthodoxy and the Anglo – Indian medical authority
agreed that sexual intercourse should occur only after the puberty of
the child bride. Yet the Select Committee of the Viceroy's Legislative
Council rejected the substitution of 'puberty' for '12 years' in the
Consent Act [1891].

My palms henna red, feet outlined with alta
A red braid in my black hair
Bridal red. Suhagin.

Though the substitution accorded with religious and medical opinion,
the legislators preferred the chronological criterion to determine the
appropriate time for sexual intercourse for Bengali girls.

Red One.
Lallesvari, Lallantika, Lallanarupaye, Lalita, Lata,
Aruna, Rohini, Sindhuri, Lola, Lohita.

The Calcutta Medical Society quite arbitarily declared that 'it is a
pretty well ascertained fact that few native girls in the country
menstruate naturally before the completion of the 12th year.' The
examples of Bengali girls who menstruated below 12 years was
declared 'unnatural', and many doctors believed that 'unaided
menstruation is unfortunately a rare event in Bengal . . . [and that] little
girls are ripened in this country for early consummation of their
marriage by excitation of their sexual instincts.'

> Mrinalini Sinha, 'Gender and Imperialism', *Changing Men*.

On my arms red bangles alternate with white
White for the widow
shaved head, only one meal a day.
Red shroud for the woman who dies before her husband
Red for the Devi
Red for the one who worships her,
the magician, the alchemist, the vamachari – follower of the way of women.

111

Parvati had no vagina so Shankar scratched her with his nail and made her a vagina. They collected the blood in a pot and dyed some cloth. Shankar accepted this as *bhagava* (sacramental ochre) because it came from Parvati's *bhag* (vulva) and from this time the Nath yogis wear this colour of cloth.

Rajasthani Nath story

'I wish I could forget about my Sanitary Napkin forever.'
STAYFREE TAMPONS

Advertisement, Femina (English edition)

If the origin of Tantrism is to be traced to the magical belief confounding the productive and reproductive processes, it is only natural to find great importance attached in it to the menstrual blood . . . certain practices, like those concerning the use of vermillion or choice of blood red colour for their clothes derive their significance from the same belief.

Debiprasad Chattopadhya,
Lokayat: A study in Ancient Indian Materialism.

Devi. Mahadevi, Sri Devi. Mahamaya.
No, I don't call you mother. Sister perhaps or lover.
Your mouth coated red – lips cheeks chin as though you had just raised your head from a bowl of blood.

Raktbhogini. Blood drinker.
I offer you red cloth, kumkum, alcohol, flowers, fire.
The open mouths of hibiscus frame your face. Red. Hungry.
The power of hunger – the second transcendent wisdom, that which brings form into being.

. . . the hibiscus is sacred to the Goddess and is the flower offered in her worship. Ayurvedic medicine prescribes it as an emmenagogue effective in promoting menses. An extract from the flower is used in preventing unwanted pregnancies, inhibiting the flow of semen in men and bringing on temporary sterility in women. Ayurvedic physicians believe that the anti-conception properties of the drug can be effective post-coitally. In one study conducted in 1974, Dr Tiwari states, 'An uncontrolled clinical trial using ethanolic extract of hibiscus flowers

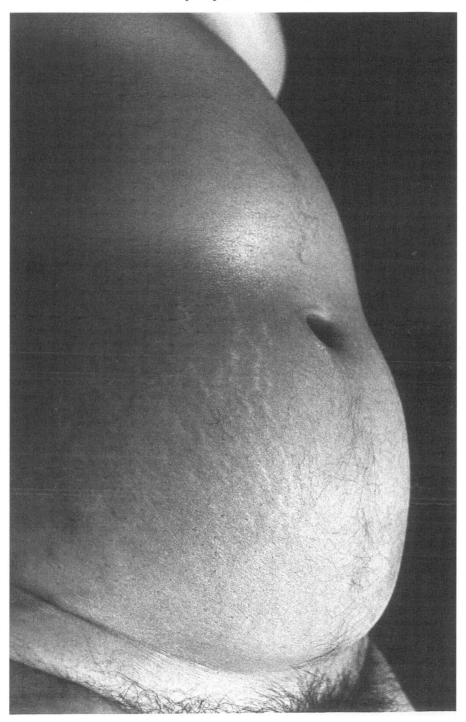

was carried out on 21 women in the reproductive age group by administering . . . 3 divided doses from the 7th to the 22nd day of menstrual cycle (a total of 229 cycles). Fourteen women did not have a pregnancy for 4 years whereas 7 women dropped out of the trial for various personal reasons.'

> Indian Council of Medical Research, *Medicinal Plants of India*.

Raktbhogini, Raktdanti, Yogmohini, Yogini, Singhini, Baghini, Taratarini,
Kapali, Kakini, Kankali, Kurukulla, Kamadudhe, Kamrupani, Kamesvari,
Kamkotini, Kamakshi, Kamakhya . . .

Mistress of blood, alchemy, death, desire.
Your names. Three. Seven. Nine. One thousand and one.
One thousand and eight.
Chanted three times. Twenty-one times. One hundred and eight times.
The chant ribbons into a spiral concentrating into seed sound
blazing forth at the navel.
Manipura chakra – city of jewels, fire centre, site of transformation
where food is turned into blood and blood into nectar

Sati's organ of generation fell at Kamakhya, near Gauhati in Assam and a temple was built there to mark the spot. It contains no image of the Goddess but in the depths of the shrine is a yoni shaped cleft in the rock adored as the yoni of Sati. A natural spring within the cave keeps the cleft moist. During Ambuvaci (July–August) after the first burst of the monsoon, a great ceremony takes place, for the water runs red with iron oxide, and the ritual drink is symbolic of the rajas or ritu of the Devi, her menstrual blood.

> Ajit Mookerjee, *Kali the Feminine Force*

'If she has called you once,' they say,
'she will call you three times.
Each year when the river runs red,
Kamakhya will summon you.'

Bare feet, bare head.
Neither vermillion nor collyrium
fasting, empty, washed clean
I make my way up the pilgrims' path

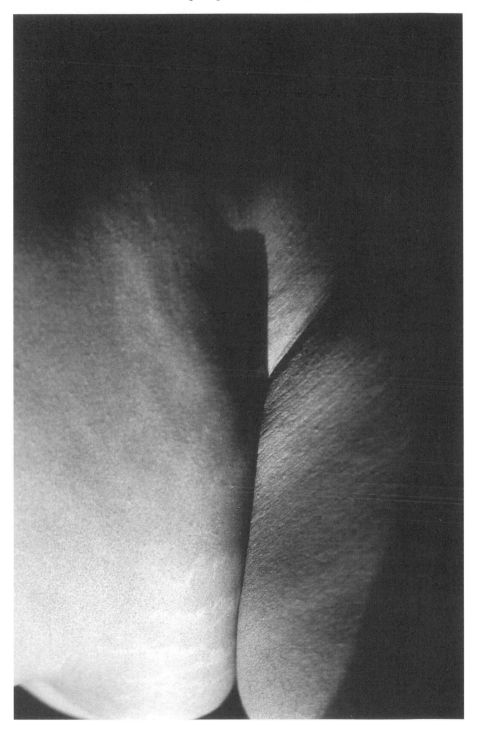

The hill springs out of a great curve of the river
Today's Brahmaputra, yesterday's Lohita
This used to be the land of mother right
Water rises up inside the sacred hill like sap
breaking the earth's surface in a hundred springs

Mayanagari – city of illusion, Kamagiri – hill of desire,
Strirajya – women's kingdom, Yoni pitha – seat of the vulva.

Indra, the king of the Gods, murdered a Brahmin Tvastr, for he feared his power. There is no sin greater than Brahminicide. In order to purify his sin, Indra appealed to the earth, to the trees and to women to each take on a third of his guilt.
The earth agreed, but said 'I fear that in the time to come I will be dug into, excavated. Hence in return I ask for a boon that whatever is dug out of me will fill up again. The sin she took became a natural fissure. Therefore, one who wishes to build an altar should not build upon a fissure or a cleft in the earth for it is the colour of guilt.

Pushed along by the press of thousands of bodies
I descend
narrow passage, dark, aromatic
sounds die away
something gathers inside, stilled

I reach out to touch the glistening black cleft
moist with oblations

The trees said 'As a boon, let us not be overcome by pruning.' Indra replied, 'From pruning shall more shoots spring up from you.' They took a third of his sin. It became sap. Therefore one should not partake of sap which is red or comes from pruning, for it is the colour of guilt.

touch my fingertips to the water surrounding her
bring the sacramental fluid to both eyes, forehead, crown

The women said, 'Let us have constant enjoyment of love in exchange, and let us have offspring from after the menses.' They took a third of his sin into their menstrual blood and became women with stained garments. Therefore, one should not sit with such a woman, nor eat her food for she keeps emitting the colour of guilt.

Taittriya Samhita

from her body to mine.
the pujari pours three drops into my cupped palm
I drink.

In Saktism the menstrual taboo is broken down and the menstrual fluid regarded as sacred. It becomes the object of veneration. A menstruating woman is placed in a special category during ritual practice. In the chakra puja of tantrikas menstrual fluid may be taken as a ritual drink along with wine . . .

Ajit Mookerjee, *Kali the Feminine Force.*

They call me Sakti
men seeking the power of women
men seeking to become women

Ramakrishna, they say,
observed monthly seclusion
bled from his armpit

offerings pile up in front of me . . .

The Tantras as a whole, Saktism especially, have been unequivocally condemned by scholars, Indian and foreign alike. It is true that . . . provision is found to have been made in the Tantras for rites which appear highly objectionable and derogatory from an ethical standpoint for they pertain to the use of what are called the five makara, as well as even more objectionable things like seminal and menstrual discharges of men and women . . .

C. Chakravarthi, *Tantras: Studies on their Religion and Literature.*

I receive my share
of the final sacrament
a strip of the Devi's menstrual cloth,
tie it securely around my upper arm

117

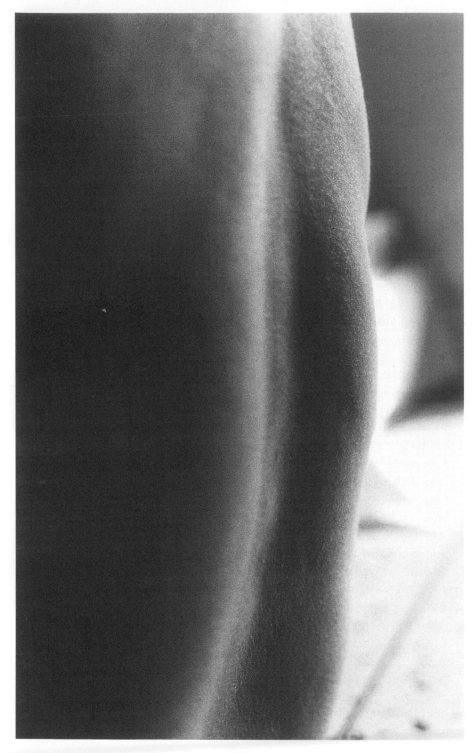

Raktpushp (Blood Flower)

a talisman
good protection against
the hungry eyes
of aspiring magicians
the frightened fascinated eyes of householders
full of remembered stories of the yoginis of Kamarupa
sorceresses who enslave men
keeping them as pigs by day
turning them back into men at night

   . . . when a drop of menstrual blood shed by the sixty-four yoginis is
   fertilized by the shadow of a hawk, a daughter is born who is an
   insatiable eater of men.

Tribal Myth

The three days of seclusion are over
three days of binding
the breath, the appetite, the wayward mind
singing songs of praise
songs which speak of the cosmos within the body –
dehatattva.
of transforming, perfecting this instrument
of grace –
kayasadhana.

   Here within my body
   are the Ganga and Jamuna,
   here are Prayag and Benares
   here are the sun and the moon
   here the pithas and upapithas
   I have not seen a place of pilgrimage
   or an abode of bliss like my body.

Dohakosa of Saraha

THIS IS THE ONLY ANSWER SCIENCE HAS

Dr Shirish Seth who performed hysterectomies on mentally retarded
girls between 12–35 years old defends the practice:
'The women were incapable of managing their periods and [made] a
mess of it . . . smeared the walls with their menstrual blood, played with
it and even ate it at times. The removal of the uterus will restore a
semblance of dignity to their lives. This surgery could be a solution to

119

the rapes and sexual harassment that mentally retarded girls are often
subjected to, and solve the problems of caretakers in maintaining
cleanliness. It will also relieve the girls of the trauma of menstruation
and of seeing so much blood every month.'
Seth points out that this practice is routinely undertaken in other
countries, including the United States, where researchers at the
prestigious Johns Hopkins University have published a paper on its
merits.

News report, *Indian Express*, Feburary 1994.

my flesh is taut, tumescent
as though the lightest touch
would cause the skin to slit open
spilling hot blood.

<u>. . . otherwise uncleanness dwells in her, and every kind of magical harm,
and in the peculiarly mysterious menstrual blood are concentrated all
these dread powers, but in it too, they are discharged.</u>

even the caress of the evening breeze
is unbearable
as if I had eaten, all at once,
garlic, onions, ginger, chillies, drumsticks,
cinnamon, cloves, meat –
those hot stimulants forbidden to widows.

<u>This according to the law is an incomparable means of cleansing the
woman, O Dushyanta; for month after month the menstrual blood
takes all the evil in them away. Indeed if a man suspects his wife of
unfaithfulness, he must confidently lie with her again after she has had
her courses, since she is thereby cleaned again, like a vessel by ashes.</u>

a mere kick of my foot, they say
would cause the ashoka tree to burst into flower

<u>. . . however, sexual intercourse with the still unclean woman is
strictly forbidden . . . to visit a rajasvala is one of the seven things
whereby a man forfeits his happiness or long life.</u>

The Mahabharat

120

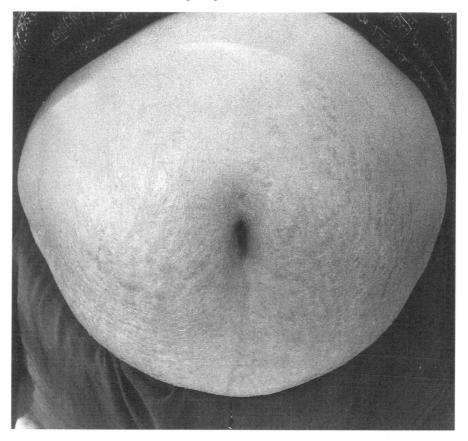

Rivers are female and menstruate in the rainy season. The mud
(*Rajas*) that is carried with their currents makes them menstruous
(*Rajasvala*). One should not bathe in them at this time, just as a man
should not have intercourse with a menstruating woman.

Dharmashastras

'Beware of the asaras,' she said,
'seven of them live inside the river.
Suhagins without husbands, married to the ocean.
They enter you at that time of the month.
Once an asara has got into your stomach
no child will ripen in your belly,
and every month when you bleed you will feel terrible pain.
Asaras were once apsaras, beautiful women

whose unsatisfied desire caused them to liquefy into a river.
If one enters you
you too will be filled with a terrible hunger.'

A woman is Ganga, Jamuna, Sarasvati
When the three sacred rivers meet,
the monthly flood rises

A restlessness comes upon her then,
She plays, plays for three days
The first day is black
the second ruby
the third yellow
bathe in this very river
to realise your own divinity
for a woman is Ganga, Jamuna, Sarasvati

No one can know a woman's pain
Perhaps only the great yogi Bhola Mahesvar
hold him in your inner self
to know the secret red jewel
A woman is Ganga, Jamuna, Sarasvati . . .

Howda Gosain, *Baul* song

The Tantrika literatures go into great details over the question of
menstrual blood. Bloods of different types of women are given
different names . . . the belief as it survives today is of course a
superstitious dross. And nothing will probably appear to our modern
taste to be more vulgar and repulsive than the elaborate Tantrika
discussions of it. There is nothing to wonder at the archaic belief
becoming a superstition today. It is simply the result of advances in
technology and knowledge.

Debiprasad Chattopadhya,
Lokayat: A Study in Ancient Indian Materialism.

For the first time in India
Introducing DAINTY CARE FOR WOMEN
The ultimate germicidal solution for menstrual hygiene.
Because sometimes feelings are too deep to be expressed in
words.

Advertisement in *Femina* (English edition)

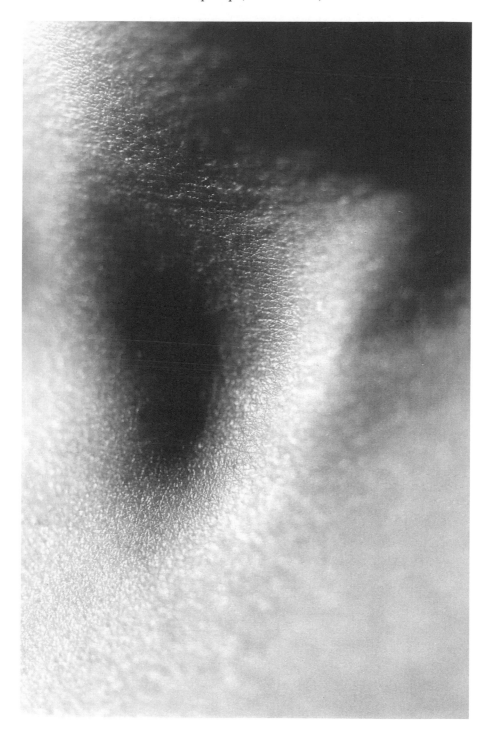

The monthly curse
legs heavy, back aching
irritable, tearful
hoping that no one in school
at the office
in the market
at home
will notice
telltale leaks, stains
used rags, cotton, towels

Calcutta had the honour of having the first medical college for teaching western medical science through the medium of English. In 1833, a committee appointed by Lord William Bentick recommended the establishment of an institution in which 'the various branches of medical science cultivated in Europe should be taught and as near as possible on the most approved European system' . . . a medical college came into being in 1835 with the main object of producing sub-assistant surgeons for employment in military and civil stations in India.

Concise History of Science in India

Freedom. Stayfree. Carefree. Whisper. . .
write the name on a slip of paper
or else speak quite softly
the man at the shop
wrapping the unmistakeable packet twice
newspaper then plastic
understands
he does not look at me

The financing of Unani and Ayurvedic medicine by the Government in the hope of finding some soul of goodness in them is precisely on a par with the same government financing archery clubs to find out the possibilities of the bow and arrow in modern warfare.

Indian Medical Gazette

They call me banjh, the one with a dry womb
in which no child grows
the midwife had said
'for red trouble

Raktpushp (Blood Flower)

brew the bark of the asoka tree
the very tree that comforted Sita in captivity
whose name means without sorrow.
There is too much heat in you'

Persistency on the part of Indian women to rely on traditional
domestic medicines and on such medical aid as they could get from
members of their own sex who dabbled in herbs and drugs, and one
could hardly have the heart to blame them for their great disinclination
to trouble with accounts of their private ills their male relatives,
burdened as they were with the cares of life, or for that refinement of
modesty which prevented them from seeking medical aid for diseases
which were peculiar to their sex.

Pearey Mohun Mukherjee, *First Annual Report*,
Countess of Dufferin's Fund, 1885.

Barren one. Widow, Witch
Banjh, Randi, Churel, Dakin, Pey. Ghoul
Hariti, eater of children
Jyestha, Alaxmi, inauspicious one
the beating, the blaming
the threats of desertion
prayers, penances, exorcisms.

Mahadevi, Jagatdhatri, Viswamata
mother of all creation
Katyayani is also your name
Katyayani, the widow
Dhumavati, the hag
seventh transcendent wisdom
the widow who dwells in the wounds of the earth
mistress of the power of poverty

[Shah notes that] the greater prevalence of mental illness is positively
linked with universal phenomena of physiological and psychological
changes occuring in females after menopause making them more
vulnerable . . .

Bhargavi V Davar, 'Mental Illness among Indian Women',
Economic and Political Weekly of India.

Ma Kali, Chandi, Chamunda, Candamari
Varahi, Sivaduti, Bhairavi
Chinnamasta, Bagala, Matangi
The fierce mothers

Majority of women in our country are housewives. In most other countries women do as much office work as men and in addition do the duties of housewives. Thus Indian women have more 'spare time'. Since majority of them have no other activities or hobbies and do not do any reading (being uneducated) they spend most of their spare time concentrating on their vaginal discharge.

O. P. Kapoor, Kapoor's Guide for General Practitioners.

Mothers who roar with laughter, intoxicated
mothers with shrunken breasts,
sunken bellies
I know you,
you who do not bear children
you who have too much heat in you

. . . her long and matted hair flowing wildly, she laughed her long and maddened laughter, her third eye scarlet, moving like a disk in her head, her greedy tongue protuding long and loose. She shone with a brightness more vertiginous than the sun or fire. She ground her huge, hard teeth, lips drawn back and streams of blood ran from the corners of her mouth. Corpses of children swung from her ears as ornaments, on her breast there hung a string of severed heads with wild and awful faces . . .

Kalika mangala Kavya

A SMILING ANSWER TO THOSE DIFFICULT DAYS!
BAIDYANATH'S SUNDARI KALP – A woman's own medicine.
There are several reasons why I am a capable, dynamic and successful woman. I am both a housewife and working woman. There used to be certain days when I felt dull, tired, drained and weak.
SUNDARI KALP changed my life
You too can gain control over those difficult days
Remain active with SUNDARI KALP.

Advertisement, Femina (Hindi edition)

I have seen her
a woman crazy with love
I saw her, right here in this world
Intoxicated, she stole the stuff of love
intoxicated, she roams these very paths

She met no mate, how did she learn to love?
a maiden, how did her womb grow full?
She gave birth to three:
Two householders, one renunciate
Creator, Preserver, Destroyer,
She, the mother of them all

Yes, I have seen her,
the woman crazy with love
The one who stole the stuff of love
I saw her roaming these very paths.

Radheshyamdas Gosain, *Baul* song

Pushp: Flower *Svayambhu Kusum*: Self-born flower *Chums*
Cheti Besi: Sitting apart *Chine se hai*: Untouchable
Door Baithna: Sitting far *Samurta*: Becoming mature
Khapuspa: Mystic flower, menstrual blood of a virgin *Periods*
Cennir: Auspicious red water *Raktachandana*: Red sandalwood
Sonita: A kind of water in the form of feeling *Being Down*
Rajas: Passion *Rajasvala*: Menstruating/passionate woman
Ras: Fluid/emotion from which *Rajas* rises, from which the embryo is
formed *Mahavari*: The great cycle *Mahina*: Monthly period
Masik Dharm: Monthly law *The Curse*

Each text a body, each body a text
names, words, sentences,
these lines encircle my body
turning in on themselves
only to open out again,
describe a new arc of yet another
overlapping circle
circle, cycle, spiral, parabola –
ribbons, rags, bonds, bandages.

PushpFlowerSvayumbhuKusumSelfbornflowerBesiSittinga
touchableDoorBaithnaSittingfarPeriodsSamurtaBecomingma
tureKhapuspaMysflowermenstrualbloodofavirginCennirAu
SonitaAkindofwaterintheformoffeelingBeingDownRajasPass
ionRajasvalaMenstruatingpassionatewomanRasFluidemotion
fromwhichRajasrisesfromwhichtheembryoisMahavariThegrea
tcycleMahinaMonthlyperiodMasikDharmMonthlylawTheCurse
PushpFlowerSvayambhuKusumSelfbornflowerChetiBesi
sehaiUntouchableDoorBaithnaSittingfarPeriodsSamurtaBec
ermenstrualbloodofavirginCennirAuspiciousredwaterRakta
chandanaRedsandalwoodSonitaAkindofwaterintheformoff
passionatewomanRasFluidemotionfromwhichRajasrisesfromw
edMahavariThegreatcycleMahinaMonthlyperiodMasikDharm
MonthlylawTheCurseKhapuspaMysticflowermenstrualbloodof
RaktachandaRedsandalwoodSonitaAkindofwaterintheform
valamenstruatingpassionaRaktachandanaRedsandalwoodSoni
formoffeelingUntouchableDoorBaithnaSittingfarPeriods
KhapuspaMysticflowermenstrualbloodofavirginCennirAuspi
iousredwaterachandanaRedsandalwoodSonitaAkindofwater
ntheformoffeelingBeingDownsvalaMenstruatingpassionatew
omanRasFluidemotionfromwhichRajasrisesfromwhichthe
isformedMahavariThegreatcycleMahinaMonthlyperiodMasikD
CursePushpFlowerSvayambhuKusumSelfbornflowerChetiBesi
PushpFlowerSvayumbhuKusumSelfbornflowerBesiSittinga
touchableDoorBaithnaSittingfarPeriodsSamurtaBecomingma
tureKhapuspaMysflowermenstrualbloodofavirginCennirAu
SonitaAkindofwaterintheformoffeelingBeingDownRajasPass
ionRajasvalaMenstruatingpassionatewomanRasFluidemotion
fromwhichRajasrisesfromwhichtheembryoisMahavariThegrea

PHOTO CREDITS

Photos on pages 106, 110, 121, 123, 127, 129 by Sheba Chhachhi, and photos on pages 113, 115, 118 by Sonia Jabbar; from *Notes to the Body*, a collaborative venture.

REFERENCES

Textual Sources

Sanskrit

Dharmashastras
Grihasutras, Vishnu Puran
Manusmriti (Laws of Manu)
Mahabharat
Samvarta Samhita
Taittriya Samhita
Vyasa Samhita

English Language

Bose, D. M., Sen, S. N., and Subbarayappa, B. V. (eds) (1971) *A Concise History of Science in India*, New Delhi: Indian National Science Academy.

Chakravarti, C. (1972) *Tantras: Studies on their Religion and Literature*, Calcutta: Punthi Pustak.

Chattopadhya, D. (1959) *Lokayata. A Study in Ancient Indian Materialism*, New Delhi: People's Publishing House.

Davar, B. V. (1995) 'Mental Illness among Indian Women' *Economic and Political Weekly of India* 30: 45.

Femina (1996–7) Bombay: Bennett Coleman and Co. Ltd.

Indian Council for Medical Research, 'Medicinal Plants of India' in N. Patnaik, (1993) *The Garden of Life: An Introduction to the Healing Plants of India*, New Delhi and London: HarperCollins.

Indian Express (1994) 'This is the Only Answer Science Has', February.

Indian Medical Gazette (1927) 62: 223 in D. Kumar, (1997) 'Medical Encounters in British India, 1820–1920', *Economic and Political Weekly of India* 32:4.

'Kalika mangala Kavya' in D. Kinsley, (1975) *The Sword and the Flute, Kali and Krishna. Dark Visions of the Terrible and Sublime in Hindu Mythology*, Berkeley: University of California Press.

Kapoor, O. P. (1976) *Kapoor's Guide for General Practitioners, Part II*, New Delhi: S. S. Publishers.

Lal, M. (1994) 'The Politics of Gender and Medicine in Colonial India: The Countess of Dufferin Fund, 1885–1888', *Bulletin of Medical History* 68: 29–66.

Meyer, J. J. (1930) *Sexual Life in Ancient India*, New York.

130

Mookerjee, A. (1988) *Kali the Feminine Force*, London: Thames and Hudson.

Sinha, M. (1987) 'Gender and Imperialism: Colonial policy and the ideology of moral imperialism in late nineteenth-century Bengal' in J. Kimmel, (ed.) *Changing Men*, London: Sage Publications.

Oral Sources

Baul songs from the author's collection, written down by Debdas Baul. The Bauls are wandering rural singer performers from Bengal, who are followers of a mystical tradition that incorporates Tantrik, Vaishnav and Sufi thought. The songs are assumed to be composed in the sixteenth century but have altered over time depending on the context.

Dohakosa of Saraha – Carya-padas or verses composed and sung by masters of Buddhist Tantrik tradition called Sidhas.

Stories, myths and personal experiences gathered from workshops with women's groups, particularly Sabla Sangh Action India and Jagori, New Delhi, and through personal communications with friends.

Additional Unreferenced Sources

Sanskrit
Devi Mahatmaya, Markandeya Puran
Durga Saptasahi
Lalita Sahsranama

English Language
Chawla, J. (1994) *Child-Bearing and Culture, Women Centered Revisioning of the Traditional Midwife: The Dai as a Ritual Practitioner*, New Delhi: Indian Social Institute.

Dasgupta, S. (1946) *Obscure Religious Cults as a Background to Bengali Literature*, Calcutta.

O'Flaherty, W. D. (1980) *Sexual Metaphors and Animals Symbols in Indian Mythology*, New Delhi: Motilal Banarasidass.

Shodhini Collective (eds) (1997) *Touch me, Touch-me-not. Women, Plants and Healing*, New Delhi: Kali for Women.

7

The Micropolitics of Biopsychiatry

CAMILLA GRIGGERS

While I fought with all my strength not to let myself sink in the Enlightenment, I saw things mocking me from their places, taunting me threateningly. And in my head foolish phrases floated around without let-up. I closed my eyes to escape the surrounding turmoil of which 1 was the center. But I could find no rest, for horrible images assailed me, so vivid that I experienced actual physical sensation. I can not say that I really saw images; they did not represent anything. Rather I felt them. It seemed that my mouth was full of birds which I crunched between my teeth, and their feathers, their blood and broken bones were choking me. Or I saw people whom I had entombed in milk bottles, putrefying, and I was consuming their rotting cadavers. Or I was devouring the head of a cat which meanwhile gnawed at my vitals. It was ghastly, intolerable.

In the midst of this horror and turbulence, I nonetheless carried on my work secretary.

(Marguerite Sechehaye, *Autobiography of a Schizophrenic Girl*, 1970)

MY GOAL IN THIS CHAPTER is to render a gender critique of the practices of the new biopsychiatry. I begin with the premise that being functional and being healed are two different things. This is a central concept that comes from the work of the French medical theorist Canguilhem (1994). In regard to the behaviour of the organism within its environment, the idea of normativity does not exclude dysfunctionality or maladaption. You can have a dysfunctional normativity; you can have a functional maladaption. My method here is to apply that idea of a normative maladaption to my reading of the new biopsychiatry as a political economy of signs and values, and as a biochemical alteration of the brain as an organ of memory and desire.

Let us begin with the observation that there are enough 'dysfunctional' subjectivities in the US to stimulate 'mental health' and psychiatric treatment as a growth industry within a depressed economy. To conceptualise rational cognition and its breakdown at such a material level, I have applied the neo-materialist method in Deleuze and Guattari's *Capitalism and Schizophrenia* (1983,1987), particularly their notion of an abstract machine as a complex assemblage of signs and matter that regulates cultural processes of subjectivisation and signification. Desire, from this materialist point of view, is not only systematically produced as (dys)functionality, but also strategically anti-produced by medical practices of diagnosis and treatment, not to mention market development and profit.

Psychopharmacology constitutes a material practice in the treatment of post-traumatic stress syndrome, major depression, manic-depression, borderline and multiple personality disorder, psychoses, and more and more frequently of late, minor depression and anxiety, funk and malaise. Women comprise a large portion of the psychopharmacological market; most of those taking the antidepressant Prozac, for example, are women in their childbearing years (Stone 1993: 91). Because memory is emotional-state dependent, psychotropic interventions in and modulations of feminine affect produce at a neurobiological level a gendered chemical prosthetic subject whose repressed memories of the nervous system's[1] circulating violences are the object of channelling, regulation, research and development. The psychopharmaceutical industry's general economy channels repressed memories of the nervous system's unspeakable yet everyday terror and modulates their return as emotional and psychic disorders.[2] Where psychotherapy modulates collective memory at the molecular level by keeping articulated memories sequestered in the private space of the clinician's office, psychopharmacology has brought a new level of understanding to the meaning of molecular politics. Working at the level of particle-signs where they are generated neurologically within the organic body, neurochemical interventions deterritorialise[3] the molecular assemblage of limbic[4] and autonomic particle-signs into blocks of memory, organised emotional expressions, and continuums of desiring-intensities. In short, neurochemical interventions both deterritorialise and stabilise blocks of becoming.[5]

According to the micropolitics theorised by Félix Guattari in

Molecular Revolution: Psychiatry and Politics (1984), the plane of consistency where a micropolitics of desire could articulate would include any mechanisms, whether biochemical, social or machinic, that stabilise deterritorialisations between social content and the machinic expression of form. His term 'desiring-machine' is meant to suggest the workings of an abstract expression-machine in the process of stabilising deterritorialisations of desire: 'The non-signifying expression-machine (on the level of the signifier) organises a system of empty words and interchangeability for all the territorialised systems of words produced by the manifold local agencies of power. (We may instance the power of the family over the production of nice speech, or the power of the school over the production of nice writing, discipline, competition, hierarchy, etc.)' (1984: 83). For Deleuze (1993), who favours the term 'assemblage' to 'machine', the key to understanding the mapping of power on to desire is to understand that 'desire only exists when assembled or machined' (1993: 136). The point then is to ask not to which drives desires correspond, but to ask into which assemblage various blocks of becoming enter. There are different politics of assemblages, and psychopharmacology's expression-machine can enter into relations with any number of them. Desire doesn't precede its social construction. Likewise, the plane of consistency articulating an assemblage of signatory and social relations does not precede the assemblage but is constituted by it (Stone 1993: 137). Since all assemblages are socially constructed, all assemblages inscribe a politics. The politics of biopsychiatry, because biopsychiatry works at the level of the individual's brain chemicals, is expressed as a neural micropolitics.

In this micropolitics, the components of desire are reterritorialised through a psychochemical-machine, whose delivery system is psychiatric diagnosis and prescription of psychotropic drugs. The components for potential desiring-assemblages include repressed memory (interiorised expressions of impressions and experiences which lack exteriorised forms of expression) and the resulting surges of repressed affect (deterritorialising velocities of asignification traversing the body's limbic system). Psychotropic medications actualise potential conjunctions between abstract systems of rational cognition and behaviour and material social systems organising a technologically and economically striated domestic space, workplace and institutional space.

On a biochemical plane of articulation, psychotropic intervention shapes an abstract feminine chemical prosthetic subject by modulating deterritorialising surges within the social body's nervous system at the level of the micropolitics of the subject. In the flow of rational consciousness both within the individuated subject and within the social body at large, *surge* can be understood as what a particular point of subjectification experiences in relation to turbulent social force. In the collective movement of particle-signs that constitutes the flow of rational significations, surge-flux threatens to change the rate or direction of the sign-flow of established meanings. In terms of the breakdown, surges of desire, affect and memory express as the frequency and amplitude of symptoms and symptom clusters, with frequency expressing as the measure of sign-flux passing through its cycle of occurrence (marking the duration and relation of affective events) and amplitude expressing as emotional intensity. Neurochemical treatments reterritorialise the frequencies and amplitudes of flux, i.e., the temporality, spatiality and intensity of the feminine subject's neural network assembling affect, memory and desire into meaningful and intense blocks of becoming. Functioning within an economy of representation, psychopharmacology channels asignifications within the body-politic on to the individual subject's wired and rewired affect. Within this juncture of psychopathology and pharmacology, the politics of interpretation takes the formal expression of the science of symptomatology – practice which is in actuality a virtual hermeneutic nightmare.

Within clinical psychology, the recent articulation of a domestic 'post-traumatic stress disorder' provides a paradigmatic example of this interpretive nightmare and its political implications, while demonstrating the way the nervous system expresses itself and recuperates its effects through the bodies of individual subjects and their breakdowns. The now accepted clinical practice of diagnosing post-traumatic stress disorder in cases of domestic and sexual abuse simultaneously recognises the nervous system's circulating violences on the homefront and screens the nervous system's everyday effects with a discourse of psychopathology (Herman 1992). Common clinical symptoms of adults suffering from post-traumatic stress syndrome, when the 'trauma-stress' was experienced within the domestic household early in their social becoming, are alarmingly profuse. They include acting out,[6] blurred boundaries, body-image disturbance, chemical dependency, cognitive deficits, depression, dissociation, eating disorders, emotional numbing, fear/paranoia, flashbacks, hearing inner voices, hypnagogic hallucinations, inability to trust, insomnia, low self-esteem, minimising, multiple and borderline personality, persistent anxiety, promiscuity, reactive affective states, recurrent nightmares, sexual dysfunction, self-injurious behaviour, somatisation and suicidality. The syndrome is often characterised by an incubation period of anywhere from ten to thirty years. If this 'disorder' is as pervasive as the general effects of the nervous system, we can only speculate how 'normative' the syndrome – which is quickly becoming *the* psychological disorder of the 1990s – actually is. Indeed, once it was recognised formally within clinical psychology, post-traumatic stress disorder began to challenge the legitimacy of many previous clinical diagnostic practices and psychopathological classifications.

In fact, clinical researchers and practitioners agree on only one thing in cases of post-traumatic stress syndrome: as one expert in the field put it, '[f]or traumatized individuals, many of the usual assumptions about symptoms do not apply. For example, the presence of hallucinations may not indicate psychosis, depression may not be major affective disorder, episodic overwhelming anxiety may not be panic, and hypomanic agitation may not be bipolar disorder' (Dominiak 1992: 89). The task of diagnosing and treating a syndrome with a variable, multisymptom and malleable presentation makes determination of 'medication-responsive primary major psychiatric illness', 'symptom management' and 'appropriate pharmacologic intervention' an unstable procedure at best. Yet currently diagnosis and treatment occur in a milieu in which one half of all patients who seek assistance from the psychiatric institution are treated pharmacologically (US Department of Health and Human Services, 1995). Because symptoms of post-traumatic stress disorder can mimic borderline states, lethal crises and psychotic reactions, clinicians are faced with the challenge of distinguishing 'agitation from hypomania, and psychosis from dissociation, other forms of dyscontrol, and abreaction' (Dominiak 1992: 108).

Everything is at stake in the initial diagnosis, since dissociation, the fragmenting of thought processes (i.e., *suppression*), is recognised as an appropriate defence mechanism *against* psychosis in situations of enduring traumatic stress, while abreaction, defined as the release of repressed emotions by acting out in words, action, or imagination the situation causing the conflict (i.e., *surge*), is identified by most clinicians working with post-traumatic stress syndrome as a crucial step in the recuperative process for traumatised individuals (Dominiak 1992: 108). This core contradiction within the regime of signs expressing as psychopathological diagnosis and 'symptom management' generates breakdowns of its own, since the psychic process which defends *against* psychosis looks like psychosis. *Surge* signs simultaneously as healing process and as the 'maladaptive' symptom authorising the neurochemical policing of memory, affect and desire. Indeed, treating abreactive surges of affect pharmacologically requires drastic amounts of sedation that not only debilitate and slow the subject in her therapeutic work but typically prove entirely ineffective in the long run in relieving the violent return of repressed and fragmented emotion and memory (Dominiak 1992: 108). Needless to say, being diagnosed and treated pharmacologically for psychosis when you're not yet psychotic is anti-therapeutic.

The standard protocol for psychiatric diagnosis – determination of the patient's symptomatology as either psychotic or non-psychotic and the decision to use only psychosocial intervention or to medicate – is challenged by the variable symptom cluster of post-traumatic stress disorder, since post-traumatic stress disorder's plane of consistency crosses many previous diagnostic categories. Clinical practitioners face the daily hermeneutic dilemma of distinguishing psychotic phenomena from symptoms that may appear to be psychosis but are instead 'attributable to dissociation, splitting, intrusive thoughts, vivid recollections, obsessionality, and extreme emotional reactions' (Dominiak 1992: 98). The distinction between functionality and dysfunctionality, which often determines more radical psychotropic intervention, is described by one clinician as the point at which adaptive defence mechanisms become 'overly rigid' or 'exaggerated' (Shapiro 1992: 35).

In addition, the clinical judgement distinguishing between psychopathological dysfunction and adaptive functionality is subject to codes of class and social status. For example, the environmental supports of the patient, including familial, social and financial resources, are a standard criterion for psychopharmacological evaluation, along with the individual's psychiatric assessment (Dominiak 1992: 108). By this standard of evaluation, the underclasses would be by definition more prone to psychotropic treatments than non-pharmaceutical ones. It's no surprise that the psychiatric network finds it easier and more efficacious to diagnose mental illness and prescribe medication than to bolster social and familial resources for the poor. In regard to mental illness among socio-economically 'underprivileged' populations, the blurred boundary between adaption and maladaption is at its most acute, while the political stakes invested in first producing and then channelling collective (mal)adaptions become most tangible.

Canguilhem's extensive critique of the categories of normality and normativity in *The Normal and the Pathological* (1994) frames this problem of diagnosis in the context of a broader understanding of health:

The normal should not be opposed to the pathological because under certain conditions and in its own way, the pathological is normal . . . Health is more than normality; in simple terms, it is normativity. Behind all apparent normality, one must look to see if it is capable of tolerating infractions of the norm, of overcoming contradictions, of dealing with conflicts. Any normality open to possible future correction is authentic normativity, or health. Any normality limited to maintaining itself, hostile to any variation in the themes that express it, and incapable of adapting to new situations is a normality devoid of normative intention. When confronted with any apparently normal situation, it is therefore important to ask whether the norms that it embodies are creative norms, norms with a forward thrust, or, on the contrary, conservative norms, norms whose thrust is toward the past (1994: 352).

One must distinguish, therefore, between the 'pathological normal' and the 'normative normal' (1994: 352). And in making this distinction, one inevitably confronts a politics of normality. In this regard, the pathology of normality can not help but be a politics of normality.[7] And a politics of normality is not the same thing as health.

This politics of diagnostic hermeneutics is particularly manifest in diagnoses of 'borderline personality disorder', a term formally used within psychopathology to designate 'troubles lying on the frontier between neurosis and psychosis, particularly latent schizophrenias presenting an apparently neurotic set of of symptoms' (Laplanche and Pontalis 1973: 54). The semiotic terrain of borderline disorder is ambiguous at best, repressive at worst. The psychosocial aetiology of the disorder is admittedly diffuse and subject to multiple determinations. Clinical research in psychopathology has shown not only childhood trauma but chronic stress to be potential antecedents of borderline personality disorder (Shapiro and Dominiak 1992: 2). Borderline personality disorder as a diagnostic category is broad, inclusive and vague. It constitutes the official 'grey' area between neurosis and psychosis, between psychosocial treatment and psychotropic medication, between out-patient treatment and institutionalisation in the practice of psychiatry. Susanna Kaysen, author of *Girl, Interrupted* (1993), an autobiographical account of her psychiatric institutionalisation at the age of seventeen, was classified as a borderline personality disorder. On looking up the classification in the *Diagnostic and Statistical Manual of Mental Disorders* twenty-five years after her discharge, Kaysen found this gloss: 'This is often pervasive and is manifested by uncertainty about several life issues, such as self-image, sexual orientation, long-term goals or career choice, types of friends or lovers to have, and which values to adopt' (1993: 150).

Kaysen comments in her moving autobiographical account that 'Often an entire family is crazy, but since an entire family can't go into the hospital, one person is designated as crazy and goes inside' (1993: 95). One is hardly surprised that in Kaysen's family, the designated crazy is the disturbed daughter. The social limit of insanity, however, hardly ends with the family. Not only is the individuation of psychopathology within psychiatry a suppression system for the nervous system at large, but the oedipalisation of the subject in psychoanalysis and psychotherapy, that is, the reduction of the identity and meaning of the social subject to her familial history, is a suppression of group psychosis and general dysfunction within the socius. Psychopathology as it is currently practised suppresses the need for group psychiatry, sociohistorical analysis, and the integration of the subject's history with the group's history.[8] On the battlefront of desire, where points of subjectification localise both sign production and the production of subjectivity, 'For desire to be expressed in individual terms means that it is already condemned to castration' (Guattari 1984: 72).

The discourse of psychopathology, technologised in its postmodern form as psychopharmacology, reproduces the distributional flow of social power by suppressing the assemblage of desiring-machines in touch with the historical social experience and memory of the group. Psychopharmacology functions as a *surge suppressor*, putting a brake on flux (any tendency to change direction, speed or intensity) within the collective flow of feminine social bodies and signs. In short, biopsychiatry puts a brake on non-majoritarian desire, which can express within the collective social flow only as *surge* – sudden accelerations of sign-flow away from established meanings. As an interpretative machine, psychopharmacology modulates the potential flux in desire and affect caused by historical social memory embodied in the individual subject. The abstract-machine of rationality as it is institutionalised in psychopharmacology modulates cognition, behaviour and desire on two planes: neurochemical and representational. The neurochemical plane regulates embodied knowledge as the subjective assemblage of memory, affect and desire; the representational plane regulates the flow of signs between the individual and the public.

On the plane of subjectification in psychopharmacology's double articulation, psychopharmacological treatment rewires the traumatised subject's faciality[9] – the elaborate system of codes that regulates signs of class, race, gender and desire – through a process formally expressed within psychiatry as 'symptom management'. Symptom management modulates subjectification by deterritorialising potential conjunctions between neurochemical processes and abstract social facialities, working at a neurobiological ground zero of social being and becoming. Psychotropic drugs enter the subject through the organic body, territorialising three neurobiological systems of the brain: the serotonergic system, the limbic system, and the autonomic nervous system.[10]

Each chemical intervention actualises potential conjunctions between adaptive defensive mechanisms presenting as 'maladaptive' symptoms and 'normative' (i.e., functional, intelligible and socially acceptable) ideation, affect and behaviour. For example, episodic violent outbursts associated with anamnesis (surges of recollection) and abreaction (release of repressed emotions) can be regulated with the anticonvulsant carbamazepine (Tegretol). Counterindications of carbamazepine include potentially hazardous side-effects on bone marrow and liver, skin rashes and lightheadedness. Carbamazepine regulates behavioural 'dyscontrol' by modulating 'epileptoid overactivity' of limbic structures, those parts of the brain responsible for generating emotional experience and memories and for influencing emotion-related behaviours (Dominiak 1992: 106). 'Emotional storms' produced by asignifying turbulences traversing the individuated and alienated subject can thus be nipped in their neurochemical bud if not in their social context. Angry women overcome by surges of rage and violent acting-out behaviour, self-mutilation and suicidal actions, caught in a cycle of dissociation and intrusive abreaction, can be suppressed at the very neurobiological root of emotion and memory and at the neurochemical point of origin of dissociation.

The most pervasive psychic defence mechanism, dissociation, appears across a vast strata of symptomatologies, including schizophrenia, borderline personality disorder, multiple personality disorder and post-traumatic stress syndrome. Dissociation is generally understood to be 'temporary alteration of the general integrative function of consciousness', characterising states ranging from splitting and psychogenic amnesia to depersonalisation and multiple personality (Shapiro and Dominiak 1992: 43). Within the micropolitics of subjectification, dissociation can be understood as the de-molecularisation of memory and affect, the reduction and separation of memory-blocks into simpler groups or single particles, and the deterritorialisation of associational affective formations. Dissociation and splitting are the fundamental symptoms of schizophrenia, the term coined by Bleuler in 1911 to designate psychoses characterised by *Zerspaltung* (disintegration and fragmentation) and *Spaltung* (splitting of thought into two groups) (Laplanche and Pontalis 1973: 408). Dissociation can also present as psychogenic amnesia, a symptom historically associated with hysteria (Shapiro and Dominiak 992: 44). While dissociation may well function as an internalised surge-suppression mechanism articulated through the subject's limbic system, in its extreme forms of expression it becomes itself 'pathological' and must, in turn, be suppressed. While antidepressants and anxiolytics (tranquillisers) suppress depression and anxiety, however, they don't affect dissociation. In cases of multiple personality disorder, lithium can be prescribed to suppress pathological dissociation expressed as 'switching', though clinicians admit that rewiring multiple personality disorder with psychotropic medication presents the risk of suppressing more regulating personalities and activating 'unwanted alters' (Dominiak 1992: 103).

In the recently articulated clinical syndrome connecting sexual abuse to post-traumatic stress disorder, popularised and legitimised within the clinical community by Judith Herman's *Trauma and Recovery* (1992), a direct relation has been recognised between experiences of victimisation and the presence of dissociation. The clinical recognition of a post-traumatic stress syndrome among the abused disputes Freud's reading of hysteria as a fantasmatic production of incestuous desire on the part of the daughter, and is an initial step towards interpreting 'hysterical' symptoms as actual outcomes of the nervous system. In cases of abuse trauma, particularly when the victim is a dependent child, dissociation is seen as an appropriate way for the mind to escape what the social body cannot (Shapiro and Dominiak 1992: 44).

What is repressed through dissociation, however, does not remain dormant but returns as a sequelae to abuse trauma: nightmares, memory flooding, somatisation, depersonalisation, and parasuicidal behaviour. In other words, dissociation (*suppression*) expresses in a wave structure with uncontrollable memory (*surge*) appearing in the form of intrusive memories, flashbacks, night terrors, auditory hallucinations and memory fragments that can generate their own psychic reactions in the fluctuations of surge and suppression. Clinical research in the area of abuse, psycho-pathology and psychopharmacology suggests that dissociative states are not usually responsive to neuroleptic intervention in the long run (Dominiak 1992: 100), while clinical practice suggests that for all dissociative phenomena, healing involves verbalisation and the integrative processing of memories and affect associated with the traumatic stress and its prolonged repression.

While dissociation, understood as the formal expression of the subject's alienation from her own memories and from social rep-resentation, cannot be successfully 'treated' with neurochemical intervention, the secondary symptoms produced by dissociation are regularly treated with psychotropic medications. Post-traumatic stress disorder, for example, like bipolar disorder, tends to express in a bimodal fluctuation of states of hyperarousal (agitation, anxiety, abreaction, anamnesis, memory flooding, flashbacks, hypomania, micropsychotic breaks, intrusive thoughts or voices, acting out, intense mood shifts, insomnia, self-mutilation and suicidal behav-iour) and states of avoidance (splitting, emotional shutdown, fugue states, minimising, denial, depression). The symptoms associated with each of these states can be treated psychotropically. Propanolol, for example, can be prescribed to suppress autonomic hyperarousal. Complications from propranolol include altered cognitive functioning, depression, delirium and hypotension (Dominiak 1992: 104).

Hyperarousal of the autonomic nervous system, which includes the sympathetic and parasympathetic systems regulating the heart, intestines and glands, can also be suppressed at the neurochemical level with benzodiazepines, or 'tranquillisers'. Benzodiazepines can produce side-effects of chemically-induced amnesia as well as over-sedation, physiological dependence, and enhancement of behavour-ial dyscontrol if taken with alprazolam (Xanax) and lorazepam (Ativan) (Dominiak 1992: 105). The traumatised subject can self-regulate hyperarousal, producing an internal calming effect by stimulating stress-induced analgesia through cutting, starvation, head banging and so on. When this circuit of self-regulated psychic pain modulation becomes 'pathological', the psychopharmacologist can prescribe naloxone – a receptor blockade with opiate antago-nists that suppresses the processing of endogenous opioids, though this intrusive form of chemical intervention (the drug must be delivered intravenously) has shown little long-term effect on subjects whose sphere of psychic and social control has already been reduced to the interiority of their own physical body, as in anorexia-bulimia and other forms of parasuicidal or suicidal self-mutilation (Dominiak 1992: 105).

The psychopharmacological production of a chemical prosthetic feminine subject recently entered a new mass culture phase with the newly developed and aggressively marketed serotonin-specific drugs – Desyrel (trazodone), Anafranil (clomipramine), and the trendy and popular Prozac (fluoxetine). Serotonergic systems of the brain interface with the autonomic nervous system. These serotonin-specific drugs suppress hyperarousal and relieve depression by blocking the absorption of excess serotonin in the brain, thus increasing serotonin levels. Billed as a miracle drug, Prozac has been attributed wondrous capabilities by the mass media, from making timid introverts socially gregarious and adept to making business women more productive and self-assured. With fewer side-effects than the tricyclic antidepressants (counterindications of Prozac include mild nausea, shakiness, insomnia and, often downplayed in the publicity literature though commonly reported by users, anorgasmia), Prozac is the 1990s psychotropic medication for women that has gone mainstream, much like Valium did in the 1960s and 1970s, grossing for Lilly nearly $1 billion of the $8 billion antidepressant market in 1992 (Breggin and Breggin 1994: 3). By 1993, profits rose to $1.2 billion. While the pharmaceutical industry claims that 'personality enhancement' with 'cosmetic psychopharmacology' promises to be the great democratiser for people made 'vulnerable' by trauma or by innate neural chemistry, psychopharmacology obviously provides a tool for reinforcing cultural norms, reproducing the nervous system's body-politic and channelling abstract machinic criteria onto real social bodies.

NOTES

1. I use the term 'nervous system' her in Michael Taussig's sense of a social economy of circulating violences. See *The Nervous System* (1992).
2. The media participates in a similar in a similar economy at the level of mass culture by channelling repressed memories of everyday terror into either sensationalised news events of a few seconds' duration or made-for-TV evening movies about incest, domestic abuse, and so on, replete with commercial breaks. Avant-garde art, literature and film work on the same cultural plane – screening the

unrepresentable – though tackling it at the level of codes of apperception (for a much smaller audience).

3. On the distinction among territorialisation, deterritorialisation and reterritorialisation, Deleuze and Guattari write that territorialisation 'reorganizes functions' and 'regroups forces' within supple, segmentary social space (1987: 320), while reterritorialisation, which implies the specific striating procedures of a state apparatus, 'is not an added territory, but takes place in a different space than that of territories, namely, overcoded geometrical space'. Likewise, 'overcoding is not a stronger code, but a specific procedure different from that of codes' (1987: 222). The striations of the state are in turn subject to decoding and deterritorialising processes, lines of flight on which 'there is always something like a *war machine* functioning (222).

4. Limbic and autonomic particle-signs are feelings of emotion and distress before they are articulated as expressions of identity. See footnote 10.

5. Because their work is materialist rather than ontological, Deleuze and Guattari (1987) privilege the notion of *becoming* over that of *being*, emphasising the process of subjectivisation in regard to specific cultural practices.

6. Mass-mediating and policising 'acting out' behaviour within the public sphere is the basis of ACT-UP politics.

7. On the 'abnormal', Deleuze and Guattari comment:

    It has been noted that the origin of the word *anomal* ('anomalous'), an adjective that has fallen into disuse in French, is very different from that of *anormal* ('abnormal'): *a-normal*, a Latin adjective lacking a noun in French, refers to that which is outside rules or goes against the rules, whereas *an-omalie*, a Greek noun that has lost its adjective, designates the unequal, the coarse, the rough, the cutting edge of deterritorialization. The abnormal can be defined only in terms of characteristics, specific or generic; but the anamalous is a position or set of positions in relation to a multiplicity. Sorcerers therefore use the old adjective 'anomalous' to situate the positions of the exceptional individual to the pack (1987: 244).

8. Analysis of the sociohistorical structures of power relating abstract forms and collective social contents at a multitude of micropolitical levels is the heart of Félix Guattari's revisionist psychoanalysis and the crux of his political critique of the psychiatric institution in *Molecular Revolution: Psychiatry and Politics* (1984).

9. The face is not a signifier of individuated consciousness but a signifying mechanism, a network of interpretations organising a zone of acceptable expressions of the signifier and acceptable conductions of meanings to signs and of signs to social subjects. See the discussion of faciality in 'The Despotic Face of White Femininity' in my

Becoming-Woman (1997), and the chapter 'Year Zero: Faciality' in Deleuze and Guattari's *A Thousand Plateaus* (1987).

10. The serotonergic system regulates neurotransmissions within the brain that rely on serotonin; a depletion of serotonin is commonly associated with depression. The limbic system of the brain is the location of emotion. The autonomic nervous system regulates involuntary body functions in cardiac, smooth and glandular epithelial tissue, such as heartbeat, intestinal and stomach contractions, and gland secretions.

REFERENCES

Breggin, Peter R. and Breggin, Ginger Ross (1994) *Talking Back to Prozac*, New York: St Martin's Press.

Canguilhem, Georges (1994) *A Vital Rationalist: Selected Writings from Georges Canguilhem*, ed. François Delaporte, New York: Zone Books.

Deleuze, Gilles (1993) *The Deleuze Reader*, ed. Constantin Boundas, New York: Columbia University Press.

Deleuze, Gilles and Guattari, Félix (1983) *Anti-Oedipus: Capitalism and Schizophrenia*, trans. Robert Hurley, Mark Seem and Helen Lane, Minneapolis: University of Minnesota Press.

Deleuze, Gilles and Guattari, Félix (1987) *A Thousand Plateaus: Capitalism and Schizophrenia*, trans. Brian Massumi, Minneapolis: University of Minnesota Press.

Dominiak, George (1992) 'Psychopharmocology of the Abused' in George Dominiak and Shanti Shapiro (eds) *Sexual Trauma and Psychopathology: Clinical Intervention with Adult Survivors*, New York: Lexington Books.

Griggers, Camilla (1997) *Becoming-Women*, Minneapolis: University of Minnesota Press.

Guattari, Félix (1984) *Molecular Revolution: Psychiatry and Politics*, trans. Rosemary Sheed, New York: Penguin Books.

Herman, Judith (1992) *Trauma and Recovery*, New York: HarperCollins.

Kaysen, Susanna (1993) *Girl, Interrupted*, New York: Vintage Books.

Laplanche, J. and Pontalis, J. B. (1973) *The Language of Psychoanalysis*, trans. Donals Nicholson-Smith, New York: W. W. Norton and Co.

Sechehaye, Margeurite (1970) *Autobiography of a Schizophrenic Girl*, New York: New American Library.

Shapiro, Shanti and Dominiak, George (eds) (1992) *Sexual Trauma and Psychopathology*, New York: MacMillan Inc.

Stone, Elizabeth (1993) 'The Personality Pill', *Mirabella*, June: 86–92.

Taussig, Michael (1992) *The Nervous System*, New York: Routledge.

US Department of Health and Human Services (1995) *1992 Ambulatory Medical Care Survey*, CD-ROM series 13, no. 4. Hyattsville, MD: National Centre for Health Statistics.

8

Hysterical Men:
Shell-shock and the Destabilisation of Masculinity

LISA L. DIEDRICH

'HYSTERIA' DERIVES FROM THE Greek word *hystera* for uterus, and is, therefore, etymologically linked with the female body. Over the centuries, this original linguistic link between hysteria and the female body has been scrupulously maintained. Despite the constantly changing definitions of hysteria and its eclectic symptoms, the cultural associations between hysteria and women have not been overturned or even significantly undermined. To use the phrase 'male hysteria', then, is oxymoronic.[1] During World War I, however, hysterical symptoms were frequently identified in soldiers who experienced trench warfare first hand. Although many psychiatrists at the time acknowledged that war neurosis was in fact 'male hysteria', the term that became common parlance, possibly because it avoided implicit feminine associations, was 'shell-shock'.[2] Within the specific context of both the homefront and the warfront of World War I, I will look at the construction of male hysteria as well as its treatments, and its relationship to constructions of masculinity and femininity. Does a recognition of hysteria in males – even if labelled 'war neurosis' or 'shell-shock' – destabilise the masculine/feminine binary categories; and, if so, is such a destabilisation lasting or simply a momentary disruption of such categories? Other binary oppositions – reason/madness, health/illness, mind/body, doctor/patient, upper class/working class, public/private – and their potential destabilisation are also relevant to the

146

discussion here. What is at stake, in other words, are the 'sociocultural categories of the normal' and how they come into being (Epstein 1995: 9). The normal, or what we take to be normal, is not an ontological, ahistorical category, but rather is discursively produced and diligently policed within time and space: that is, the normal has a history and a geography. How do we decide, Julia Epstein wonders in her book *Altered Conditions*, 'what counts as normal and what we label as abnormal?' (1995: 8). '[T]he very idea of normativity is coercive', Epstein maintains – with a nod to the work of Michel Foucault, who saw health care in general and the clinic in particular as one example of a disciplinary practice in which 'useful' and 'intelligible' bodies – i.e., 'docile bodies' – are constituted (Epstein 1995: 8; Foucault 1977: 136).

The dichotomy between modernity and postmodernity is also implicitly contested in the 'abnormal' occurrence of hysteria in males in World War 1. World War I is often described, historically speaking, as the quintessentially modern war. *In The Great War and Modern Memory*, Paul Fussell writes:

What we can call gross dichotomizing is a persisting imaginative habit of modern times, traceable, it would seem, to the actualities of the Great War. 'We' are here on this side; 'the enemy' is over there. 'We' are individuals with names and personal identities; 'he' is a mere collective identity. We are visible; he is invisible. We are normal; he is grotesque. Our appurtenances are natural; his, bizarre (1975: 75).

In addition, literary modernism was at its peak during the war, and many writers who experienced and wrote about the war were influenced by modernism. According to Allyson Booth, 'the Great War was experienced by soldiers as strangely modernist and . . . modernism itself is strangely haunted by the Great War' (1996: 6). Yet the Great War's link to historical and literary modernism does not preclude an analysis that foregrounds postmodernist theory and its emphasis on the destabilisation and denaturalisation of cherished binary categories. As David Harvey notes in *The Condition of Postmodernity*, 'No one exactly agrees as to what is meant by the term ['postmodernism'], except, perhaps that "postmodernism" represents some kind of reaction to, or departure from, "modernism"' (1989: 7). Postmodernism, it seems to me, is not *either* a reaction to *or* a departure from modernism; it is *both*. Modernism itself is not a discrete theoretical or historical category of analysis; it carries within it an 'inner dissonance', an antagonism which is articulated in postmodernism (see Young 1995: 54). In other words, it might be said that the seeds of postmodernism were planted in the trenches of Mons, Loos, the Somme, Arras, Verdun and Ypres. In order to ground my theoretical and historical discussion, I will refer to two works of fiction – Pat Barker's *Regeneration* (1991) and Virginia Woolf's *Mrs Dalloway* (1925), neither of which is a war novel in the conventional sense, that is about strategy and military battles won and lost; rather World War I gives structure to these narratives without being their prevailing content.[3]

HYSTERICAL WOMEN:
THE FEMALE BODY AS SYMPTOMATIC

Hysteria is linked not only etymologically but also culturally to the female body, because the female body in relationship to the normatively defined male body is seen as pathological, symptomatic by its very nature. In other words, 'illness affects and defines [woman's] whole being' (Doane 1986: 173). Hysteria is a quintessentially feminine disease and, as such, refers 'more to an image than an illness' – the image being that of the feminine (Foucault 1965: 139). The symptoms and significations that concatenate around the sign of hysteria are constantly shifting; and just as the symptoms are polymorphous and hyperbolic, so too are hysteria's meanings and manifestations. Foucault writes of modern interpretations of hysteria:

It was not so much a question of escaping the old localization in the uterus, but of a diverse, polymorphous disease dispersed throughout the entire body. A disease was to be accounted for that could attack the head as well as the legs, express itself in a paralysis or in frenzied movements, that could bring on catalepsy or insomnia: in short, a disease that traversed corporeal space so rapidly and so ingeniously that it was virtually present throughout the entire body (1965: 145–6).

Hysteria's habit of mimicking other diseases, moreover, makes hysteria not simply one disease, but many, if not all, diseases (Smith-Rosenberg 1985: 203; Foucault 1965: 148). Hysteria, in other words, might be described as a performative disease.[4] This characteristic mimicry or performativity links hysteria to conceptions of femininity, if we consider femininity not as an ontological category inherent to female bodies, but as a social construction to which 'real' women can never quite conform or measure up. Femininity itself, then, is mimicked or performed, though never fully or finally achieved (Butler 1990). If the female hysteric is said to mimic or perform a disease, then does the male hysteric, in a sense, mimic and perform not only a disease but femininity as well? Can the male hysteric, in other words, be said to be in drag symptomatically?

Before addressing questions concerning the male hysteric, however, I will first consider briefly some of the ways in which the female hysteric has been perceived and treated beginning in the Victorian era. Though hysteria, as I've said, often mimics the symptoms of other diseases, by the nineteenth century the etiology of such symptoms was usually diagnosed not as organic but as psychological. Most nineteenth-century physicians who attempted, therefore, to diagnose the disease according to the symptoms may have been deceived because the disease they encountered was 'not essence; it [was] a ruse of the body' (Foucault 1965: 148). The deceptiveness of hysteria contributes to the sense that the hysteric is a fraud, and a self-centred, willful fraud at that.[5] In her book *Disorderly Conduct: Visions of Gender in Victorian America*, Carroll Smith-Rosenberg describes the adversarial – even hostile – power relationship that often developed between the (male) physician and his hysterical (female) patient (see also Bernheimer 1985: 6). 'These hysterical women', according to Smith-Rosenberg, 'might . . . be only clever frauds and sensation seekers – morally delinquent and, for the physician, professionally embarrassing.' Smith-Rosenberg continues:

Except when called upon to provide a hypothetical organic etiology, physicians saw hysteria as caused either by the indolent, vapid, and unconstructive life of the fashionable middle- and upper-class woman, or by the ignorant, exhausting, and sensual life of the lower- or working-class woman. Neither was a flattering etiology. Both denied the hysteric the sympathy granted to sufferers from unquestionably organic ailments (1985: 204–5).

Many physicians and others believed that the hysteric's loss of self-control and self-discipline selfishly disrupted the normal functionings of the family and denied her 'natural' role in it. In order to 'cure' hysteria, many physicians preached the platitudes of self-discipline and stressed the moral imperatives of woman's 'natural' role in the family. The hysteric must learn, in other words, 'to undertake the arduous and necessary duties of wife and mother' (Smith-Rosenberg 1985: 205), and, by doing so, exhibit 'the self-control, self-discipline, self-denial, and will power' that 'constitute the symbolic substance, the implicit meaning of the pursuit of health' (Crawford 1984: 76–7).

Faced with hysteria's disruptive, excessive character, physicians in the late nineteenth century often administered S. Weir Mitchell's 'rest cure'. According to Mitchell's rest cure, the patient first had to agree to cooperate fully with her physician, relinquishing absolute control to him and disregarding her own feelings, questions, and concerns. 'Bed rest for six weeks to two months', 'seclusion, and excessive feeding' were the hallmarks of a cure that hoped to sub-due the hysterical woman's unruly body and mind (Bassuk 1986: 141). Just how successful Mitchell's rest cure was at treating hyste-ria is unknown, but his belief that the hysterical woman had lost all self-discipline and must succumb to the mastery of her physician as a pathway to cure was a pervasive ideology. Mitchell himself believed that the rest cure not only should be administered in cases of hysteria, but that all 'women should model their lives on the principles underlying the rest cure' (Bassuk 1986: 143).

THE HYSTERIC AS PROTO-FEMINIST

Because the nineteenth-century hysteric lacked the self-discipline considered appropriate to women, she may be said to have resisted the limited roles allowed for women. By disrupting the family, the hysteric in a sense freed herself from domesticity. According to Smith-Rosenberg, 'The hysterical woman ceased to function with-in the family. No longer did she devote herself to the needs of others, acting as self-sacrificing wife, mother, or daughter: through her hysteria she could and in fact *did* force others to assume those functions' (1985: 206). Hélène Cixous, furthermore, has stressed the feminist revolt which is implicit, if not explicit, to hysteria. Hysterics, like Freud's Dora, are, to Cixous, proto-feminist heroines making 'permanent war' against phallogocentrism (Cixous and Clement 1986: 287). In her introduction to *In Dora's Case*, a collec-tion of essays on Freud, hysteria and feminism, Claire Kahane notes:

Although Freud's assertion that hysteria afflicted *both* men and women was a liberating gesture in the nineteenth century, contemporary fem-inists are reclaiming hysteria as the dis-ease of women in patriarchal culture. *Dora* is thus no longer read as merely a case history or a frag-ment of an analysis of hysteria but as an urtext in the history of woman, a fragment of an increasingly heightened critical debate about the meaning of sexual difference and its effects on representations of feminine desire (1985: 31).

Many commentators have noted the widespread incidence of hysteria among highly intelligent nineteenth-century women like Virginia Woolf and Charlotte Perkins Gilman. In his 1895 collaboration with Freud on the subject of hysteria, Josef Breuer, relates, to cite another example, the now famous case of Anna O., who, in real life, was Bertha Pappenheim, a 'willful, energetic, intuitive, and compassionate person' of exceedingly high intelligence (Hunter 1983: 467). Constricted by her role as daughter in a conservative Jewish household, Pappenheim exceeded those bounds by engaging with Breuer in what she described as a 'talking cure', later recognised as the birth of psychoanalysis. 'Psychoanalysis', therefore, according to Dianne Hunter, 'can be seen as a translation into theory of the language of hysteria.' Hunter asserts as well that, '[b]oth psychoanalysis and hysteria subvert the reigning cultural order by exploding its linguistic conventions and decomposing its facade of orderly conduct' (1983: 485 and 486). In other words, hysteria, by giving expression to women's rage at her repressive socio-psychological experiences, and psychoanalysis, by listening to that rage and translating it into theory, challenged, at least to some extent, the dichotomous relationship between the normal and the pathological within specific cultural contexts.

In opposition to Cixous and others who portray hysterics as heroic proto-feminists, Catherine Clement argues that although the hysteric undoubtedly disturbs the phallogocentric economy, she does not ultimately overturn it in any meaningful way, but rather remains, in Toril Moi's words, 'efficiently gagged and chained to her feminine role' (Moi 1985: 192; Cixous and Clement 1986; Clement 1980).[6] Clement believes that by opting for, in Lacanian terms, the imaginary over the symbolic – the pre-linguistic over the linguistic realm – for expressing her dis-ease, the hysteric's disturbance can only be directed inward not outward via language, and, thus, is actually easily monitored and maintained by the social order. The hysteric cannot stand outside the phallogocentric social order to make her protest; thus, any analysis of her rebellion must include effects in both the private and public spheres. Clement writes, 'If one would only consider the feminine situation in the context in which it is inscribed, and not by itself, all alone, removed. The same goes for women as for madmen: in a *manifest* position of exclusion, they keep the system together latently, by virtue of their very exclusion' (1980: 134). The hysteric's revolt, in other words, does not overturn but reinforces the phallogocentric economy and the unequal masculine/feminine dichotomy on which it is based. '[R]esistance as Foucault notes, 'is never in a position of exteriority in relation to power' (1978: 95).

Recognising the limitations of hysterical resistance, however, is not to deny that for individual women in specific historical and cultural contexts, hysteria was a means of opting out of an intolerable, though socially sanctioned, situation. As I turn now to soldiers in the trenches during World War I, we shall see similarly courageous, though in many respects also nonetheless futile, attempts to contest an equally intolerable situation.

THE FEMINISATION OF THE SOLDIER

The Great Adventure. They'd been mobilized *into holes in the ground so constricted they could hardly move. And the Great Adventure – the real life equivalent of all the adventure stories they'd devoured as boys – consisted of crouching in a dugout, waiting to be killed. The war that had promised so much in the way of 'manly' activity had actually delivered 'feminine' passivity, and on a scale that their mothers and sisters had scarcely known. No wonder they broke down.*

(Pat Barker, Regeneration, 1991: 107–8)

Ironically, S. Weir Mitchell developed his rest cure in 1872 in order to treat soldiers suffering from battle fatigue. However, as Ellen Bassuk notes, although '[t]heoretically used to treat both men and women, most patients described in the literature were nervous females who were suffering from battle fatigue on the home front' (1986: 141). Nonetheless, the connection between 'battle fatigue' on the warfront and on the homefront is not simply coincidental, but crucial. Women in western society are perceived as 'naturally' passive and are expected as noted above to selflessly assume their 'naturally' ordained roles as wife and mother, placing their family's needs above their own. Similarly, the soldier, particularly during wartime, must also subsume his[7] individual will to the needs of his platoon and his country. The ideal of self-sacrifice holds true for the wife and mother as well as the soldier. Moreover, a soldier's body, like a woman's body, is the object and instrument of extreme discipline – 'an infinitesimal power over the active body' – that constitutes such bodies as both 'useful' and 'intelligible' within society (Foucault 1977: 137).[8]

Despite being subjected to extreme disciplinary training in order to subordinate his individual will to the social will, the soldier engaged in warfare prior to World War I was seen neither as passive nor as feminine, but as active, masculine and, of course, heroic. In the trenches of World War I, however, this heroic image of the soldier was turned on its head. The situation of the soldier in the trenches, as Pat Barker makes clear in the above quote, was imitative of the domestic situation for women. In the trenches, soldiers were immobilised and forced to wait passively for something to happen to them. Trench warfare was defensive, not offensive, in character; siege-like conditions were maintained on both sides for days, even months. In his important book on the war entitled *No Man's Land*, Eric J. Leed asserts that '[i]n this war the reality was immobility enforced by the technological domination of defensive firepower. This fact had great significance for a redefinition of the soldierly character, which in this war could have little in common with the aggressive, offensive image that had traditionally defined the soldierly role' (1979: 101). Thus, the 'offensive personality' associated with the soldier in particular and the masculine in general was replaced by a 'defensive personality' associated with the feminine. This 'defensive personality' contributed to the incidence of war neurosis among trench soldiers: 'passivity', Claire Kahane writes citing Alan Krohn, 'has been a consistently central component of hysteria' (1995: 9).

The psychiatrist and anthropologist W. H. R. Rivers, the real-life protagonist of Barker's novel *Regeneration*, studied the incidence of neurosis among various branches of service. Rivers found that pilots, who were highly mobile and actively engaged in their battles, showed the least incidence of neurosis; while those in the balloon service, who floated above the front as observers of enemy activities and who were, thus, highly vulnerable to enemy artillery, were far more susceptible to neurosis than pilots or even their fellow soldiers in the trenches (Rivers 1932; Leed 1979; Barker 1991). According to Leed, 'The happiness of the hero lay . . . in adventure and self-transcendence,' both of which were impossible to achieve while passively waiting for death wallowing in trenches or floating above a battlefield (1979: 135). The quite common phenomenon of 'living burial' – being, literally, buried under mud, debris, and bodies following an explosion – was perhaps the most extreme and gruesome example of the trench soldier's enforced immobility and passivity in the face of death. Leed notes that the hysterical paralysis that resulted from 'premature burial' 'earned its own pathological category as the "burial alive neurosis"' (1979: 22–3).

153

SILENT PROTESTS

The world of war was not a world of freedom.
(Eric Leed, *No Man's Land*, 1979: 96)

Although raised in a modern western culture that strictly delineated and constantly reinforced as 'natural' distinctions between masculine activity and feminine passivity, soldiers during World War I were paradoxically confined to a situation that belied the autonomy and mobility essential to their society's construction of masculinity. Like many middle- and upper-class Victorian women confined to their households, many soldiers found confinement in the trenches intolerable and their means of expression circumscribed. Due to cultural constructions of masculinity that condemned fear as unmanly, as well as the hierarchical structure of military command that condemned dissent as insubordinate and undisciplined, many soldiers, according to Elaine Showalter, were 'found, like women, to express their conflicts through the body' (1985: 171; see also Leed 1979: 164 and Gilbert 1983: 447–8). Mutism and speech disorders, symptoms commonly identified with hysteria in women, were epidemic among soldiers during World War I. Showalter asks, 'What had happened to make these men so unstable, so emotional, in a word, so feminine?' and answers that 'powerlessness [can] lead to pathology . . .' (1985: 190).

But did all men at the front experience war similarly? Most assuredly not. According to Paul Fussel, 'There was the wide, indeed gaping distinction between officers and men, emphasized not merely by separate quarters and messes and different uniforms and weapons but by different accents and dictions and syntaxes and allusions' (1975: 82): that is, one might say, differences of voice itself. Not surprisingly, then, W. H. R. Rivers and other doctors studying war neurosis noted that it manifested itself differently in officers and enlisted men. Rivers explained that enlisted men, whose recourse to autonomous action was most limited, exhibited disorders that he identified as 'hysterical' and were most often expressed 'in some definite physical form, such as paralysis, mutism, contracture, blindness, deafness, or other anaesthesia'. Officers, on the other hand, typically exhibited disorders that Rivers categorised as neurasthenic, including relatively minor physical symptoms such as 'lack of physical and mental energy, . . . disorders of sleep and of the circulatory, digestive, and urogenital systems [and] . . . tremors, tics, or disorders of speech'; as well as mental symptoms including 'depression, restlessness, irritability, and enfeeblement of memory' (1922: 207–8). Since, indeed, most officers were middle or upper class and most enlisted men were working class, Rivers considered class difference significant in the aetiology of neurotic symptoms.[9] Mutism, for example, was far more common among enlisted men, according to Rivers, because it symbolised the conflict between wanting to speak and knowing that if one does the consequences will be disastrous; mutism, in other words, reveals an 'anxiety about the voice itself' (Kahane 1995: viii). Moreover, cognisant of the discussions of eugenics circulating at the time, Rivers also suggested that, being 'more widely educated than the private soldier', the officer's 'mental life is more complex and varied, and he is therefore less likely to be content with the crude solution of the conflict between instinct and duty which is provided by such disabilities as dumbness or the helplessness of the limb' (1922: 209). For Rivers it is only 'natural' that working-class soldiers should express their neurosis through their bodies while upper-class officers should express their neurosis through their minds. But disentangling cause and effect – class association from wartime experience, the natural from the social – as Rivers attempts to do in congress with the pseudo-science of eugenics is surely impossible here. Pat Barker's fictional character Second-Lieutenant Billy Prior dramatises and calls into question the upper class/working class, mind/body dichotomies Rivers perpetuates. Prior, from a working-class family, is also an officer. When Rivers first meets Prior he is suffering from mutism as a result not only of his horrific experiences in the trenches, but also, according to Rivers, as a result of the conflict of being an officer who is also working class. Prior is an important liminal figure in Barker's book (he is also, significantly, bisexual); his father ruefully describes his son to Rivers as 'neither fish nor fowl' (1991: 57). Septimus Smith, Virginia Woolf's shell-shocked character in *Mrs Dalloway*, is also described in liminal terms: 'on the whole, a border case, neither one thing nor the other' (1925: 93). In World War I categories of gender, class, and sexuality were often transgressed, yet still we must question again whether such transgressions represent a radical rupture of the social order or simply a temporary disruption articulated through the loud silences of society's liminal figures.

OLD VS. YOUNG/HOMEFRONT VS. WARFRONT

If I were fierce, and bald, and short of breath,
*   I'd live with scarlet Majors at the Base,*
And speed glum heroes up the line to death.
*   You'd see me with my puffy petulant face,*
Guzzling and gulping in the best hotel,
*   Regarding the Roll of Honour. 'Poor young chap,'*
I'd say – 'I used to know his father well;
*   Yes, we've lost heavily in this last scrap.'*
And when the war is done and youth stone dead,
*   I'd toddle safely home and die – in bed.*

(Siegfried Sassoon, 'Base Details', 1917)

The trench soldier's feeling of powerlessness, his inability to speak out against appalling conditions that annihilated his autonomous self, did not mean, however, that his silent protests were a form of resistance only directed inward. As Sassoon's poem quoted above makes plain, World War I, like most wars but more so, was implemented by older men and waged by young men. Again we see a mind/body dichotomy: the old men, their bodies no longer powerful, nonetheless, omnipotently send young men, in their prime physically, to die for what they (the old men) deem worth fighting for. Young men were pawns in the war games being played by older men, and, like many women in Victorian households,[10] their only recourse was hysteria (or, for a few, like Sassoon and Wilfred Owen, hysteria as well as – significantly – writing). Barker dramatises this mythic conflict when she has Rivers meditate on a stained-glass window depicting the story of Abraham and Isaac, which Rivers understands as *the* bargain on which civilisation is based:

If you, who are young and strong, will obey me, who am old and weak, even to the extent of being prepared to sacrifice your life, then in the course of time you will peacefully inherit, and be able to exact the same obedience from your sons. Only we're breaking the bargain, Rivers thought. All over northern France, at this very moment, in trenches and dugouts and flooded shell-holes, the inheritors were dying, not one by one, while old men, and women of all ages, gathered together and sang hymns (1991: 149).

As Barker makes clear, the young men in the trenches of World War I had become nothing more than objects of exchange between the fathers of civilisation; their bodies unto death were their dowry. Much of the bitterness of the men in the trenches, therefore, was not directed at the enemy, who were also trapped in

156

trenches, but at the 'managers' of the war, the staff, as well as those who enjoyed 'security and comfort' and could not understand the suffering of the men at the front (Leed 1979: 94; see also Fussell 1975).

Those on the homefront who enjoyed 'security and comfort' were not only the powerful old men directing the war's operations and sending young men off to die, but 'women of all ages', many of whom encouraged their sons, brothers, friends and lovers to join the war effort.[11] Moreover, with so many men away at the front, women replaced them in all sorts of occupations and took up other jobs made necessary by the war, as, for example, munitions workers, nurses and ambulance drivers. In other words, they entered the public sphere in significant numbers for the first time in history. '[A]s young men became increasingly alienated from their prewar selves, increasingly immured in the muck and blood of No Man's Land,' Sandra Gilbert writes, 'women seemed to become, as if by some uncanny swing of history's pendulum, evermore powerful' (1983: 425; see also Woollacott 1993: 129). While men were immobilised in the trenches in a situation domestic in character, women were mobilised on the homefront and 'allowed an expanded range of escape routes from the constraints of the private family' (Leed 1979: 45). Women were not only employed at home, however, they were also frequently employed as nurses and ambulance drivers, who, if not at the front itself, were within close enough proximity – within, in fact, 'the forbidden zone' directly behind the lines – to witness its devastation, to be threatened by its dangers, and, in some cases, then, to write about their experiences.[12] In her essay 'Corpus/Corps/Corpse', Jane Marcus says these '[y]oung, healthy, well-educated women became the charwomen of the battlefield, the cleaners of the worst human waste we produce, the symbolic bearers of all its pollution and disease' (1989: 126). Though women have always been the symbolic bearers of pollution and disease, never before has this role been quite so public nor quite so cross-class. Furthermore, many men were returning home from war – if they returned at all – mute and mutilated and finding women surging with energy and confidence born of newly earned economic power. The war had, in other words, destabilised the categories of masculine and feminine. Sandra Gilbert finds the army nurse/soldier patient relationship to be symbiotic, and a particularly telling example of the collapse of the masculine/feminine binary: 'her evolution into active, autonomous, transcendent subject is associated with his devolution into a passive, dependent, immanent medical object' (1983: 435). In *Regeneration*, Pat Barker portrays the new found freedom of a group of women munitions workers. Symbolically, their work transforms their skin into an eerie, otherworldly yellow, making them appear somehow unnatural, other than women. One of the women mourns not the death of her husband at war, but his impending return home, explaining that when war broke out in Europe and her husband went off to fight, 'peace broke out' for her at home (1991: 110).

Much of the resentment felt by soldiers in the trenches towards those on the homefront was bred of an inability to communicate their experiences of war to those not directly involved: 'its conditions were too novel, its industrialized nastiness too umprecedented' (Fussell 1975: 87). The experience in the trenches was not a 'typical' war experience, if any war experience can be said to be 'typical'; it was, simply put, not heroic. The soldiers who experienced the horrors of World War I, for the most part, did not return – at least in their own minds – as the heroes those on the homefront willed them to be.[13] Their experience on the battlefield, in other words, was reduced at home to an heroic cliché. Many found that the experience of war, like that of madness, was beyond language, bracketed off from the realm of reason and everyday life. 'Faced with annihilation and death,' Margaret Higonnet writes, 'language finds itself in crisis' (1993: 211). Eric Leed compares the soldier to an initiate into a secret society; the soldier, like the madperson and the initiate, is a liminal being upon his return to 'civilization'. 'The experience', Leed writes, '. . . is primarily a nonverbal, concrete, multichannel learning experience that can never adequately be reproduced in mere words' (1979: 74). Siegfried Sassoon, through his poetry and his declaration calling for an end to the war which was published in the London *Times* in July 1917 and which opens *Regeneration*, confronts the heroic image of war and the travesty of a war prolonged by those with no experience of it: 'I believe that I may help to destroy the callous complacence with which the majority of those at home regard the continuance of agonies which they do not share, and which they have not sufficient imagination to realize' (quoted in Barker 1991: 3).

The gulf between those who went to war and those who stayed home and the adversarial atmosphere it engendered did not miraculously disappear with the cessation of hostilities. Virginia Woolf's novel *Mrs Dalloway* published in 1925 and narrating the events of one particular day in 1923 reveals a lingering liminality felt by veterans of World War I in relation to the rest of society. Ostensibly, the book is about Mrs Dalloway's preparations for a rather posh party, but this narrative is bracketed by another narrative that follows the trials and tribulations of Septimus Warren Smith, who is suffering hysterical symptoms as a result of his experience at war, and his compassionate but plaintive wife, Rezia. Just as nineteenth-century women with hysteria disrupted the proper functioning of the family, Septimus's shell-shock – long after the war has ended – continues to disrupt and destabilise the fabric of the Warren Smiths' domestic life. Septimus is unable to fulfill his societal duties and obligations as the 'man of the house'; he is unable, as a man was expected to do at the time, to care for his wife emotionally and economically: 'Didn't one owe perhaps a duty to one's wife? Wouldn't it be better to do something instead of lying in bed?' (Woolf 1925: 102). 'In essence the traditional figure of the veteran', remarks Eric Leed in what could be a description of Woolf's Septimus Warren Smith, 'is derived from everything that is presumed to lie "outside" the boundaries of domestic existence' (1979: 195). After the war, veterans, unable to reintegrate themselves into the normative roles set for them by society, continued in increasing numbers to suffer from war neurosis while the public's patience with such suffering abated as the war became for them, though not for the soldiers who had fought and suffered traumatic experiences, a distant and entirely assimilated memory. At Mrs Dalloway's party some of the guests, including Dr William Bradshaw, who treats shell-shock with a rest cure, appear to be discussing the 'Report of the War Office Committee of Enquiry into "Shell-Shock"', which had been published by the British Army in 1922 and 'recommended a "cure" for shell-shock that was clearly underpinned by coercion and violence' (Ouditt 1994: 194–5). Which brings me, finally, to a discussion of the methods used to treat shell-shock during the war and after; many of these methods being clearly reminiscent of the efforts to cure (female) hysteria.

DIAGNOSING AND CURING SHELL-SHOCK

In his book, *A War Imagined* (1992), Samuel Hynes describes the mood in Britain at the brink of war in 1914. According to Hynes, there were many in Britain who welcomed the war not only to repudiate German aggression, but also in the hopes that war would return Britain to its Victorian apex. It was a nostalgic longing for an age when Britain stood tallest and most civilised among nations, before her colonies, her workers, and her women began to agitate for change, and, as a result, to turn, or threaten to turn, British society on its head.[14] The Britain of 1914 was feared by many to be weak and decadent; and this fear of a soft, effeminate society influenced the way war was imagined, at least initially. Such factors also played a role in the 'medicocultural diagnoses'[15] and treatments of shell-shock. Many officers and army doctors in Britain, as well as the other nations involved in World War I,[16] were reluctant to acknowledge shell-shock as a legitimate neurosis deserving of special treatment. In this view, shell-shock was the result not of the extreme and traumatic conditions of trench warfare, but rather of a particular soldier's weakened moral capacity or his wilful and criminal insubordination. At best the shell-shocked, or hysterical, soldier was seen, like female hysterics of the late nineteenth century, as a self-indulgent, cowardly malingerer, at worst as a moral and physical degenerate, whose masculinity was called into question. Characterised as effeminate, the soldier suffering from shell-shock was also often accused of homosexuality.[17] Moreover, influenced by Social Darwinist and eugenic theories circulating at the time, some attributed shell-shock to 'hereditary taint', and encouraged stricter recruiting practices to weed out 'unsuitables' (Showalter 1985: 170)[18]

According to this 'moral view of neurosis' – what Foucault would describe as 'the psychological effect of a moral fault' – shell-shock was to be handled not with sympathy but with discipline; a discipline that '[b]efore seeking to relieve . . . inflicts suffering within the rigor of a moral necessity' (1965: 158 and 182). Such disciplinary therapy, whose purpose was to punish transgression and re-exert control over a body out of bounds, could be quite cruel, nothing short of torture in some cases. British doctor Lewis Yealland, for example, enthusiastically encouraged the use of electroshock to 'cure' cases of shell-shock. In a horrific scene in *Regeneration*, Barker re-enacts an actual treatment described in Yealland's own writings in which he administers electroshocks to various parts of a mute patient's body, including the mouth and throat, until his speech faculty returns (1991: 224–33). As Barker's narrator explains, 'in every case the removal of the physical symptom was described as a cure', and, therefore, '[m]ost of [the] patients would be out within a week' (1991: 224). Relapse and suicide rates, not surprisingly, were inconsequential to doctors like Yealland.

Disciplinary therapy, however, did not necessarily have to include electroshock and other forms of violence. Its main purpose, whether more or less physically violent, was to encourage a soldier to function in ways deemed normative to his soldierly role and to the dictates of masculinity. The medical response, in all its forms, to male hysteria, in other words, represents a frantic attempt to reinstantiate the 'sociocultural categories of the normal' even in the face of a war that exposed over and over the ontological emptiness of such categories. In *Mrs Dalloway*, two different doctors – Holmes and Bradshaw – are consulted regarding Septimus's condition. Dr Holmes is of the opinion that nothing whatsoever is the matter with Septimus and suggests Septimus take 'a day off with his wife and [play] golf. [And] [w]hy not try two tabloids of bromide dissolved in a glass of water at bedtime?' According to Dr Holmes 'health is largely a matter in our own control' (1925: 101). Dr Bradshaw, on the other hand, does at least recognise the seriousness of Septimus's condition. He maintains that in order to cure shell-shock one has to re-establish the patient's sense of proportion. According to Bradshaw,

Health we must have; and health is proportion; so that when a man comes into your room and says he is Christ (a common delusion), and has a message, as they mostly have, and threatens, as they often do, to kill himself, you invoke proportion; order rest in bed; rest in solitude; silence and rest; rest without friends, without books, without messages; six months rest; until a man who went in weighing seven stone six comes out weighing twelve (1925: 109–10).

Bradshaw himself has a solid sense of proportion; he understands the difference between madness and reason, and has the authority and wherewithal as a respected citizen and physician to see to it that his patients learn – through discipline – the difference as well.

In contrast to disciplinary therapy, psychoanalysis provided an alternative interpretation of the aetiology of shell-shock and recommended different methods of treatment. W. H. R. Rivers was the pre-eminent psychoanalyst treating shell-shock during World War I, and his writings on war neurosis – as well as Pat Barker's novelisation of his practice at Craiglockhart Military Hospital near Edinburgh – reveal his view that shell-shock was not a result of moral weakness, but an understandable – even natural – response to a soldier's feelings of powerlessness, and a bodily manifestation of the conflict between the instinct of self-preservation and soldierly duty. In his practice, Rivers utilised Freud's theory of forgetting, which he found to be 'the most striking and characteristic feature of [Freud's] psychology' (1922: 166).[19] Like Freud and

Breuer, Rivers employed a 'cathartic method' for treating hysteria. He advised his patients not to repress traumatic war experiences under a cloak of emotional self-restraint requisite to masculinity, and helped them (through conversation, dream analysis and, less frequently, hypnosis) to remember their traumas in order that they might experience an abreaction of their 'strangulated' affect. Hysterical symptoms, according to Rivers, were often not a direct result of a traumatic experience itself, but a result of the individual repression of the experience as well as the collective silence surrounding male hysteria, which explains why many cases of shell-shock were still being diagnosed after the war. Rivers recognised the connection between repression and masculinity in general and between repression and military discipline in particular; in other words, as Barker explains, soldiers in World War I had 'been trained to identify emotional repression, as the essence of manliness. Men who broke down, or cried, or admitted to feeling fear, were sissies, weaklings, failures. Not *men*' (1991: 48).

Disciplinary therapy was by its very nature based on an unequal doctor/patient relationship; doctors, like Yealland, assumed a position of omnipotence and absolute superiority – physical and moral – over their patients. Psychoanalysts, like Rivers, on the other hand, did not attempt to dominate their patients, but encouraged a 'collaborative' means to cure. In *Regeneration*, Barker focuses extensively on the doctor/patient relationship. Rivers is portrayed as a man of great empathy, even to the point that, while treating Sassoon's 'anti-war complex' his own views of the war and his contribution to the war effort are called into question; he experiences, in Freudian terms, something of a countertransference.[20] 'In a sense, then,' Showalter writes, 'Rivers caught Sassoon's anti-war complex in the process of treating it' (1985: 188). With Rivers's psychoanalytic therapy, we see, therefore, a destabilisation of the doctor/patient dichotomy, a blurring of the distinction between the two positions whose distance is maintained and reinforced in disciplinary therapy.

REGENERATING MASCULINITY AND OTHER CONCLUSIONS

There is little question that Rivers's approach to treating shell-shock was more benevolent than the disciplinary methods of Yealland and others. Nonetheless, both approaches ultimately served the same purpose; and psychoanalysis, ironically, served that purpose more authoritatively, more effectively: during the war, to return the soldier to combat, and, after the war, to return the veteran to his 'rightful' position in the family and society. In other words, those doctors treating shell-shock served a normalising function; they attempted to re-establish the soldier's or veteran's sense of duty to his country, his platoon, and his family; to reinstill self-discipline; ultimately, to regenerate his masculinity. Treatments for shell-shock 'cured' the symptoms not the causes; men, whose masculinity was allegedly restored, were sent back to the trenches where they were once again placed in intolerable and life-threatening situations. A soldier's masculinity/potency was emphasised so that he could be returned to a situation in which he was once again feminised and made impotent. In the treatment of shell-shock, 'reason' must triumph over 'madness', masculine duty over hysterical (feminine) resistance; but the madness of the trenches – the madness of a society that must rigidly maintain at all costs the masculine/feminine binary – remained unchallenged, at least within the context of the clinic.

Again, as we saw when looking at the nineteenth-century female hysteric, one must consider the long-term effects in both the public and private spheres of such hysterical modes of resistance. In *Mrs Dalloway*, Septimus hurls himself out of a window to his death to elude the treatments of Drs Holmes and Bradshaw, and, thus, remains a 'border case': 'even Holmes himself could not touch this last relic straying on the edge of the world, this outcast, who gazed back at the inhabited regions, who lay like a drowned sailor, on the shore of the world' (1925: 103). Woolf does allow Septimus's death to intrude upon, to disrupt Mrs Dalloway's party; and Mrs Dalloway herself feels some kinship with Septimus, understanding that his 'death was defiance' (1925: 204). Alone for a moment, away from her guests, Mrs Dalloway realises, 'She felt somehow very like him – the young man who had killed himself. She felt glad that he had done it; thrown it away while they went on living.' Septimus's suicide momentarily, then, destabilises Clarissa Dalloway's world, society, the symbolic order. The moment quickly dissolves, however: 'But she must go back. She must assemble. She must find Sally and Peter. And she came in from the little room' (1925: 206). The social manifestations of Septimus's action are short lived; only Septimus's world is permanently transformed, turned upside down. Likewise, Siegfried Sassoon's rebellion, though less self-destructive than Septimus's suicide, is also ultimately subdued. As Elaine Showalter notes,

> His therapy was a seduction and a negotiation; his return to France, an acknowledgment of defeat. Obviously it was better for the authorities to have treated his pacifism as an anti-war complex, to have framed his rebellion as nervous breakdown, and to have isolated him in a mental hospital, than to have allowed him to find the political and collective audience for his ideas that might have helped him resist (1985: 187).

Rivers, who is still conflicted over the war and who believes that Sassoon is returning to France with a death wish, nonetheless discharges him to *duty*. As we have seen, World War I did destabilise many binary categories – the world *was* turned upside down – but soon enough it was turned right side up again and those binary categories which had been subverted were re-established with a vengeance. Whether female or male, hysteria as resistance challenges, but does not ultimately undermine our cherished categories.

We may interpret this conclusion as simply an understanding that hysterical resistance is at once 'kinda subversive and kinda hegemonic'.[21] But, it seems to me far more useful if we employ a more radical, more persistent critique of the project of modernity and its dependence on dualisms and its emphasis on progress: that is, if we employ what Derrida (1994) calls in a much different context, a 'counter conjuration', that recognises, as I mentioned at the outset, that modernity contains within it an 'inner dissonance', that the notion of progress depends on a fear of and a desire for regress, and that the transgressive – that which is shameful, vulnerable, and, yes, hysterical – is always already embodied within the normative. It is not only, then, our persistent regeneration that matters, but also our equally persistant degeneration. The promise of postmodernism is not to celebrate degeneration over and above regeneration, illness over and above health, madness over and above reason, but to overcome through an *embodied* deconstructive theory and practice the need to divide one from the other and instantiate it as normal.

NOTES

Thanks to Sara Ahmed who read and commented on an earlier draft of this essay, and to Margrit Shildrick and Janet Price for the opportunity and encouragement.

1. It should be noted, however, that Freud and, before him, Charcot both insisted that hysteria was not found only in women; 'men too were susceptible to the disease, albeit in much lower ratios than women' (Micale 1995: 25).

2. The term 'shell-shock' was coined in an article in the British medical journal *The Lancet* in February 1915 by Dr Myers (Showalter 1985: 167).

3. Sharon Oudit explains that Virginia Woolf's 'war books' 'do not deal with trenches, bayonets and barbed wire, or even hospital discipline, munitions making or conditions on the home front. Woolf, in her writing, exploits the metaphorical over the metonymical potentialities of language. Rather than trammeling her characters in an associative sequence involving their appearance, possessions, friends and politics, she develops a narrative perspective which defamiliarises this realist mode of presentation' (1994: 164). Woolf's writing is subtlely political and deceptively scathing social commentary. 'From her first book to her last,' writes Kathy J. Phillips, 'Virginia Woolf satirizes social institutions . . . by means of incongruous juxtapositions and suggestive, concrete detail, which can be interpreted as metaphor' (1994: 48). See also, Longenbach (1989) and Booth (1996).

4. In his historiography of hysteria entitled *Approaching Hysteria*, Mark Micale notes that, '[o]f all the arts, theater proved most amenable to the representation of hysteria'. Micale continues:

   The late nineteenth century witnessed a flowering of European drama, featuring many memorable female characters and bringing fame to numerous stage actresses. As Gail Finney has shown, the hysterical heroine flourished. It is easy to see why. The theater is a public and highly performative artistic medium while hysteria is the most extroverted of psychopathologies, its own act and audience' (1995: 198).

5. In *Madness and Civilization* (1965), Foucault notes the parallels between hysteria and hypochondria.

6. Along with Clement and Moi, both Elaine Showalter and Mary Russo agree that it is problematic and somewhat simplistic to see the hysteric as, first and foremost, a feminist heroine. Russo writes: 'Historically, Clement is right: hysterics and madwomen generally have ended up in the attic, or in the asylum, their gestures of pain and defiance having served only to put them out of circulation' (Showalter 1985: 161; Russo 1986: 222). But, nonetheless, Russo goes on to explain that those hysterics who performed their disease and were photographed at Charcot's clinic at Salpêtrière, though 'seen but not heard', 'nonetheless, . . . used their bodies in public, in extravagant ways that could have only provoked wonder and ambivalence in the female viewer, as such latitude of movement and attitude was not permitted most women without negative consequences' (1986: 222).

7. I am using the masculine pronoun exclusively here only because I am specifically talking about soldiers during World War I, all of whom were men (unless, of course, one considers those exceptional though oft-documented cases of women who cross-dressed and fought as men).

8. In *Regeneration*, Pat Barker gives a humorous example of the way women's bodies and soldier's bodies are similarly disciplined. In a sexual encounter between Second-Lieutenant Billy Prior and Sarah Lumb, she struggles to take off his puttees, is unable to do so, and giggles, 'They're like *stays*.' Prior responds, 'Don't tell the War Office. You'll have a lot of worried men' (1991: 216).

9. In *Approaching Hysteria*, Mark Micale points out that recent studies looking into the occupations of past hysteria patients have discovered that domestic servants in fact appear to have suffered quite frequently from hysteria. Micale contends that this was due to 'close daily contact with their social superiors'. He writes:

    Just as certain 'aristocratic' ailments of the eighteenth century descended to the middle classes early in the nineteenth, so perhaps a more medicalized self-consciousness began to form later in the century among working class people living in bourgeois environments. A kind of psychological gentrification occurred wherein servants, who attended their bourgeois and upper-class employers in sickness and health, developed the illness behaviors of their social superiors (1995: 159–160).

    While I find Micale's interpretation of 'psychological gentrification' compelling, I'm not certain it goes far enough. Domestic service has all of the characteristics I have mentioned as contributing to hysteria: namely, passivity and powerlessness. It would seem in these cases, as well as the cases that I have been looking at, that hysteria is likely a form of resistance to one's passive and powerless position. This, of course, doesn't exclude an element of 'psychological gentrification'.

10. Toril Moi describes Dora as a pawn in a game being played between two powerful men, her father and Herr K., the husband of her father's mistress. 'The father wants to exchange Dora for Frau K. ("If I get your wife, you get my daughter"), so as to be able to carry on his affair with Frau K. undisturbed. Dora claims that her father only sent her to psychiatric treatment because he hoped that she would be "cured" into giving up her opposition to her father's affair with Frau K., accept her role as victim of the male power game, and take Herr K. as her lover' (1985: 182).

11. Women in Britain, for example, often handed out white feathers to young men not in uniform to encourage them to join the military. In *Regeneration*, Barker mentions this custom just once without explanation, though subtly revealing its insidiousness: one of Rivers's patients, who has suffered the unimaginable trauma of landing face

166

down after an explosion in the rotting gut of a dead German soldier and, as a result, cannot even eat, is eventually discharged from the army and on his first trip out in civilian clothes is handed two white feathers (1991: 174).

12. It is not only women's war experience itself, but also the writing of that experience which collapses binary categories. According to Margaret Higonnet,

> The woman writer who trespasses onto the territory of war fiction transgresses many taboos. First and most important, she articulates knowledge of a 'line of battle' presumed to be directly known and lived only by men. Women, many still believe, should remain 'behind the lines' at the 'home front', as the symbolic preservers of peace and of the race (1993: 206).

For an extensive analysis of women's World War I writing, and a much-needed addition to Fussell's important study, see Tylee (1990).

13. The experience of American soldiers in Vietnam seems parallel here; except, of course, not only did the soldiers themselves question the myth of the heroic soldier, but so too did many folks at home. See, for example, O'Brien (1990).

14. For a discussion of the intersection between the suffrage movement in Britain, the modernist art and literary movement, and the politics of the Great War, see Longenbach (1989). Longenbach explains that many intellectuals 'came to the aid of their country, embracing violence and war as a mystical cleansing, rejecting the feminist, pacifist, and socialist reforms needed at home to agree to internationalist slaughter of a whole generation in the name of democracy' (1989: 134).

15. The term is Julia Epstein's (1995: 20).

16. Leed's *No Man's Land*, in fact, focuses most heavily on German soldiers' experiences of World War I.

17. The fact that Sassoon and Wilfred Owen, the two best known World War I war poets, were homosexual and were both hospitalised for shell-shock is certainly intriguing, but hardly indicates a trend. While *Regeneration* touches on homosexuality only peripherally, Barker's second volume, *The Eye in the Door* (1993), of her trilogy (the Booker Prize-winning *The Ghost Road* (1995) completes the trilogy) deals more explicitly with efforts to ferret out homosexuals servings in the British army and government, who were deemed a 'threat to the empire' – a potentially **deadly** 'contagion' – during World War I and its aftermath. In *Mrs Dalloway*, it is hinted as well that Septimus Warren Smith is homosexual, and that his hysteria was brought on by the death of his beloved commander.

18. One rather interesting suggestion circulating in Britain at the time was that bizarre, un-English first names might be a marker for 'hereditary taint'. Pat Barker alludes to this in a humorous discussion of Sassoon's first name, Siegfried; and Virginia Woolf was possibly

also aware of such theories choosing the first name Septimus for her shell-shocked character (who is loosely based on Sassoon).

19. In his book *Instinct and the Unconscious*, Rivers writes: 'It is a wonderful turn of fate that just as Freud's theory of the unconscious and the method of psycho-analysis founded upon it should be so hotly discussed, there should have occurred events which have produced on an enormous scale just those conditions of paralysis and contracture, phobia and obsession, which the theory was especially designed to explain' (1922: 164).

20. Barker's portrayal is based on Rivers's own writings in which he analyses a dream of his that he interprets as a questioning of his own position regarding the war. In *Conflict and Dream*, he writes, '[t]he incidents of the dream thus symbolized a movement, directed from without, in the pacifist direction . . .' (1932: 170–1).

21. In an essay entitled 'Queer Performativity', Eve Kosofsky Sedgwick offers a critique of the ways in which scholars have theoretically appropriated Judith Butler's notion of performativity. Sedgwick is unimpressed with most of these theoretical appropriations in that they do not go beyond showing the ways in which a certain type of performativity is both 'kinda subversive and kinda hegemonic'. In the hopes of using Butler's theory more radically, Sedgwick herself attempts to explore performativity as a means of 'understanding the obliquities among *meaning, being,* and *doing*'; and she looks specifically at shame as an affect that produces and delineates identity – often a particularly queer identity (1993: 2).

REFERENCES

Barker, Pat (1991) *Regeneration*, New York: Dutton.

Barker, Pat (1993) *The Eye in the Door*, New York: Plume.

Barker, Pat (1995) *The Ghost Road*, New York: Dutton.

Bassuk, Ellen L. (1986) 'The Rest Cure: Repetition or Resolution of Victorian Women's Conflicts?' in Susan Rubin Suleiman (ed.) *The Female Body in Western Culture: Contemporary Perspectives,* Cambridge, Massachusetts: Harvard University Press, pp. 139–51.

Bernheimer, Charles (1985) 'Introduction Part One' in Charles Bernheimer and Claire Kahane (eds) *In Dora's Case: Freud-Hysteria-Feminism*, New York: Columbia University Press, pp. 1–18.

Booth, Allyson (1996) *Postcards from the Trenches: Negotiating the Space Between Modernism and the First World War*, New York and Oxford: Oxford University Press.

Breuer, Josef and Freud, Sigmund (1895) *Studies on Hysteria*, New York: Basic Books.

Butler, Judith (1990) *Gender Trouble: Feminism and the Subversion of Identity*, New York: Routledge.

Cixous, Hélène and Clement, Catherine (1986) *The Newly Born Woman,* trans. Betsy Wing, Minneapolis: University of Minnesota Press.

Clement, Catherine (1980) 'Enslaved Enclave' in Elaine Marks and Isabelle de Courtivon (eds) *New French Feminisms,* trans. Marilyn R. Schuster, Brighton: The Harvester Press Ltd., pp. 130–6.

Crawford, Robert (1984) 'A Cultural Account of "Health": Control, Release, and the Social Body' in John B. Mckinlay (ed.) *Issues in the Political Economy of Health Care,* New York and London: Tavistock Publications, pp. 60–103.

Derrida, Jacques (1994) *Specters of Marx: The State of Debt, the Work of Mourning, and the New International,* trans. Peggy Kamuf, New York: Routledge.

Doane, Mary Ann (1986) 'The Clinical Eye: Medical Discourses in the "Woman's Film" of the 1940s' in Susan Rubin Suleiman (ed) *The Female Body in Western Culture: Contemporary Perspectives,* Cambridge, Massachusetts: Harvard University Press, pp. 152–74.

Epstein, Julia (1995) *Altered Conditions: Disease, Medicine, and Storytelling,* New York and London: Routledge.

Foucault, Michel (1965) *Madness and Civilization: A History of Insanity in the Age of Reason,* trans. Richard Howard, New York: Vintage Books.

Foucault, Michel (1977) *Discipline and Punish: The Birth of the Prison,* trans. Alan Sheridan, Middlesex: Penguin.

Foucault, Michel (1978) *The History of Sexuality Vol. 1: An Introduction,* trans. Robert Hurley, New York: Vintage Books.

Fussell, Paul (1975) *The Great War and Modern Memory,* London: Oxford University Press.

Gilbert, Sandra M. (1983) 'Soldier's Heart: Literary Men, Literary Women, and the Great War', *Signs* 8 (3): 422–50.

Harvey, David (1989) *The Condition of Postmodernity: An Enquiry into the Origins of Cultural Change,* Oxford: Basil Blackwell.

Higonnet, Margaret R. (1993) 'Not So Quiet in No-Woman's Land' in Miriam Cooke and Angela Woollacott (eds) *Gendering War Talk,* Princeton, New Jersey: Princeton University Press, pp. 205–26.

Hunter, Dianne (1983) 'Hysteria, Psychoanalysis, and Feminism: The Case of Anna O.', *Feminist Studies* 9 (3): 464–88.

Hynes, Samuel (1992) *A War Imagined: The First World War and English Culture,* New York: Simon and Schuster.

Kahane, Claire (1985) 'Introduction Part Two' in Charles Bernheimer and Claire Kahane (eds) *In Dora's Case: Freud-Hysteria-Feminism,* New York: Columbia University Press, pp. 19–32.

Kahane, Claire (1995) *Pasions of the Voice: Hysteria, Narrative, and the Figure of the Speaking Woman, 1850–1915,* Baltimore and London: Johns Hopkins University Press.

Leed, Eric J. (1979) *No Man's Land: Combat and Identity in World War I,* Cambridge: Cambridge University Press.

Longenbach, James (1989) 'The Women and Men of 1914' in Helen M.

Cooper, Adrienne Auslander Munich and Susan Merrill Squier (eds) *Arms and the Woman: War, Gender, and Literary Representation*, Chapel Hill: University of North Carolina Press, pp. 97–123.

Marcus, Jane (1989) 'Corpus/Corps/Corpse: Writing the Body in/at War' in Helen M. Cooper, Adrienne Auslander Munich and Susan Merrill Squier (eds) *Arms and the Woman: War, Gender, and Literary Representation*, Chapel Hill: University of North Carolina Press, pp. 124–67.

Micale, Mark S. (1995) *Approaching Hysteria: Disease and Its Interpretations*, Princeton, New Jersey: Princeton University Press.

Moi, Toril (1985) 'Representation of Patriarchy: Sexuality and Epistemology in Freud's Dora' in Charles Bernheimer and Claire Kahane (eds) *In Dora's Case: Freud-Hysteria-Feminism*, New York: Columbia University Press, pp. 181–99.

O'Brien, Tim (1990) *The Things They Carried*, New York: Penguin.

Ouditt, Sharon (1994) *Fighting Forces, Writing Women: Identity and Ideology in the First World War*, London and New York: Routledge.

Phillips, Kathy J. (1994) *Virginia Woolf Against Empire*, Knoxville: University of Tennessee Press.

Rivers, W. H. R. (1922) *Instinct and the Unconscious: A Contribution to a Biological Theory of the Psycho-neurosis*, Cambridge: Cambridge University Press.

Rivers, W. H. R. (1932) *Conflict and Dream*, London: Kegan Paul, Trench, Trubner and Co. Ltd.

Russo, Mary (1986) 'Female Grotesques: Carnival and Theory' in Teresa de Lauretis (ed.) *Feminist Studies/Critical Studies*, Bloomington: Indiana University Press, pp. 213–29.

Sassoon, Siegfried (1983) *The War Poems*, London: Faber and Faber.

Sedgwick, Eve Kosofsky (1993) 'Queer Performativity: Henry James's *The Art of the Novel*', *GLQ* 1 (1): 1–16.

Showalter, Elaine (1985) *The Female Malady: Women, Madness and English Culture, 1830–1980*, London: Virago Press.

Smith-Rosenberg, Carroll (1985) *Disorderly Conduct: Visions of Gender in Victorian America*, Oxford: Oxford University Press.

Tylee, Claire M. (1990) *The Great War and Women's Consciousness: Images of Militarism and Womanhood in Women's Writings, 1914–64*, Houndmills: Macmillan.

Woolf, Virginia (1925) *Mrs Dalloway*, Middlesex: Penguin Books.

Woollacott, Angela (1993) 'Sisters and Brothers in Arms: Family, Class, and Gender in World War I Britain' in Miriam Cooke and Angela Woollacott (eds) *Gendering War Talk*, Princeton, New Jersey: Princeton University Press, pp. 128–47.

Young, Robert (1995) *Colonial Desire: Hybridity in Theory, Culture and Race*, London and New York: Routledge.

9

The Death of the Clinic?
Normality and Pathology in
Recrafting Aging Bodies

ROMA CHATTERJI, SANGEETA CHATTOO
and VEENA DAS[1]

IN HER INFLUENTIAL 'Manifesto for Cyborgs', Donna Haraway (1990) considers what she calls informatics of domination and the related move from biology as clinical practice to biology as inscription. Communication technologies and biotechnology are crucial tools, she says, which are recrafting our bodies. Thus, 'It is time to write the *Death of the Clinic*. The clinical methods require bodies and work; we have texts and surfaces. Our dominations don't work by medicalization and normalization any more: they work by networking, communications, redesign, stress management. Normalization gives way to automation, utter redundancy.' (Haraway 1990: 194).

This is an attractive argument: surely the emergence of biology as inscription is altering the institutional biomedical spaces within which bodies are recrafted and Haraway has captured an important moment of rupture. Yet we feel that by assuming a complete transition from the birth of the clinic to its death, Haraway ignores the processes through which the clinic is maintained as an idea and a practice in day-to-day functioning in different societal contexts. Further, the sharp dichotomies proposed by her between birth and death, clinical practice and inscription, organism and biotic component (among many others), do not allow for an analytical space within which we could see how the new ideologies of domination through information, require and use bodies and work. Hence the relations between different forms of biopower and the different sites on which these are actualised are left unexplored. A good example that comes to mind is the emergence of the new era of recombinant vaccines through the new techniques of molecular biology which literally recraft the relation between the body of the pathogen and the body of the recipient of the vaccine. Yet, Emily Martin (1995), who has explored the functioning of the metaphor of immunity in American society through a multi-sited ethnography and looked at the discourse on vaccines, has not a single word to say on the access to bodies through which large-scale field trials are currently being conducted on experimental groups, and without which the deployment of these vaccines on normal populations would not be possible.

Our argument is not that new forms of domination have not emerged but that there are intricate relations between inscriptions, documents, bodies and work which make a narrative of complete transition from earlier to new forms of biomedical power difficult to maintain. Some of these relations are reconfiguring the clinic in new ways[2] – in other cases medicalisation and normalisation are actualised on bodies that cannot be recrafted through information or biotechnology. A particularly important case we feel is that of aging bodies, for though research on Alzheimer and other age-related disorders is currently addressing the problems of genetic markers of these diseases,[3] the current practices in the management of such disorders is premised on ideas about the normal and the pathological derived from the disciplinary perspective of geriatric medicine. Not that geriatrics as a clinical specialty enjoys the same authority in all societies: but some notions of a moving norm that would define pathologies in old age as posing a unique set of problems not shared by the average adult seem to enter the clinical discourse on aging across societies. The institutional forms which such ideas take vary – one may say that the relation between verbalisation and spatialisation is strongly influenced by the socio-political context in which the work of the clinic takes place. Further, the ideologies of gender enter the clinic in the management of aging in unexpected ways. In some contexts old age seems to obliterate the differences that were carefully maintained between bodies seen as gendered: in other cases notions of gender define sharply the way in which disability is experienced. We hope to address these issues in a comparative perspective in this chapter.

THE ETHNOGRAPHIC SITES

Our ethnography is based upon intensive fieldwork conducted in a general hospital, the Sri Maharaj Hari Singh hospital (henceforth SMHS) in Srinagar in India in the years 1985 and 1986 by Sangeeta Chattoo and in Regina Pacis, a nursing home (*verpleeghuis*), in Arnhem in the Netherlands by Roma Chatterji in the years 1986 to 1989.[4] The politico-economic context as well as the administrative culture of the two clinical sites is very different although both places embody some notion of the welfare state as it shapes entitlements towards the aged and the sick.[5] In the Indian case, the general hospital provides medical services which are either free or heavily subsidised by the government.[6] Because of the demand on its services the hospital has to cope with a large number of patients but the inadequacy of resources results in overcrowding and perpetual shortages of staff, equipment and medicines. During the period of fieldwork it was found that the average number of patients seen by a single doctor in the Out Patients' Department (OPD) in a single morning was 21; on an average a doctor was able to spend about ten minutes on an outdoor patient. The hospital also admitted patients as indoor patients. It had 680 beds distributed over 20 wards. In contrast to the public hospitals the private hospitals in the city were far better equipped to provide medical care but were expensive; therefore the SMHS hospital was frequented primarily by people belonging to poor or lower middle-class strata. The hospital did not have a separate geriatric ward.[7] Old people were treated on an acute care model for the specific disorders that they reported. This often meant that a person may be discharged from one ward because he or she is declared cured of the particular disease for which he or she was admitted, but may soon report again with a different disorder in a different OPD. As we shall see later, this kind of management of age-related disorders in the hospital sometimes puts different demands on men and women because of their respective positions in family structures, and consequently they see the clinic and its services in a very different light. It is also the case that the hospital presents patients with a certain set of possibilities which are also shaped by their experiences as not only old but also as gendered bodies.

In the Netherlands the nursing home has been expressly designed as a care institution offering intensive long-term nursing care to people with chronic and terminal illnesses.[8] At the time of its inception in the early 1960s the nursing home was seen as being complementary to the hospital, which dealt primarily with acute

173

forms of disease through specialised well-defined medical interventions. Over the years the nursing home has acquired an identity of its own, provided in part by the disciplinary perspective of geriatric medicine. Regina Pacis is a 'combined' facility with both somatic and psycho-geriatric sections. Each section is divided into three wards with approximately thirty-five residents in each. The majority of the residents are women. The length of stay of residents varies between several months to about two years – a few of the residents have been in the nursing home for more than ten years. Though it is implicitly acknowledged that the impaired elderly admitted here are not likely to live long, this is never articulated in the official ideology. Officially the staff see themselves as building a place of hope. Hence those admitted are referred to as residents rather than as patients but the daily practices construct them as patients. These paradoxes pervade our own writing and the reader would notice a frequent slippage between resident and patient: a slippage we feel is necessary to convey the ambiguity of the situation. Much of this ideology derives from the vision of aging and death articulated in the discipline of geriatrics and embodied in the organisational style of the nursing home.

Geriatrics was able to make a claim for itself as a clinical discipline in the Netherlands (as in many other countries) by its reconfiguration of the standards of normalcy that were to be applied to the aging person.[9] It was argued that aging is generally accompanied by an irreversible loss of physiological functions including the increasing vulnerability of the immune system. This results in the simultaneous occurrence of multiple pathologies which doctors have to cope with not as one disease at a time, but as the simultaneous presence of a multiplicity of ailments, many of which are in chronic form. Further, geriatricians argue that much of the symptomatology of old age presents itself in an altered form, so that you require a specialised medical gaze to recognise it. For instance, such easily recognisable symptoms as fever or pain may not occur even with the onset of serious disease: conversely the patient may experience annoying symptoms such as generalised aches and pains or fatigue which may be attributed by the doctor to the process of aging rather than to a recognisable disease entity. Thus old people may have to handle suspicions that they are malingering or simply being difficult if either members of the family or the care takers are not attuned to the special nature of the problems faced by them. The consequences of this disciplinary perspective are very different for the organisation of care in the nursing home in the Netherlands as compared to the hospital in India. In the Netherlands, the nursing home functions within a medical paradigm that strives to manage the pathologies of old age rather than to achieve cure. Thus the nursing home is designed to provide an environment within which an alternate community of old persons could be built within which the impaired elderly could lead 'normal' lives. This is especially so when their normal environments have become hostile or dangerous, threatening them with isolation and debility. This perspective results in a shift from the patient being seen as a bearer of a disease as in acute care model to his or her being seen as a whole person to whom a new environment has to be provided.

MEDICAL JUNK AND OBSOLESCENCE IN THE FAMILY

Due to the different kinds of organisational styles described above, the medical gaze constructs old people in entirely different ways in these two institutional settings. For the doctors in the SMHS hospital, who are struggling with shortage of resources and of personnel, the patients above the age of fifty who come with varied complaints are 'medical junk' unless a specific and treatable disorder can be identified. However, very often the doctors are faced with old patients who come with generalised body aches, chest pain, breathlessness, loss of appetite, or lack of sleep. The staff of the hospital tries to get rid of these patients in the OPD by prescribing pain killers or vitamin pills – placebos given to many old people who are considered to be malingerers. But the verdict of the doctor is often not acceptable to the old person as the following case shows.

A seventy-year-old man, a regular patient in the OPD came to the doctor's chamber complaining of his usual difficulties – lack of appetite, inability to digest food properly, general aches and pains, feeling of weakness and other such multiple pathologies. The doctor tried to placate him with the usual placebo, but the old man was convinced that his condition necessitated admission to the hospital. The doctor explained that he did not need hospitalisation as he was not suffering from any particular disease. The man kept pulling out old prescriptions and results of diagnostic tests to say that he did suffer from diseases such as high blood pressure – he was therefore entitled to be admitted. Finally he burst into tears and wailed, 'Doctor sahib, I am a very poor man. I have nowhere

175

to go, no one to take care of me. Where shall I go? Please have mercy on me.' The doctor got furious and raised his voice, 'For all these complaints you should go to the governor. This is a hospital not an alms house. It is meant to treat the sick. Don't waste my time. There are other patients waiting.'

For this patient, who was destitute and had no family to support him, struggling at the edges of survival, the hospital was a final court of appeal. Through the staff of the hospital this patient was addressing the State. If he had become useless for his family, unable to labour and provide for himself then surely the State as *mai bap* (mother and father) had a responsibility to provide for him But he could find no other institution where he could be heard. Hence the hospital was his last resort. As one of the non-medical staff, an attendant, put it: 'This hospital is a court where the poor man's appeal is heard – justice is given to him.' Such an interpretation is often heard in public hospitals in India, and though the doctors are not able to provide space to all who come with such demands, the very lack of a professional administrative culture allows the biomedical space to become an extension of other kinds of public spaces – thus bending the biomedical space towards a different imaginary. In this as well as other such hospitals one often finds that destitute people who were admitted for some complaint and do not have anywhere to go afterwards may sit in the courtyards outside hospitals either begging or providing some services in the informal economy that comes to flourish around the hospital compound. The non-medical attendant may not have been fully correct in saying that justice is given to the poor in the hospital but as a public space the poor feel that here they have a right to be heard. The voice is not always plaintive as in this case: sometimes it takes on an angry pitch (cf. Cohen 1995). In a later section we shall argue that women, who are functioning within the ties of family and kinship and are thus constrained by norms of modesty, can take on this voice much less frequently than men.

The medical staff in the nursing home in the Netherlands would not use a term such as 'medical junk' to describe old people who present multiple pathologies. The issue of how to deal with those who have become obsolete for the family, however, appears in a different guise. Take the case of Mr Rijder, an Alzheimer's disease patient who was admitted into the nursing home after a series of compromises to make care arrangements for him had failed to work. The 'case' of Mr Rijder began in 1985 when the district nurse of the Department for Old People for the *Basis Gezondheit*

Dienst (Basic Health Service) was asked to visit the Rijder family. The problem centred around Mrs Rijder, who could not cope with the changes entailed by her husband's increasing dementia. She complained that Mr Rijder did nothing but sit in the living room or stand in the balcony. He followed her around like a child and got in her way. If he tried to go out he would get lost. The district nurse who had visited the family reported that he was having increased memory and orientation disturbances. He was restless and had developed a tendency to wander and was showing aggression towards his wife. Mr Rijder himself had denied that there was any problem with him. Various solutions were suggested, including home help, which were not acceptable to Mrs Rijder because she felt that this would interfere with her domestic arrangements.

For a while Mr Rijder was admitted to a *Dag Opvang* (day centre) which was less oriented towards a therapeutic facility and more towards recreation. Initially he could join in the conversations of the group especially about his years in military service though he was not fit enough to engage in other activities of the group such as billiards. In a short time, though, his condition deteriorated further and it was felt that he could not fit into the group any more. Such created environments for old people are premised on the idea that they (the old) can be given a norm around which to engage their environment: for instance in this case none of the old people admitted in the day care centre were fit enough to work and were seen to be in need of the stimulation of social contact, but they had to be psychologically capable of maintaining social interactions among each other. Thus anyone who became incapable of maintaining the norms (in this case the norms necessary for conversation) had to be excluded and often had to move further on his or her institutional career as a patient. Mr Rijder's deteriorating memory and lack of orientation was perceived as a threat to the functioning of the group.

Finally in 1987, the social worker of the nursing home felt that Mrs Rijder could not deal with the problem anymore. She was also apprehensive that the frequent demands made by Mrs Rijder on her son and daughter-in-law because of Mr Rijder's condition could threaten their son's marriage. She was, however, still reluctant to move him to the nursing home as she felt that he was still conscious of his surroundings and would find the environment of a psychogeriatric ward traumatic. A further series of compromises were tried such as temporary admission while Mrs Rijder took a vacation. It became clear, however, that in no way could the nursing home shield Mr Rijder from the trauma of separation from his home environment. In one instance while he was in the nursing home on a temporary basis, he tried to escape by climbing out of a open window and was rescued with great difficulty. Two weeks after this incident he was moved to the nursing home as a permanent resident but died one month later after a stroke.

Despite the care with which Mr Rijder's move to the nursing home was planned there is no way to describe his admission in the nursing home except as that of having experienced social death. One may be tempted to read the disciplinary regime of the panopticon in this incident but one has to remind oneself that Mr Rijder's family could not find any way of coping with his aging body, his loss of self, and the disorder this introduced into their lives. Mr Rijder was brought to the nursing home accompanied by his wife, son, daughter-in-law and grandson, and a pretence was maintained that he was just there to check out the place. We would like to loop back to the description of this day in one of the earlier papers of Chatterji (1996).

We all left the activities room together. Mr Rijder was walking towards us from the corridor. He asked the social worker where 'they' had gone. 'Gone home', she replied. He asked again. It had not registered with him. She said again, 'They have gone home.' He looked surprised and then said to me (i.e. to Roma Chatterji) – 'Will you walk?' We walked down one of the corridors of the ward. At each window he would stop, test the frame with his hand to see if he could open it and look out. Then he would say 'Not this one and not this one either.' He had not forgotten his attempted escape after all.[10] We went back to the living room where the social worker sat waiting for us. 'Can you take me home? I have to go home. I have nothing here', he said, pointing to his clothes. The social worker said that he had to stay here and have his supper, that his wife had gone to their son's house and was already asleep. 'I must go home on the bicycle then' he said, 'you have a car. Will you take me home?' ' I have to stay here as well', she said. 'I must get out' he said.

Looking at these two cases, we can offer none of the comforting contrasts between the individualism of the West and the holism of India. In both cases we are faced with a scene of social death for the impaired elderly. The old man in the SMHS hospital is encountered by the fieldworker, alone in the hospital, trying to subvert its admission policies by demanding the right to be cared for. While he weeps and implores the doctor for some compassion, his voice can also take on an angry pitch at the denial of his rights. It finds a responsive echo in the support his narrative receives from the people gathered in the hospital. In contrast, the welfare state in the Netherlands already provides that entitlement to the impaired elderly, but for all the compassion and care with which the admission of the elderly such as Mr Rijder is organised, we cannot fail to recognise the sense of rejection, betrayal and the courting of death on his part. In one sense what we are finding here is the most ordinary of sufferings implicated in the very corporeality of our beings[11] – so how are we to account for the loss of voice in the latter case and the emergence of a new pitch in the voice of the old man in the former? Let us look a little more closely at the notion of social death.

Walter Cannon's now famous paper on 'voodoo death' written in 1942 proposed the idea of death by suggestion which occurred through the onset of shock in victims at whom a fatal bone had been pointed (Cannon 1942). If we look at the circumstances which surround this event, we find that for the relatives of the person his death is seen as inevitable after the fatal bone has been pointed. They begin preparations for mourning and Cannon seems to suggest that the shock of experiencing himself as already dead leads to the physiological features of the drop in blood pressure, weak and irregular heartbeat, and other related symptoms for the victim. While we may not fully understand the chain of events here, the sociological features of such an event do not seem limited to so-called primitive societies. In the case of Mr Rijder, the process of leave-taking seems to have implied his social death for the family. At one stage of the plans for moving Mr Rijder, his wife remarked that it was like taking him to the churchyard (for burial). The social worker commented that it was very difficult for Mrs Rijder for it was as if she were a widow and yet not a widow.

The nursing home becomes a recipient of the social cast offs. But unlike diseased persons, who may be temporarily cast off from society in order to be resocialised into its norms of health, the old cannot be reclaimed back into society. The clinic then becomes a space where a different normality is created, but by its very separation from the rest of society and its simultaneous dependence upon the societal norms of personhood, it cannot offer back the self to the old impaired person. Further the maintenance of an ideology of hope at all costs repackages such emotions as that of anger or grief as medical symptoms to be treated. Therefore for the residents who have experienced or are experiencing a form of social death, the very bureaucratisation of care and the emphasis

179

upon the obligations to maintain sociality becomes a theft of their voice.

The hospital in Srinagar, on the other hand, due to its very lack of both resources and professional management, has to willy-nilly allow the community to enter the hospital. This is evident not only in the fact that much of the care, even for seriously ill patients, is provided by members of the family due to the shortage of nursing staff, but also that the voice of the old person, whether in its pitch of anger or pathos, is not, or cannot be, shut off by the application of bureaucratic procedures. We do not want to suggest that this is purely a matter of lack of resources on the part of the hospital – it seems more likely that the shape of the biomedical culture has itself been formed by the different theories of the self that under-lie the institutions in these two societies. Hence, paradoxically the institution that defines old people as medical junk finds itself unable to contain the voice of the old who bear loud and clear testimony to the social death that they are facing. Conversely the institutional set up of the nursing home in the Netherlands repack-ages this voice in terms of the symptomatology of the aging process – it protects the family from having to face this inevitable deterio-ration of relationships with the old, packaging it within the bureau-cratic rules and records and thus does not allow a different pitch of voice to emerge.

In the next section we explore the manner in which the bureau-cratic record, *viz.* the case file, becomes a testimony to the truth of weakness, loss and disability, especially used by women in the Indian context against the demands put on their sexual and repro-ductive bodies by the patriarchal masculine practices of the family. This deflection of the record from its original intention shows that medical objects are not constructed by the enunciative modalities in expert cultures alone – they also circulate and take on new meanings in the hands of the patients.

THE RECORD AS TESTIMONY

We begin by describing the case of Saleema Shah, who though only in her late forties, was struggling to have her disabilities recog-nised. She was castigated by her husband as a malingerer who was constantly running to the hospital to escape the burden of house-work. This was itself a cover for the more unspeakable complaint that she was denying him sexual access and that she was failing in her duty of providing him with an heir.

Saleema was a widow with three children from her earlier marriage. She married her present husband out of economic necessity since her brother was unable to support her. Her present husband, a contractor in the Forest Department and quite well off by local standards, agreed to marry Saleema (according to her own account) only because he wanted an heir. He was considerably older than herself, had been married four times and had divorced each of his earlier wives because of their inability to bear him an heir. Within the norms of marriage and sexuality among both Muslim and Hindu families, it would be rare for a man to entertain the notion that his potency or virility may be the cause of his childlessness: blame always comes to be attached to the woman. In any case, Saleema conceived three times but each time she miscarried. Her frail health, frequent pregnancies and the heavy load of domestic work she had to bear made future pregnancies extremely dangerous for her. Subsequently she developed menorrhagia and had to consult a gynaecologist, which in itself she considered shameful in the tightly controlled norms on women's sexuality.[12]

Gynaecologists and obstetricians (the doctors of women's diseases in local parlance) are perceived to be primarily concerned with conditions of pregnancy and childbirth. If older women consult such doctors it is presumed that they are sexually active. There is much conflict within families among elderly couples over the man's demand for sexual access to his wife's body and the wife's reluctance to engage in sex because of her fear of ridicule. Moreover, an older woman visiting a doctor concerned with affairs of pregnancy and childbirth may come under suspicion that she is trying to get an abortion from a pregnancy resulting from an adulterous relationship. Thus Saleema was frequently shamed as an 'old woman' having to frequent a 'lady doctor'.

The gynaecologist diagnosed an ovarian cyst and advised a bilateral oopherectomy and hysterectomy. Her husband refused to give consent to an operation that would leave her sterile as he still hoped that she would be able to bear him a son. After all he had married her only because, with her proven fertility, she was likely to fulfil his ambition of having an heir. So he gave her an ultimatum – if she went ahead with the operation, he would divorce her. Saleema could not undergo such an operation without her husband's consent: though in law it is the patient's consent that is needed for a surgery, most public hospitals dealing with poor or illiterate women treat them as legal minors. In Saleema's case, she also had the fear that her operation would somehow provide legal

181

grounds for her husband to get a divorce without the obligation of providing her maintenance since she presumed that the marriage had been based upon her proven childbearing capacities. It matters little that such an apprehension did not have formal legal grounds: after all it was her vision of how the law operates that mattered here. So she refused to undergo the operation and continued to lose blood and turned anaemic.

As her condition deteriorated, it was discovered that she had advanced carcinoma of the breast and this time she was persuaded by the doctor to undergo a mastectomy. After the operation she was put on hormonal treatment which caused premature menopause. Her domestic situation worsened, for now that her reproductive powers were of no use to her husband, it was her domestic labour that became the subject of contention. Though prosperous, he treated her purely as a source of cheap labour.

Less than an year later Saleema was back in the hospital complaining of headaches, dysphagia, giddiness and general malaise. The doctor's report said that she had developed secondaries in both the lungs and possibly in the brain. A brain scan showed multiple intra-cerebral metastases. She was put on a combination of radiotherapy and chemotherapy. Saleema would come to the OPD for her radiotherapy accompanied by the children of her first husband. While the hospital provided subsidised services, not all drugs were available free of cost. Her husband never accompanied her to the hospital nor did he offer to pay for her medication. In fact he accused her of malingering, of using her illness as an excuse to escape housework. He even accused her of concocting the story of going to the hospital while she went elsewhere for some clandestine engagements.

In the face of these accusations, Saleema began to treat the medical record as the repository of her truth. She would insist that every visit should be clearly mentioned on her record along with the details of what her illness was and what medication she was required to take. Since patients in the hospital had not only access to the record but were also always in possession of it, the medical dossier became her shield against the cruel accusations of malingering and lying levelled against her. She produced it before her husband as if in a court of law as 'proof' of the severity of her illness.

In some ways this case may be seen as a further illustration of the dialogic nature of illness narratives. As Good (1994: 173) writes:

Illness is not only constituted in the 'wandering viewpoint' of the individual – the sufferer, a family member, a care provider. It is also multiply constituted in ways that are often conflicting. Illness is essentially dialogical. It is 'synthesized' in the narratives of Turkish families, fraught with gender and kinship politics. It is objectified in a specific form of disordered physiology in case presentations and conversations among physicians. But such objectification may be resisted or subverted by patients, by legal advocates, or by agents of insurance companies who authorise or refuse payments for specific treatments, all negotiating with one another in constituting the medical 'object' and in addressing the material body. Thus, while core symbols in medical lexicon may indeed condense or hold in tension a powerful network of meanings, the process of synthesis is not only semiotic but social, dialogical, imaginative, and political. And so too should be our analysis.'

Thus while Saleema's case is shot through with the politics of kinship and gender, what we see most clearly is her attempt to contest the meaning of her life as it is fixed by the sexual and reproductive contract that she has entered with her husband. In this the medical record and the objectification of her condition turn out to be her allies, recruited by her *against* the definitions provided by her husband of her illness (or rather lack of it). Much before Saleema comes to recognise that she is suffering from a terminal disease, she has also, like Mr Rijder, to face her social death. Her social death lies in the recognition that her body is nothing other than a reproductive machine for her husband, and her tragic efforts to push her body to bear more children conjoin the obligation to reproduce with the move towards dying. The sense of loss comes for her not from a desperate holding on to youth but by the relentless pressures put by her husband to make her body function as if it were simply a materialisation of his wishes rather than her life, or her form of dying. In whatever feeble way, the hospital appears to her as the producer of a truth that has the authority to contest the false imputations put on frail and aging women by the patriarchal masculine demands.

In the feminist literature both in the West and in India, we get an argument against the medicalisation of women's bodies on the grounds that the State is only interested in reducing women's fertility as a means towards population control (see Hartman 1987; Nair 1992; Ravindaran 1993; Sen and Snow 1994). There is indeed some merit in bringing to light the coercive practices of the State in relation to fertility control programmes. One cannot, however, overlook the fact that the contest is not always between the State's control over the bodies of women and their own rights over it, but often between the rights *men* exercise over the women's reproductive bodies in the setting of the family and the relief women seek for their frail bodies from the intervention of the medical profession. This is particularly important to realise for women who are subjected to repeated child bearing and who seek the authority of the clinic to authorise their experience of aging. Unlike other experiences of aging that we describe in this paper in which the gendered differences become muted, here gender is at the core of the problem. The desire of the male for possessing the reproductive powers of the woman is structured for her by the possibility of her imminent death in the act of fulfilling his desire.

When presenting cases of this kind one often senses the exasperation on the part of feminist scholars and activists as to why women submit to these definitions of their bodies and their selves. Countless studies can, however, be quoted to show that a form of resistance that seems easy from the outside is extremely difficult to live out for women like Saleema who are constrained by lack of both material and symbolic resources and hence themselves collaborate in the production of their misery by their bodily practices (cf. Das 1994) . It is this aspect of the problem that invites us to see the clinic not only as a site for the exercise of domination but also as a site in which women search for alternative definitions of their bodies.

THE MEDICAL DOSSIER:
THE TECHNICAL AND THE SOTERIOLOGICAL

In one of the most important contributions made in recent years to our understanding of pedagogic practices in medical schools, Byron Good shows how soteriological concerns suffuse medical care. He writes, 'I suggested that the juxtaposition of the rational-technical or physiological with the existential or soteriological is essential to our understanding medicine as a symbolic formation' (1994: 84). As an example, he gives an account of a case, described by a student as 'interesting', when an AIDS patient had steroid psychosis with a frightening shift of personality. The patient went about threatening people that he would bite them or scratch them and give them AIDS. When asked whether the student thought that the patient was acting out unspoken fears, the student replied: 'Yes, very much. I mean he was totally uninhibited, I mean I'm sure that he was expressing a lot of fear of dying . . . while this was happening he was essentially saying all the things that he could never say normally.' In the discussion of the case, however, the resident who presented it slid over the frightening details and instead concentrated on what might have caused the psychosis. As Good argues, we see in this case how an irruption of the fundamentally moral dimension of illness into the rational-technical sphere is contained by the routine medical procedures which are used to manage the rupture of the commonsense reality of the hospital rather than opening it up to moral reflection.

In the case of Regina Pacis, the shadow of death and loss is ever present, but since the self-definition of the nursing home is that of building a system of hope, fears of death and loss are very difficult to express both for the residents and the care givers. This fear is often displaced in the bureaucratic activity of record keeping on the part of the care givers, but it makes for dramatic interruptions in the routine of the nursing home when death in its gross physicality has to be faced.

The rights over the medical dossier have been much discussed in the Netherlands and especially the question as to whether the medical record is to be treated as the property of the patient, the care takers who document the information it contains, or the institution. One feature that clearly emerges from this discussion on right of access over medical files is that it is not thought of as a composite whole. Thus the institution has access to the whole file but there are several regulations which limits its rights to circulate the information contained in it. The patient, on the other hand, has access to only that part of the medical report which is used by the multidisciplinary team, but not to the doctor's observations on the patient's condition that may be reported in the file. The patient has a right to change or correct information that pertains to his or her personal or social situation but not the details of the medical history. Also direct access to medical data like X-ray reports or results of tests may be denied to the patient. This is obviously very different from the way in which medical reports are used in the hospital in Srinagar, where not only do patients maintain their own records but often use them to claim entitlements in the hospital or as proof of disability in the dense politics of the family. In accordance with this acute care model, the case file in the hospital records each illness in the form of a separate and independent event in spite of the fact that many of its elderly patients suffer from complications resulting from bronchial disease, stroke, cardiovascular disease, diabetes, hypertension, and so on.

In contrast, with its perspective of defining the impairments of old age as 'normal' to the aging process, Regina Pacis treats the whole person rather than individual parts of the body as undergoing these impairments. The case file reflects this construction so that it tries to create a record of the continuous history for the patient (or rather the resident), including his or her social and psychological profile. The multidisciplinary model of care in the nursing home, and the team approach whereby each patient has an individual care plan tailor made for him or her, requires a systematic flow of information among the specialists of the team. Systematic record keeping becomes a necessary prerequisite for this kind of functioning.

In the medical system in the Netherlands, records mediate every step in the patient's institutional trajectory – from the initial diagnosis to his or her death. One may say that they constitute the person as a case – as Chatterji has written elsewhere the patient acquires a 'shadow self' or a 'file self' (Chatterji 1996; Cohen 1994). In a sense the medical records constitute the person as a case so that she may be incorporated within the problem-solving mechanism of the medical bureaucracy. The medical dossier therefore contains old medical records, private correspondence between doctors concerning the case, old letters from the patient or friends and family – in short, anything that may be seen as relevant for understanding the patient's psychological or physiological conditions. This could be said to constitute the archival section of the file. This section is accessible only to the doctor in charge and is protected from the scrutiny of other care givers by the subsection on Medical Secrecy under the Act of Person's Registration 1983. In contrast to the archival part, the working files on the patient that record day-to-day activities are actively used by the nursing staff and may be found duplicated in a number of different sections of the nursing home. For instance, the social worker's case file that contains information on the patient's social, medical and nursing status, on the basis of which the patient is admitted to the nursing home, is kept in the social worker's office, but copies of these are also filed with the nursing dossiers that are kept in the ward. The dossiers kept in the wards contain the details of day-to-day functioning including a record of accidental falls, medication, temperature, urine and faeces charts, a diary with dates for family visits, appointments with the barber, hairdresser or priest, and preparation and disposal of the body after death.

We give an extract from the nursing dossier of a dementing patient in the nursing home to show how the person is constructed through the everyday practices of nursing.

5/1[13] The gentleman has come from Day Care. There was no family member who could accompany him. His wife is terminally ill.
The gentleman walks with a stick. Needs help with washing and dressing.
16/1 The gentleman has washed and dressed himself.
17/1 Has a red patch on left ankle.
27/2 Was very angry this morning because he was made to take a shower and wanted to hit one of us (nurses).
6/3 Slept well. Has gone home to his wife who is dying.
(This man's son-in-law had not wanted him to be present at his wife's death bed. The ward-in-charge had overruled his request and had taken him home to visit.)
7/3 No perceptive reaction to the fact that he went home yesterday. His wife is dead. Could not understand it at first. Visited the morgue later. Was very sad after that.
9/3 Spoke about his wife's funeral. Is very conscious of it all.

Byron Good (1994) has analysed the importance of *writing* in medical pedagogy. He argues that learning to write and speak are central to the early years of medical education. Writing structures the conversation with patients: it is the critical dimension for formulating the patient as a project for treatment. In the acute care model of disease, it is assumed that disease has its own natural course and the medical record should reflect the working of the disease in the patient. For all the criticisms one may make of this model one has to remember that sick persons have a stake in getting cured and in many cases such objectification works to achieve the goal of cure. Further, as we saw in the case of Saleema, the very objectification of disease was what she craved for.[14]

In the case of the nursing home, however, the purpose of the record is not so much to document the natural course of the disease as to structure the work of the nurses and the multifunctional team of care givers. In the process the ideology of treating the patient as a whole person in fact has the opposite effect of fragmenting the patient into a series of functions and of impaired body parts. For many purposes the medical file replaces the self of the patient. In the case of patients who are dementing and therefore no longer in control of their past, the file serves to orient the staff towards the wishes of the patient – such at least is the mythology. However, soteriological concerns break into this carefully constructed myth of rational technical efficiency, especially when they are faced not only with the process of dying but with the gross physicality of death.

As part of the mythology sustained in the nursing home, it is believed that death is a significant component of the home's self-identity, but that it is to be seen not just as an ending but as something which would bring life to a meaningful close. In the daily bodily practices of the nursing home, however, death becomes not something which lies in the future but that which is an invisible presence that helps to foreground the immediate present. People who enter the nursing home undergo a process of social death, as we saw: dislocated from a meaningful past and facing a future that threatens further loss. Entry into the nursing home for them is an end of sorts. But for the nursing home staff it is a new beginning – a new life for the patient in a new environment. Great effort is therefore made to establish a new set of relationships by involving the family in the decisions on care arrangements and in giving great thought to the placement of the resident in the wards. The therapeutic network around the patient establishes him or her in an immediate present that simultaneously defers the end. What is very hard for the care takers to bear is not simply the daily process of witnessing bodily pain and having to keep records of deterioration without the redemptive promise of cure at hand, but the idea that the moment of death involves a conscious choice for many of the residents in whom they have invested so much time and patience. In the nursing home pain is a sign of life: it is when the patient goes beyond pain that the rational technical mode of functioning breaks down as the following case shows.

Mrs Hatinga, a long-term resident in the nursing home, was dying a painful and lingering death.[15] She had been a difficult patient, irascible and moody, quick to pick quarrels with other residents and nurses alike. However, the very length of her stay in the ward had made her part of the ward family. In her own way she had become very attached to some of the nurses – a feeling that was reciprocated and sealed through the bodily practices of daily care on the part of the nurses.

In February 1987 she reached the last stages of the dying process. She would lapse into periods of unconsciousness: she could not speak and had to be fed through a nasal tube. The attendant doctor wanted to respect her wishes expressed in her living will and so instead of any aggressive life-saving treatment he gave her high doses of morphine to ease her pain. He had decided to allow her to die since active medical intervention would at best have had a very temporary palliative effect. The nurses who were attending on the patient however could not qute bear to see the patient simply go without efforts to save her. Chatterji was witness to the following exchange.

Staff Nurse to Doctor (in an angry tone, almost shouting): All you do is increase the morphine dosage. You should be phoning the hospital. They must insert a tube to drain the fluid in her stomach.
Doctor: It will not help her now. She is going to die whatever we do. And I know she would not want an undignified death. She would want to be left alone.
Staff Nurse: So you keep telling me but we should be doing something. It is not good for the junior nurses to see the morphine dosage being increased like this. Suppose she just sinks . . . they will think it is the morphine.

(During this entire exchange a trainee nurse was crying uncontrollably).[16] For the staff nurse, morphine was associated with the unspoken fear of euthanasia. Pain, even the insufferable pain that Mrs Hatinga was experiencing, was preferable to death induced by morphine. Pain for the nurse was an expression of life and active medical intervention symbolised hope – hope for life even if it meant temporary deferment of death.

In writing about the great transition that took place in the eighteenth century in Europe due to the disappearance of famines and epidemics, Foucault (1973) writes that power which had earlier been governed by the need to ward off death now becomes occupied with the production, regulation and maintenance of life. How much of Foucault's contention that death has been effectively expelled from Western modernity is governed by the *wish* to either leave behind death as a problem of other centuries or as a problem of other societies? In the context of the nursing home we saw that while the care takers may be seen as those who are engaged in the maintenance and regulation of *life*, in fact this is done only if we see death as the absconding presence in the institution, which comes to hide itself in the routinisation imposed by the bureaucratic practices of the home. But these bureaucratic practices break down as in the case of Mrs Hatinga, or are felt to be incommensurate with the task of dealing with the social death of the new entrants, in the case of Mr Rijder. The carefully kept records of each and every function and scar seem to be desperate attempts to fill up the suffocation of speech, rather than triumphs of rational technical management.

CONCLUDING OBSERVATIONS

What are the lines that could connect the practices in these two institutional sites and do these pose any new question to feminist understandings of bodies and power? It seems to us that in his characterisation of clinical discourse, Foucault emphasised the formation of various enunciative modalities which manifest not the unity of the subject but his dispersion.[17] In this respect, he says the term *'le regard medical'* (the medical gaze) used in his *Birth of the Clinic* was not a happy one (Foucault 1973: 54). In making up the object called 'clinical discourse', he separated out those who have a *right* to speak and the institutional *sites* from which they speak. What was not included in this dispersion from our point of view is the speech that breaks through in these very institutional sites without the agents having the authority to speak. What we are suggesting is that the clinical discourse excludes not only the subjugated knowledge of the traditional healers or midwives, who are *disempowered* by the new medical regime, but that it also excludes the speech of those who come to have a stake in the institutional sites of biomedicine, but whose experience of the clinic is not encoded in the theory of the clinic because it cannot be configured under the notion of resistance. By their very nature the enunciative modalities we have been describing appear in fragmented forms. Sometimes they do not even have the coherence to make up a narrative, as in the case of Mr Rijder, or in the case of the elderly destitute in India who loudly makes claim to the resources of the hospital, or even the staff nurse who can articulate her anxiety about euthanasia only through the hysterical pitch of her voice. The loss of narrative, however, is not the same as the loss of voice – the pitch of the voice itself becomes a testimony to the dislocation felt in these institutional contexts. To be sure, Foucault makes a gesture towards the low-ranking knowledges of the psychiatric patient, the ill person, the nurse and the doctor (see Foucault 1980: 98), which are seen as parallel and marginal to the knowledge of medicine but through which criticism performs its work. This gesture, from our point of view, is a limited one: it allows for such voices only in the mode of criticism, but not as essential to the functioning of the biomedical spaces themselves.

Should a theory of the clinic encode the appropriation of the biomedical categories by not only those who speak from their positionality in expert cultures but also those, like Saleema, who carry the record of their illness as an objective, official truth to contest the oppressive practices of the family? Or the experience of the trainee nurse who cries uncontrollably at the sight of a dying patient for whom nothing can be done? What is the stake that postmodernism or feminism might have in more refined theories of biopower articulated from the site where the impaired elderly live out a social death? What is the meaning or significance of the dying space across these widely separated cultures? We suggest that, first, the biology and social embeddedness of women create a configuration that makes it imperative for us to understand and encode their experience of social death in our formulations on the clinic.

First the question of biology. Due to the demographic transition in the Western countries the life expectancy of women has outpaced the life expectancy of men. This means that there simply are a larger number of women among the impaired elderly in the Western societies. It is not accidental that the majority of the residents in Regina Pacis are women. There is, however, no straightforward line that divides the experiences of men and women in this zone, where life is experienced as already lived, and hence no single identity politics that can be recovered from this situation. But, second, the institutional division of labour results in more women being in care-taking roles as nurses or social workers.[18] It is on the basis of their experience of the daily care of the bodies of the aged that they form relationships in the nursing home. While the daily tasks of record keeping provide a structural frame through which they relate to the elderly residents, the intimacy of the bodily contacts leads to an articulation of emotion when faced with a crisis, for which the technical rationality, on which the routine is based, has no place. This means that the corporeal connectedness between the patient and care taker, especially in long-term relationships, creates a different kind of intimacy than the notion of 'medical gaze' allows. One might even say that Foucault's bodies acquire a face (visage) when we envisage the clinic to include the experiences of the care takers and the reality of bodily intimacy created through care.[19]

Both Foucault (1972; 1974) and Kierkegaard (1978) before him, formulated the radical idea that more and more talking is a way of silencing that which required a voice. For Foucault the confessional techniques led to two different technologies of power – one which silenced through repression (as in the case of madness) and the second which silenced through fabrication of the object (as in the case of sex).[20] One can see an analogy here between sex and aging: it is the fabrication of aging as an object in the nursing home on which the medical gaze imposes a bureaucratic rationality through 'too much talk'. In this context the hospital in Srinagar provides a different perspective altogether, precisely because aging has not been fabricated as a separate object of clinical discourse there. This does not mean that what we see in the hospital is some kind of an idyllic scene for the treatment of the impaired elderly: instead the hospital appears as a kind of crossroads where elderly patients bring their disappointments with the family and with a callous society for an authentication of their experiences with aging and with disability. Thus they appropriate the biomedical discourse and its sites within their own life worlds. What is common to both the situations, though, is the bearing of witness by the old to the infidelities of those on whom they depend, including some-times their own bodies. In this witnessing we can see in some places the silencing of the voice by the noise of bureaucratic rationality, and in other places the repression of the voice by the masculine patriarchal authority of the family.

We do not wish to discount the warning given by Haraway with which we begun. Indeed the dying space for the elderly may itself be transformed as new technologies for recycling of bodies and body parts become more normalised. For the moment though, the question we would extract from the situations we have been describing is this. Following Foucault and several others, we have begun to understand the dispersion of the subjects and objects of clinical discourse over different sites and in different enunciative modalities. We now understand that many objects exist only in the mode of circulation as Marx showed with his analysis of com-modities. But what theory would be adequate to describe objects when they are on the point of disappearance? In creating a space in the clinic for such disappearing objects as memories, desires, bodies and aspirations, are we writing the *Death of the Clinic* or encoding its *birth* in a different language? In concluding with a question rather than an answer, we think of Dostoevsky's heroes for whom the urgency of a situation, however urgent, is ignored, for they must first look for the question which is still more pressing. And in a different register we evoke an entire tradition in Indian literature in which the female voice finds its place in the narrative as that which tears from a situation the question that it contains.

NOTES

1. Research in the Netherlands was supported by the IDPAD (Indo Dutch Programme on Alternatives in Development) and in India by a Junior Research Fellowship of the University Grants Commission. We owe a special debt to Klaas van der Veen for his help in the research in the Netherlands. It is a pleasure to acknowledge the generosity of patients and medical staff in both places.
2. In this context, see for instance, Das (1996), Lock (1996) and Rapp (1988) among several others.
3. See Potter et al. (1993).
4. For detailed ethnography of the SMHS hospital see Chattoo (1992) and for Regina Pacis, see Chatterji (1991).
5. On the role of the welfare state in relation to health and care of the aged in the Netherlands see de Swaan (1988, 1990).
6. For an understanding of the health system in India, see the recent contributions of Nichter and Nichter (1996).
7. The use of the past tense does not imply that there has been a shift of policy towards management of geriatric patients. The rise of militancy and the accompanying terror unleashed both by the militants and the security forces in Kashmir in the 1990s disrupted medical services in the state. Sangeeta Chattoo's family had to flee Kashmir and she has not been able to return to her field site.
8. Detailed ethnographies of the institutions for the care of the elderly in the Netherlands are Ten Have (1979) and van der Wulp (1986).
9. For an account of the development of gerontology in the Netherlands, see Munnichs (1984).
10. This refers to his earlier attempt to escape during his temporary admission.
11. See Kleinman (1988); Good, Brodwin, Good, and Kleinman (1992) for the understanding of pain through the medium of illness narratives.
12. On the relation between shame and sexuality in the Indian context, see Viswanathan (1994).
13. The first number refers to the date and the second to the month. We have retained the cryptic style of the nursing record.
14. It should be noted, though, that efficacy is a culturally embedded notion. Experience in rural India shows patients prefer to go to quacks even when they give them allopathic medicines at high costs rather than to the Primary Health Centre (PHC), where they may get medication free of cost, because they feel that the doctor does not have the time to listen to them in the PHC. This has enormous costs for the health system since patients end up getting expensive injections that are little more than placebos but carry the risk of infected needles and syringes.
15. On the breakdown of narrative in the last phase of chronic illness, see Good et al. (1994).

16. For an interpretation of laughing and crying as indications of displaced intentionality see Plessner (1970).
17. The masculine pronoun is indeed correct here because female experience is not encoded in describing this dispersion as we argue.
18. For an excellent description of an emergency psychiatric unit from the perspective of the care takers, see Rhodes (1991).
19. Due to lack of space we have been unable to describe similar relations of intimacy created through care giving in the case of the SMHS hospital but we wish to note that it was not the nurses but female family members who washed and fed the elderly who were undergoing treatment for chronic ailments. This often created a special relationship between one member of the family and the patient.
20. See Caputo (1993) for an excellent discussion on the relation between power as repression and power as fabrication in the context of healing.

REFERENCES

Cannon, Walter B. (1942) 'Voodoo death', *American Anthropologist* 44: 169–81.
Caputo, John (1993) 'On not knowing who we are: Madness, hermeneutics, and the night of truth in Foucault' in John Caputo and Mark Yount (eds) *Foucault and the Critique of Institutions*, Pennsylvania: The Pennsylvania State University Press: 233–62.
Chatterji, Roma (1991) *The Welfare State from the Outside: Aging, Social Structure, and Professional Care in the Netherlands*, IDPAD (Indo Dutch Programme on Alternatives in Development) report. (In collaboration.)
Chatterji, Roma (1996) 'An ethnography of dementia: The case study of an Alzheimer's disease patient.' Paper presented to the Sociological Research Colloquim, University of Delhi.
Chattoo, Sangeeta (1992) 'A Sociological Study of Certain Aspects of Disease and Death: A Case Study of Muslims of Kashmir'. Unpublished Ph. D. dissertation of the University of Delhi.
Cohen, Lawrence (1994) 'Old age: Cultural and critical perspectives', *Annual Review of Anthropology* 23: 137–58.
Cohen, Lawrence (1995) 'Toward an Anthropology of Sensuality: Anger, weakness and Alzheimers in Banaras, India', *Medical Anthropology Quarterly* 9(3): 314–34.
Das, Veena (1994) 'Moral Orientations to Suffering: Legitimation, Power and Healing' in L. C. Chen, A. Kleinman and N. Ware (eds) *Health and Social Change: An International Perspective*, Cambridge: Harvard University Press.
Das, Veena (1996) 'The Transplant of Organs: Gift, Sale, Theft?' Paper presented to the SSRC (Social Science Research Council) conference on

'*Culture and Biomedicine*', held at the University of Cambridge, July 2–6.

de Swaan, Abram (1988) *In the Care of the State: Health Care, Education, and Welfare in Europe in the Modern Era*, Oxford: Polity Press.

de Swaan (1990) *The Management of Normality: Critical Essays in Health and Welfare*, London: Routledge.

Foucault, Michel (1972) *The Archeology of Knowledge and the Discourse on Language*, New York: Harper and Row.

Foucault, Michel (1973) *The Birth of the Clinic: An Archeology of Medical Perception*, New York: Pantheon.

Foucault, Michel (1974) *The History of Sexuality: An Introduction*. Vol.1, New York: Pantheon.

Foucault, Michel (1980) *Power/Knowledge: Selected Interviews and Other Writings* ed. Colin Gordon, New York: Pantheon Books.

Good, Byron (1994) *Medicine, Rationality and Experience*, Cambridge: Cambridge University Press.

Good, M. J., Brodwin, T. Good, B. and Kleinman, A. (1992) *Pain as Human Experience: An Anthropological Perspective*, Berkeley: University of California Press.

Good, M. J., Munakata, M. J. Kobayashi, T. Mattingly, C. and Good, B. (1994) 'Oncology and narrative time', *Social Science and Medicine* 38, 6: 855–62.

Haraway, Donna (1990), 'A Manifesto for Cyborgs: Science, Technology, and Socialist Feminism in the 1980s' in Linda J. Nicholson (ed.) *Feminism/Postmodernism*, New York: Routledge, pp. 190–233.

Hartman, Betsy (1987) *Reproductive Rights and Wrongs: The Global Politics of Population Control and Contraceptive Choice*, New York: Harper and Row.

Kierkegaard, Soren (1978) *Two Ages: The Age of Revolution and the Present Age,* Princeton: Princeton University Press.

Kleinman, Arthur (1988) *The Illness Narrative: Suffering, Healing, and the Human Condition*, New York: Basic Books.

Lock, Margaret (1996) 'The quest for human organs and the violence of zeal' in Veena Das, Arthur Kleinman et al. (ed) *Violence, Political Agency and the Self*, forthcoming.

Martin, Emily (1994) *Flexible Bodies: The Role of Immunity in American Culture from the Days of Polio to the Age of Aids*, Boston: Beacon Press.

Munnichs, Joep (1984) *Voorzieningen voor Ouderen: Visie op Ouderdom*, Deventer: van Loghum Slaterus.

Nair, Sumati (1992) 'Population Policies and the Ideology of Population Control in India', *Issues in Reproductive and Genetic Engineering* 5, 3: 237–52.

Nichter, Mark and Nichter, Mimi (1996) *Anthropology and International Health: Asian Case Studies*, Netherlands: Gordon and Breach Publishers.

Plessner, Helmut (1970) 'Lachen und Weinen' *Philosophische Anthropologie* (by Helmut Plessner), Frankfurt/Main: Suhrkamp, pp. 11–171.

Popper, H. R. B. Nelson, S. Das, R. Siman, et al. (1993) 'The Involvement of Proteases, Protease Inhibitors, and an Acute Phase Response in Alzheimer's Disease', *New York Academy of Science.*

Rapp, Rayna (1988) 'Chromosomes and Communication: The Discourse of Genetic Counselling', *Medical Anthropology Quarterly* 2, 2: 143–57.

Ravindaran, T. K. S (1993) 'The politics of women, population and development in India', *Reproductive Health Matters,* vol. 1.

Rhodes, Lorna A. (1991) *Emptying Beds: The Work of an Emergency Psychiatric Unit,* Berkeley, University of California Press.

Sen, Gita and Snow, Rachel, (eds) (1994) *Power and Decision: The Social Control of Reproduction,* Cambridge: Harvard University Press.

Ten Have, H. (1979) *Het Verpleeghuis: Veld van Onderzoek,* Deventer: van Loghum Slaterus.

van der Wulp, J. C. (1986) *Verstoreng en Verwerking in Verpleeghuizen: Belevingswereld en conflicten ven hnen die Verdere Leven ineen Verpleeghuis Doorbrengen,* Nijkerk: Intro.

Viswanathan, Kalpana (1994) 'Shame and Control: Sexuality and Power in Feminist Discourse.' Paper presented at the conference on *'Femininity, the Female Body and Sexuality in Contemporary Society'* held at the Jawaharlal Nehru Memorial Museum and Library, Delhi, November 21–24.

10

The Broken Heart

LYNDA BIRKE

What the eye doesn't see, the heart doesn't grieve.
(Christian Barnard, the first surgeon to carry out a heart transplant,
speaking of his extramarital affairs[1])

THINK OF WHAT THE heart symbolises. If I tell you that I have suffered a badly broken heart, you will not (I hope) rush me into a
coronary care unit at the local hospital. I imagine that, rather, you
would be concerned about my emotional well-being. Friends tell
me that I wear my heart on my sleeve, meaning that I show my feelings easily. My heart may, or may not, be in writing today. If not, I
can always go and eat a hearty meal. This set of meanings of the
word of heart carries a great deal of cultural baggage; they lie at
the centre of all that we are – the heart of the matter.

Yet the heart, in biomedical discourse, is nothing more than a
pump – a sophisticated one, to be sure, but just a pump. If it is
broken, it can sometimes be mended through bypass surgery, or
transplants, just as broken machinery can be fixed. This kind of
heart was once central to meanings of life and death, in that doctors
defined death when it stopped beating. But even that centrality
has now disappeared. In the age of transplant surgery, the brainstem is more important, and hearts may go on beating even after
brain death. As definer of life, the heart is redundant, and death
has been relocated.

In this chapter, I want to explore some of these meanings that
we give culturally to the heart – and to what can 'go wrong' with
hearts. I have chosen to focus on the heart because it is so rich in
meanings: sharply contrasted narratives attest to the powerful

symbolism of the heart as bearer of emotions, and to the power of mechanistic descriptions of bodily function within biomedical science. Ostensibly signifying the same part of the body, these two narratives are worlds apart. My own narrative seeks to reflect this tension: it is peppered with metaphors of the symbolic heart, in various guises. And it repeatedly draws on the persistent mechanical metaphor of biomedical texts – the pump. In examining these worlds, I will explore themes that thread through recent theorising about 'the body' to illustrate what I consider to be some of its shortcomings. 'The body', in this renewed interest, is deeply inscribed with cultural meanings; gender, race, and other social markers are etched deep into its surface. But there they seem to remain – for the newly theorised body seems to have little or no interior. A heartless beast, indeed.

1. THE HEARTLESS BODY?
SOME TROUBLING DUALISMS

A starting point for recent social theorising about the body is the recognition that bodies have hitherto been seen as pre-social, a biological given (Grosz 1994; Gatens 1996). Earlier feminist theory, for example, made this assumption in the distinction between 'sex' and 'gender', in which 'sex' was seen as the basis on which gender builds. In turn, gender was socially constructed, and bodies were largely ignored.

Yet the body is a means of expression, for example in how we use it (as in dance) and clothe it: it thus comes to represent culture and our individuality within it (Falk 1994). Recent theorising returns to the body, while trying to avoid seeing it as given. Elizabeth Grosz, for example, notes the importance of understanding the significance of the body for women's experiences, and attempts to develop a 'corporeal feminism', which acknowledges the importance of the body instead of denying it. She emphasises the 'body as social and discursive object, a body bound up in the order of desire, signification, and power' (1994: 19). Undoubtedly, our experiencing of our bodies *is* bound up in culture: bodies signify. Nevertheless, in much of this new work, the human body enters social theory largely as a surface on which 'identities' can be written. Even those studies that examine the senses (e.g. Classen 1993; Synnott 1993) continue to focus on their social contingency. The body as a material part of social processes is often neglected, and its interior almost entirely ignored.

But bodies have a habit of making their material presence felt. What was awkward for those who insisted on social construction was the sheer impossibility of dealing with pain or bleeding, with the general messiness of bodies. Pain and bleeding are not themselves culturally innocent: 'blood' carries a wealth of meanings, as does pain (Scarry 1985). Blood also has a reality that goes beyond signification. Every month my body bleeds – real blood, the dark-red stuff of veins. My heart, meanwhile, goes on pumping, supplying oxygen even to my darkest recesses.

It is those darkest recesses, the body's interior, that seem to be neglected in much recent theorising about the body.[2] The interior seems to be relegated to the category of other, to be explored only within the remit of 'biology'. It is an example of the persistent dualism of nature and culture; the body's insides belong to biology, while its surface can now be described in terms of cultural inscription. That dualism gained new momentum during the Enlightenment, as the study of 'man' developed alongside the 'human sciences'. Once separated, the boundaries were policed to ensure a future for the 'study of man' (Horigan 1990): they still are. Whatever was categorised as 'biology' became the preserve of natural sciences, with their peculiarly reductionist approach: 'biology', subsequently, was studiously avoided by scholars in other disciplines – including that of feminism.

In Val Plumwood's work on the relationship between feminist and environmental ideas (1993), she notes that nature/culture itself is one instance of a more widespread use of dualisms such as self/other. These dualisms are hierarchical, and gendered: masculinity tends to be associated with mind (not body), rationality (not emotion), with human (not animal). Plumwood argues that what these dualisms share is a common ancestry in a master/slave narrative: mastery *over* is built into the binaries to begin with. She acknowledges that the meanings attached to binary terms such as nature or culture are always multiple and shifting. 'Biology' and 'the body' are equally unfixed. But, she argues, 'the strategies of mastery are still played out between the mastering one and dualised other' (1993: 191). It is the relationship between the two which remains. Deeply intertwined with this master/slave dialectic is the history of rationality: the rational mind must rule over the vagaries of the irrational body.

We must not lose the messy materiality of bodies and their interiors in the new theorising. It is, of course, the interior which carries the blood, which seems to produce pain during childbirth or menstruation. And at the heart of the interior *is* the heart itself. The body's interior, moreover, is similar among us all (irrespective of those claims about aristocratic blue blood).

One reason why bodily insides seem to slip out of the pages of theory is that we are heirs to the distinction between biology and not-biology (the latter includes human sciences, social studies, and much of feminism). 'Biology' is out there, in the form of nature or the environment; or, it is in here, my bodily insides. 'Biology' becomes the other to social theory, that which can be left out of analysis or left to other disciplines. Moreover, once 'the biological' moves beyond the realms of social or theoretical analysis, then it easily becomes seen as fixed. Where does that leave the responsive actions of the nerves, or of the immune system? Where does that leave the complex development of the foetus from a fertilised egg? Or the changing rhythms of a beating heart? Even in new developments in theorising about the body there seems to be a level of 'biology' that is beyond analysis.

Being rather stubborn about my liking for 'biology', even in the face of trenchant criticism, I find this omission amazing. Am I alone in finding it fascinating to read about how organs develop? How hearts beat? And am I alone in finding it extremely odd that postmodern cultural critics – including feminists – lose their interest in deconstruction when (and if) they pass through the body's boundaries? Once inside, then we seem to have to fall back on to the unproblematised narrative constructions of science. For how else can we describe the beating heart?

2. CONTRASTING NARRATIVES: THE DIS-EASED HEART

Metaphors of the Heart

In medical writing, the heart is little more than a pump. We have become familiar with the images of heart failure through popular television series, such as *Casualty*, or ER. In most episodes, there is a cardiac arrest, to which staff come running; someone wields electroshock plates to kick-start the errant organ. We watch, expectant, as the heart monitor registers the irregularities. We know how to interpret the steady electronic line. Such stories remind us how used we have become to the drama of heart failure. They also dramatise the heroic stuff of modern medicine. Like Dr Frankenstein wielding electric shock, the modern hero in white coat will – we hope – save the patient. Meanwhile, the technology reads us the story of what is happening within. The heart responds – or it does not.

As the heart becomes a pump, so medical practice, accordingly, treats body parts as simply replaceable bits of machinery. A faulty heart can be replaced. And here is a step on the path towards a medical division of labour; where once a person was held to be sick, by the late twentieth century, it is tissues and organs which are diseased.[3] We no longer have only doctors; we now have cardiac specialists. The solution is to remove the diseased or contaminated organ, to regain bodily purity. It also leads to a growing market in body parts (Kimbrell 1993) – be they organs for transplant, blood, sperm, or even eggs or embryos.

In these discourses of biomedicine, there is a repeated pattern of dualism – whole/part, normal/pathological, health/disease, mind/body, rational/irrational. Crucial to these is the normal/ pathological binary; the pathological, the diseased, is something to be guarded against in preventive programmes, or to be excised in surgical interventions. The diseased heart is monitored, under constant surveillance for potential breakdown. By contrast, the normal heart is largely an unmarked category (or at least unremarked). Becoming ill with coronary heart disease (CHD) leads to increased medical surveillance. Yet surveillance requires vigilance. Writing about environmental hazards, Beck (1986) argues that we live now in a 'risk society' – one in which we are increasingly faced with risks beyond our control. Perception of these (such as radiation and pollution) shapes our relationship to scientific expertise, because these risks are so uncertain and unpredictable that we can no longer turn to scientific experts for knowledge. Within the risk society, we must act as individuals to minimise risks to our health. Increasingly, we are told to monitor our own bodies. We should, for example, avoid too much of the wrong sort of fat in our diet if we want to reduce the risk of CHD.

It is, moreover, the heart itself which is the focus of much of the surveillance of health to which we are subject. The normal heart may be an unmarked category of biomedicine, but we lay persons are still encouraged to work at the process of prevention. In the very processes of bodily discipline, the heart is a focus of attention. We must eat the right foods; we must take exercise. Think, for example, of the growth in 'keeping fit': a key notion in 'keeping fit' is that the heart is 'toned up'. When I asked a fellow hiker (in the US) which was the best route up a mountain, she asked me whether

I wanted 'a good cardiac workout' or a more gentle path. The cultural imperative now is to keep our hearts in good shape, and the heart monitor becomes important equipment for that surveillance.

Yet the irrational body – the other half to the (rational) mind – includes the heart, which is at once both symbolic (and symbolic of emotionality, not reason) *and* material. What medical practice around heart disease focuses on is precisely the unpredictability (irrationality) of a heart gone crazy. In a heart attack, the electrical excitability of the heart and the contraction of its muscular walls are both wildly out of control. The messages of both prevention ('look after your heart') and of treatment (surgery) are about control and management. And alongside the eternal vigilance to ensure our pumps are working well, there is that darker, more irrational, set of images. This is the heart of emotions, of love and passion – an altogether different kind of beast. Not surprisingly, this story of the heart is rich with metaphor and allegory.

In my Heart of Hearts, I . . .

. . . may choose to believe that the heart is more than merely a mechanical device. I may believe the more romantic metaphors, as I write this paragraph on Valentine's day. Hearts are symbols of love, and of emotions. And not only symbols, for one's heart may literally beat faster at the sight of someone to whom one has 'lost one's heart'.

As a cultural symbol, the heart is rich indeed. Moreover, in the cultural association of women with emotionality, the symbolic heart becomes gendered. I have, for example, a photograph of a late nineteenth-century illustration, in which a beautiful, but dead, young woman lies draped suggestively on a mortuary table; she is bathed in light.[4] The (male) doctor has begun his dissection, and holds aloft her heart. Here, the heart epitomises the seat of her femininity and beauty – even while it represents the act of anatomical dissection that lies at the heart of the mechanical model.

The heart has a long history as a signifier. Anne Sauvy (1989) has examined its iconography in religious texts, over four centuries. A predominant image is that of a large central heart, surmounted by a head; within the icon of the heart and in the surround are other images. In some, these represent salvation, with the holy spirit ensuring the devil's departure. Others represent temptation or evil-doing; here, the devil stays within the heart, while the trivial temptations of secular life occupy the surround. The heart, in this iconography, becomes either the 'abode of Satan or the temple of God'.

Such images have a long, and persistent, history; indeed, Sauvy notes their use by Christian missionaries even today. While both men and women are represented, some versions imply different roles: one series, from the late nineteenth-century shows, for instance, 'les visages d'hommes y surmontent les cœurs mauvais, tandis que les visages des femmes se sont associés à l'attrition, à la contrition, à la perseverance' ('faces of men are above the bad hearts, while faces of women are associated with attrition. contrition and perseverence': Sauvy: 205).

These images also, Sauvy notes, carry clear messages of imperialism. In versions produced for missions in Asia, the devil is both black and horned, while angels are feminine, long-haired, and white. The face above the heart changes: in the image depicting a heart containing the devil's temptations, the face above is clearly Asiatic (series produced in Madras, 1906). In another series, in Malaya, the face of 'Contrition' is indubitably European. Such texts continue to be produced in many languages, Sauvy points out. Writing in the late 1980s, she notes that the existence of apartheid ensured that two versions were produced for South Africa at that time: both use racist imagery. Even when both angels and devils are white, only the angel is blond (Sauvy: 273).

Such images of the heart may seem irrelevant, perhaps quaint, especially in the context of medical discourses of heart transplantation (also begun in South Africa!). But they are powerful symbols, standing not only for meanings of 'the heart', but also incorporating a whole series of binaries. Among other things, the heart in these iconographies stands *both* for the interior of the person (emotions and desires contained within) *and* for the embeddedness of those representations within a wider, external, world. That is, the figures contained within the heart are simultaneously assumed to be manifest in the world outside the body – in the form of the devil, for instance. This ambiguity of the symbolic heart, as both inside and outside the body, is a theme to which I will return below.

While reading Sauvy's text, I recalled a TV programme I watched in the US a few years ago – one of those evangelist kinds. The preacher told how, driving along an interstate, he had experienced a great pain in the middle of his chest. He pulled over, worried about a possible heart attack. But, he then realised, 'this was Satan tempting him' from within his (literal) heart: so, he told Satan where to go, by running up and down the roadside. Satan presumably vacated his heart: he evidently did not need cardiac resuscitation before his televised appearance.

To my Heart's Content: Metaphors in Medicine

The heart, then, is a powerful metaphor in many texts, carrying with it sexism, racism, and the history of colonial conquest. In the narratives of biomedicine, we meet quite different and largely mechanical images. If it is 'only' a pump, moreover, there should be no particular ethical concerns about moving it from one machine to another. In this case, the machines in question are a dead human body and a living one. Such rhetoric is relatively recent. Prior to successful heart transplants, the heart 'was seen as the centre of the soul' (Adrian Kantrowitz, US heart surgeon, 1996). As hearts became exchangeable, so a new definition of death developed – and the heart became 'just a pump'. Kantrowitz described how the use of anencephalic infants[5] (born without a brain) as organ donors for transplant surgery facilitated this rede-finition: 'Just because the heart [of the anencephalic infant] beats doesn't mean it's a living human being,' he said.[6]

I want now to shift registers and move directly into the language of science (as I was trained to do) and its accounts of how circula-tory systems develop. The heart develops from a convoluted muscular tube; this suffices for fishy needs, but for land animals a more powerful pump is needed. Frogs, for instance, have three-cham-bered hearts, while mammals have four. Tiny animals have tiny hearts; but they must beat faster. A shrew's heart at rest beats ten times a second.

Hearts must contract in coordinated fashion. To achieve that, the heart's cells are linked tightly together, and the electrical pace-maker kick-starts the cycle of contraction, the familiar heartbeat – dub-dub, dub-dub. Most of the time, this goes unnoticed – it beats away at its heart content. Sometimes, we do notice: we pay attention to it if we want to know how fit we are, or if we confront something that scares us. Then, the blood pounds in our ears.

I can engage with recent feminist and postmodern theory 'to my heart's content'. But it is much harder to make links to the kinds of scientific discourses in which I was trained. So let me go back to the paragraphs I have just written. Here is the language of certainty, and of causality – 'this is what happens'. It is also the lan-guage of mechanism – muscular tubes, pumps, failure to contract, cycles of contraction, pacemakers. There is also the language of medical success, of triumph over the killer CHD: bypass surgery, coronary angioplasty, transplants. We could illustrate with labelled diagrams, or histograms showing epidemiological data; the frequency of CHD by social class, for example, or of heart disease as 'responsible for nearly 50 per cent of deaths'.

The descriptions of science also operate with what Donna Haraway (1991) calls the 'god-trick' – the twin myths of objectivity and the passive voice. Experiments simply happen; there is no one there. Or, as Haraway later points out (1997), the witness of scientific work '. . . must be invisible, that is, an inhabitant of the potent "unmarked category", which is constructed by the extraordinary conventions of self-invisibility' (1991: 23). The significance of this invisibility in the early development of modern science is a point to which I will return below.

The passive voice is central to scientific texts, and it has to be actively worked at by its authors – it is a difficult kind of narrative to maintain (see Latour 1987). Scientists are trained to avoid any implication of agency in their writing – their own agency, or that of nature. But that cannot always be done. Here, for instance, is an example in which the heart is clearly trying to escape the strictures of scientific writing: 'When atrial contribution and the A wave kick are lost . . . there is an increase in the mean left atrial and pulmonary venous pressure *in an attempt to maintain* the same level of end-diastolic pressure and cardiac output' (Parmley 1979: 1064; emphasis added). The heart 'tries to maintain' pressure, even though it is only a pump.

Whatever the claims to represent reality, scientific narratives are just as replete with metaphor as the religious ones. Plumbing metaphors abound around hearts:

Despite [its] punishing workload, the heart loyally thumps three billion times in a long life, forcing blood along 60,000 miles of pipes – a plumbing system longer than the road networks of Wales and Scotland put together . . . A giraffe needs a frighteningly high blood pressure to service its lofty brain – and so must construct extra strong pipes to avoid blowouts (Young 1992).

Young gives these examples in a review of a text book about the circulation of the blood; its author, he notes, found inspiration 'around the house' for the plumbing analogies. It is a book, moreover, which transgresses the boundaries of what can go into a science text: 'It is certainly the only physiology book I know that includes instructions for cooking its principal subject matter,' notes Young (1992).

The plumbing metaphor reinforces the image of an organ that is quite simple, like a pump. It is reminiscent of both industrial power (an image often evoked in popular biology text books), and of simple domesticity. Even blocked arteries seem to resemble the way the kettle furs up if the water is hard. You do, of course, need the plumber's help when things go wrong, but you can do most of the maintenance yourself and stop the kettle furring.

What about gender? Is the scientific heart as replete with gender metaphor as the symbolic heart? The visual images in medical texts are rarely overtly gendered, in the way that (say) the images of religious symbolic hearts are gendered. But the written narrative of scientific accounts is different; behind the objective stance and passive voice lurks a familiar metaphor. Here, we find that the ventricles (the lower two chambers of the heart) are made of different stuff from the atria (the top two chambers). In Parmley's text, we read for example that: 'The atria are thin-walled shallow cups . . . [which] serve a reservoir function. [Later in the heart's cycle of contraction] the atria serve as a conduit for the continuous flow of blood from the veins to the ventricles' (1979: 1063). The text goes on to tell us that the ventricles are pumps (though the left differs somewhat from the right), whose job is the ejection of blood.

The metaphors become clearer in texts written for lay readers. Again, the blood seems to flow through the atria, although these 'shallow cups' can help a bit by squeezing blood through the 'doors' of the heart valves, and into the ventricles. And now the gendered reading of the narrative becomes clearer. The ventricles, we can learn, respond to 'the swelling surge of blood' by beginning their muscular contraction. The pressure 'forces blood upward and thrusts open the semilunar valves . . . The right ventricle ejects . . . blood into the pulmonary artery' (Davis and Park 1984, in a chapter entitled 'A Surging Pump'). What we have in these narratives, then, is a virile ventricle, forcing and thrusting; it is, accordingly, always well-muscled. By contrast, the atria are conduits, or rooms, receiving blood, perhaps helping a bit by squeezing. To function, it seems, the heart has to be a happily heterosexual union of virile ventricle and acquiescent atrium.

Sometimes, however, even the happy heart needs a bit of marriage guidance. The Davis and Park text notes that:

The parasympathetic nervous system acts as the heart's physiological conscience. It slows the heart, counseling it to save energy. Sympathetic nerves do the opposite. They quicken the heart in answer to the challenges that come rushing on the wings of daily experience. Heat, light, love, danger – such stresses force the sympathetic nerves to step in and spend some of the energy the parasympathetics have been husbanding (Davis and Park 1984: 65).

Gendered metaphors abound, it seems, in these narratives.[7]

Like domestic plumbing and happy marriages, the beating heart can go wrong. It needs nourishing and has its own blood supply. If this gets blocked, the muscle cells can be starved. The heart fails to contract properly. A heart attack follows. Because the heart is little more than a pump (it doesn't carry out any complex biochemical jobs, unlike the liver), it can be repaired relatively easily. Bypass surgery detours the damaged blood supply; coronary angioplasty enlarges the vessels; transplants may replace the whole heart. And now, with xenotransplantation (the use of organs from other species), we can use a heart from a pig. It is, we should remember, only a pump, wherever it comes from.

Opening our Hearts: Surgical Successes?

Partly because of the power of the (symbolic) heart as metaphor, the discourses of biomedicine must work hard to persuade us to open our hearts to the scalpel. In a study of people undergoing coronary bypass surgery, Radley (1996) describes the joint investment, by patient and staff, in particular medical ideologies. So, success may be claimed, while problems (such as postoperative pain) are played down. Radley notes: 'In the case of coronary grafting, this [ideology] is specific in its use of 'plumbing' metaphors to do with the blocking and unblocking of arteries. It also shares certain features with surgery in general in its parallel with the repairing, rebuilding or remodelling of machines' (Radley 1996: 133)

Yet even while medical literature describes the body as a set of replacement parts, surgically moving organs around is troublesome for our sense of self and identity. Cultural beliefs about selfhood may conflict with notions of body parts. Medical personnel put great stress on objectification – the heart as 'only a pump'. Yet recipients of transplanted organs experience conflict between this mechanistic/reductionist view of the body and wider cultural beliefs (Sharp 1995; Joralemon 1995).

Both altruism and individual rights are central to the rhetoric of organ transplantation; these, argues Joralemon (1995), serve the purpose of becoming a cultural suppressant of psychological rejection analogous to the medical role of immunosuppressing drugs. Patients may even believe that they have acquired the characteristics of the donor (Basch 1973; Houser et al. 1992) – claims which have occasionally been sensationalised in the media (e.g. Jeffreys 1996).

'Domino' procedures (in which one patient receives a heart-lung transplant from a cadaver donor, while his/her original heart is transplanted into another recipient) raise these issues sharply. In this case, the donor of the heart remains alive, leading to people having conflicting feelings about the fate of their heart (Sharp 1995). Sharp's study illustrates how concepts of gift-giving may become understood and used in changing social relationships. Thus, some families of donors may seek out recipients of organs, describing the search as looking for 'their new families'.

Xenotransplantation, as a specific form of transplant surgery, poses the questions of self-identity and rejection particularly strongly. Xenotransplantation raises the possibility of using organs such as hearts from specially bred donor animals. In 1996 a biotechnology company called Imutran announced that it had developed a pig which had some genes derived from humans; as a result, the recipient's body should not reject the donor heart so readily, the scientists reason.[8] Advocates of transplantation from animal donors typically stress the supply shortfall of human hearts, which animal organs could potentially fill. Yet their ready acceptance may not be shared by others, even by other health professionals – one survey in Australia of attitudes of nursing staff suggested that approximately two-thirds disagreed with the use of organs from animals (Mohacsi et al. 1995). Nevertheless, the Nuffield Council for Bioethics evaluated the various issues involved in xenotransplantation (Report, March, 1996) and concluded – with caution – that clinical trials and use of animal organs would be acceptable.

I want to examine the question of xenotransplantation in more detail, to focus on the ways in which particular discourses are used. The discourses of scientific medicine, emphasising the mechanical power or failure of the heart, are prevalent. But other metaphors coexist with the plumbing, particularly in public statements to the media.

The Heartless Pig

The breeding of the first transgenic pigs for possible transplantation provoked much debate in the media (see for example, 'Ethics of Heartless Pigs': letters to the *Guardian*, 28 August 95). Thus, a spokesman for the British Union for the Abolition of Vivisection asked whether xenotransplantation will 'now force us to consider what it means to be human' (Malcolm Eames, *Guardian*, 25 August 95). Other commentators focused on the ethics of breeding animals for such purposes, or on what might happen to the human patient after surgery. There are clearly many concerns expressed in these questions, including concerns about using tissue from non-human animals.

By contrast, the scientific discourse accompanying the new technology minimises concerns about crossing species boundaries. One justification made in the public debates was that pigs are used for meat; why, therefore, should we not take their hearts into our bodies in some other way? Doctors, moreover, have been using pig insulin and pig heart valves for some time: 'morality cannot be tissue specific', argued Imutran's research director (David White, quoted in *Daily Mail*, 13 September 95).

Scientists have long been fascinated by the possibility of moving an organ from one organism to another. Earlier attempts to do so, however, were fraught with problems. Despite the linguistic insistence on the heart as being 'only' a pump (and the Cartesian heritage of animal bodies as merely mechanism) the mechanism repeatedly broke down in spectacular ways. An organ moved from one species to another rapidly becomes black and swollen as the recipient's body rejects it. Between species, the differences are greater, so the rejection is more spectacular.

These narratives, particularly those focusing on xenotransplantation, seem to ignore or play down important cultural meanings and symbolism. Transplantation within humans raises questions about the meaning(s) of death, and corporeality. Thus, contrary to medical belief about the heart as just a pump, lay statements about heart transplants might emphasise cultural symbolism, rendering transplant 'sacrilegious' (Calnan and Williams 1992). Xenotransplatation raises many more issues, not only about animal corporeality but also about the specific origin of the tissue. The pig is often seen as an 'unclean' animal, for example. Mary Douglas's analysis in *Purity and Danger* (1966) suggests that dirtiness, impurity and danger are linked to 'matter out of place', to the transgression of cultural categories. So, even if pig meat 'counts' as matter in place when it is eaten, pig hearts in a human thorax do not.

Transplantation – whether from human or pig – becomes dangerous because it implies some kind of hybridity, a potential mixing of bodily parts between two bodies. Media discussions of xenotransplantation reveal cultural anxieties about bodily mixing; if people are anxious about becoming like the person from whom their new heart derived, then how much greater will the anxiety be if the heart comes from another species? To cross species boundaries is to create a monster.[9]

The media accounts show a persistent tension between hybridisation (mixing of body parts) and purity (keeping bodies unadulterated). So, although the creation of transgenic pigs for xenotransplantation seems, on the face of it, to be a form of hybridisation, there is also a discursive move in media stories towards a narrative of purification.[10] That is, the mixing involved in xenotransplantation becomes possible in these stories only if we purge at least some of the pig's alienness. Thus, the 'scientific' narratives create a move towards purification by describing the transplanted organ as 'part-human' (because the animal carries copies of genes originating from human tissue). If so, then the transgression of species boundaries is less blatant. Thus, one British newspaper described how 'scientists at Cambridge have produced the first pig with a human heart' (*Daily Star* 12 March 93). Moving such a 'human' heart into a human then seems more acceptable.

Purification is aided further in media accounts by embedded discourse of 'natural' defences against 'alien' or 'foreign' organisms, which must be overcome by scientific subterfuge. By inserting a human gene, the scientists create pig hearts which 'fool' the human body into acting as though the heart were human. The hearts are thus (discursively) purified of their pigness, their alienness. The discourse of purification, moreover, is reminiscent of the biblical reference to the pure at heart – a moral injunction reproduced in the iconographies of the symbolic heart that Anne Sauvy analysed. In the images she describes, the purification takes the form of angels ousting the devil in heroic conquest. In modern media accounts of 'scientific breakthroughs' it is scientific heroism that leads to the creation of pigs with an (angelic?) 'human' heart. These are not trivial words: the metaphors are very powerful. To speak of the human heart here is to purify the organ (discursively, at least) of pigness, even while translating it into humanness.

3. LEARNING BY HEART:
GENDER AND RACE IN SCIENTIFIC
METAPHORS

Thus far, I have sketched the contrasting narratives of the emo-
tional/symbolic heart, and of the mechanical heart. Both, as we
have seen, are deeply interwoven with metaphor. Indeed, part of
the process of knowledge construction is the use of language,
including metaphors. In the next two sections, I want to extend the
connections to gender, race and other categories of exclusion.
Partly I will do so through a brief glance at the history of discoveries about the heart. From there, I will move on to how we 'get
to know' the heart today. To know the heart at the end of the
twentieth century requires that we have faith in the machines that
promise to tell us what is happening within.

The metaphoric descriptions of the heart and circulation pervading scientific texts are mechanical or domestic – the plumbing
metaphor. Generally, the heart as seat of the emotions does not
appear in scientific texts – unless, that is, the texts are written for
popular consumption. In that case, the miracles of modern science
are prominent, but tinged with heartfelt gratitude. Here, for example, are some extracts from a popular science book, which begins:
'The heart is a life-giving pump, a simple machine with a sacred
mission. Its labor is brute, its fabric coarse, yet the heart connects
and sustains the body's work . . . The heart is the center of life . . .
[which] William Harvey[11] . . . deemed . . . "the sovereign" of the
body. The heart kindles and keeps life's flame – and so inspires
man's awe . . . [1] (Davis and Park 1984: 7).

This brute labourer, wearing a coarse coat, brings to mind the
thumping machines of the Industrial Revolution; yet, it is also
sacred, sovereign, and awe-inspiring. Thus, the same text elsewhere
describes how blockage of the coronary arteries leads to a heart
attack: 'The coronary arteries are a crown that keeps the heart
alive. Blocked, they prove the king all too mortal' (Davis and
Park1984: 47). Either way, the metaphor is gendered male.[12]

The relationship of the heart to the rest of the body is, moreover, one of 'centre' which sustains the 'body's work' in many
representations. This powerful image is part of the widespread
metaphor of production, which peppers not just popular accounts,
but also many elementary physiology books. In her important
book, *The Woman in the Body* (1987), Emily Martin reminds us of
the persistence of that metaphor: just as the pituitary was dubbed

the 'master gland' of the endocrine system in many such books, so the heart becomes the powerhouse which supplies the fuel to the body's periphery. The reader must locate herself, somehow, into this narrative of industrial production. It is, after all, supposed to be a description of the *human* body. Or perhaps she cannot . . .

Moreover, capitalist societies have long outgrown the kind of industrial production evoked by these images. As Donna Haraway notes (1991), Starwars is a more appropriate metaphor for the late twentieth century, while OncoMouse might represent our passage to the twenty-first (Haraway 1997). Dispersal and fragmentation, the terms of postmodernism, are more appropriate images to describe the internal universe of the body than the hierarchical powerhouse. And, as the discourses of centrality lose their power to describe, so it becomes easier to imagine losing – or moving – our literal centre in transplant surgery. To return to the theme of the heart, I want to retreat from the eve of the new millennium for a moment, and look at the early modern period – to the beginnings of what we now call the scientific method to detect the imprint of gender and race on the mechanical models of modern medicine. During the early seventeenth century, William Harvey carried out a great number of experiments on the circulation of the blood in both living and dead animals. He developed a research programme at Oxford, which flourished to become part of a new emphasis on experiment. Indeed, he could be said to have been one of the 'founding fathers' of modern science. Steven Shapin notes how Harvey thought it 'base' to learn about nature through books (as classical philosophy had done); far better, he averred, to use 'the book of Nature' (1996: 68).

Reading Nature's book, however, meant interpreting the text in terms of mechanism, captured in the rhyme coined by appreciative colleagues:

> *There thy Observing Eye first found the Art*
> *Of all the Wheels and Clock-work of the Heart:*
> *The mystick causes of its Dark Estate,*
> *What Pullies Close its Cells, and what Dilate,*
> *What secret Engines tune the Pulse, whose din*
> *By Chimes without, Strikes how things fare within.*
>
> (cited in Davis and Park 1984)

It was during this period that experimentation became consolidated as the *modus operandi* of science. Moreover, it became consolidated as a specifically *public* enterprise (Shaffer and Shapin 1985). Experiments could be seen by anyone; but not everyone could act as responsible and reliable witness – not everyone's word could be trusted, but only that of what Donna Haraway calls the 'modest witness' (1997). This figure is inevitably male and European. The modesty, suggests Haraway

is one of the founding virtues of what we call modernity. This is the virtue that guarantees that the modest witness is the legitimate and authorized ventriloquist for the object world, adding nothing from his mere opinions, from his biasing embodiment. And so he is endowed with the remarkable power to establish the facts (Haraway 1997: 24).

Thus, the distancing objectivity of modern science became built into the act of witnessing. So, it was Harvey s 'observing eye' which 'first found' the clockwork of the heart, according to contemporaries. But the early modern period was also a time of great social turmoil; gender and race (among other categories) were at issue. Haraway (1997) argues, drawing on Elizabeth Potter, that these categories were *being contested* in the development of experimental method in the seventeenth century. The modesty, required of the witness, became increasingly linked to the (masculine) mind. It was the basis of the dispassionate stance.

I have outlined this here because I want to emphasise the significance of important medical discoveries about the heart and circulation in the historical development of the scientific method. Not only the pattern of circulation, but also the first attempts at transplant were done in this period (for example, by means of attempts at blood transfusion in the late 1660s: Guerrini 1989). That we can distance ourselves to look 'objectively' at the clockwork heart, that we can accept the metaphor of mechanism, depends on that history.

Gender and other categories of relation were deeply embedded in the very scientific methods of experimentation that were at the birth of modern science. The modest witness had to belong to certain categories of class, gender, sexuality: as Haraway wryly notes, God forbid the experimental way of life have queer foundations (1997: 30). Among other organs, the pumping heart is not innocent of gender, nor race, nor colonialism, in its metaphorical associations.

Moreover, dualisms such as mind/body and culture/nature also became consolidated during this period. And this is where I suggest the heart plays a significant role. The two metaphors – of the heart as seat of emotions versus mechanical pump – must become separated if (masculine) mind is to gain greater ascendance. By separating mind from body, bodily invasion (in the form of surgery, for example) is made easier. The medical discourses of plumbing work to persuade us – literally – to open our hearts to the scalpel. But if we understand the heart to be the centre of our emotions – the heart and soul of who we are – then we would be much more reluctant. Thus, the separation of images of the heart is intertwined with mind/body dualism, itself deeply gendered.

4. ENTERING THE INTERIOR

I have argued that much social theorising on the body treats the body as surface, on which culture inscribes meanings. Yet bodily interiors do occasionally find their way into theory. One example is the immune system, whose discourses have been analysed by Donna Haraway (1991) and Emily Martin (1994). The immune system was, until quite recently, described in terms of defences, with the body portrayed as a fortress, keeping out invaders (Martin 1994). But, as Martin points out, this kind of discourse has given way in the last few years to images of an immune system which can be 'tuned up', or given a workout. This is not a fortress system, but one that is constantly in touch with, and responding to, the outside.

The heart is perhaps more ambiguous. It is at once 'part of the plumbing', and something which can be tuned up. It is at once merely a pump, and a part of the complex systems and feedback controls of late twentieth-century integrated circuits (to paraphrase Haraway). It is precisely that ambiguity which allows the heart metaphorically and literally to link the apparently diverse discourses of emotionality and pumps; emotional events can, after all, alter heart rates (see Bendelow and Williams 1995). Indeed, it is just that effect that is important when animals are brought into hospital wards for therapeutic purposes: stroking the animal reduces heart rate and thus helps to reduce the risk of another heart attack.

How, then, do we get to know the interior? My phrase, 'entering the interior' is meant to evoke images of colonialism, with its multiple associations, rather as the metaphor of mapping (for example, 'mapping genes' in the Human Genome Project) carries a history of navigation and conquest (see Haraway 1997). After all, to enter the body's interior from the cultural spaces of feminist theory seems to me to be a great expedition into the unknown for feminism.

To enter the interior means relying on the texts (written or graphic) of biomedicine. Historically, the earlier means of getting to know the heart clinically included anatomical observation (visual), combined with taking the pulse of living patients (tactile). By the eighteenth century, sound could be added, by tapping the patient's chest; that technique was refined by the early nineteenth century, with the invention of the stethoscope. But it was not until the twentieth century that visualising the beating heart inside a living chest became possible, with the invention of the X-ray machine.

What focuses our attention today, however, is the trace of the ECG (electrocardiograph). Electrical signals pass across a screen: that is the heart. The familiar sound accompanies the blips on the oscilloscope screen – or, in the television dramas, silence accompanies a flat line. And we know how to interpret it. In his analyses of science, and its authority as knowledge, Bruno Latour advises us to look at the 'inscription devices' of labs. It does not matter what aspect of nature you are looking at, he argues,

The only way [the scientists] can talk and not be undermined by counter-arguments as plausible as their own statements is if, and only if, they can make the things they say they are talking about easily readable . . . the final end product of all . . . inscription devices is always a written trace that makes the perceptive judgement of the others *simpler* (1983: 161; emphasis in original).

What I want to emphasise here is how we have learned culturally (not least through TV dramas) to 'read' the ECG trace. It is an inscription device, in Latour's sense, although not always located in an experimental laboratory. If the hospital doctors want to convince us that our hearts are 'normal' they have only to point to the trace. They don't even have to be in the room at the time (and with the advent of new communications technology, they may even be in another part of the world).[13] The ECG machine, as an inscription device, does two things. First, it provides the readable format, the written trace (although we have to learn to interpret it, according to specific conventions). Second, it profoundly restructures the social relations between doctor and patient, and between patient and machine. Doctors no longer 'read' the body of the patient; instead they read the output from electronic devices. But this entry to the interior is what we might expect of late capitalism: we do not exchange beads with the indigenous peoples, but communicate with them at a distance. Moreover, as the technology allows more probing expeditions into the interior, so we come closer to the hybridity of the cyborg (Haraway 1991). We seem to become part-human and part-machine, if only for a moment.

Another way of conceptualising the process by which we 'come to know' the inside, draws on Actor Network Theory (ANT).[14] This seeks to establish interconnections between 'actors' in a controversy, say; but these actors are not only human, so disregarding the rigid nature/society divide. What scientists are trying to do in working out controversy is to enrol other actors, to persuade them. This might include the enrolment of animals, or machines, as part of the social/cultural processes. In the case of heart monitors, it is the machine itself that constitutes one of the actors in the drama, through which the doctors maintain the power to define normal/pathological, health/sickness, and so on. In the case of transgenic pigs created for transplant surgery, the pigs themselves might be seen as benevolent actors, 'helping' the surgeon – or the patient.

We might also think of the heart itself as an actor. It is an actor which can be enrolled – by means of keeping fit, for example – but it is also one which can resist – as shown by changes in the heart-beat for instance. So, coming to know the inside of the body (in this case, the heart) requires a complex process of establishing net-works between, say, a doctor, a patient, her heart, and the machine to which the heart is connected. It is this complex network, not the person by herself, which 'reads' normality or pathology into the ECG trace.

That we might think about the heart as an actor was brought home to me by a webpage I found, entitled 'Women Lead with Their Hearts: A Women's Empowerment Seminar'.[15] Below the title is the ubiquitous ECG trace, followed by a subhead, 'The Science of the Heart'. The text goes on,

women naturally lead with their hearts. It's why women are good care-givers, managers and friends. But all too often the heart is perceived as a weakness, not as a source of wisdom and power . . . Scientific dis-coveries over the past thirty years have revealed that the heart has a unique intelligence unto itself. The heart is central to a whole array of processes that affect brain function, personal effectiveness and overall well-being . . . The Institute of HeartMath's . . . pioneering *research* shows a relationship between feelings in the heart and mental/emo-tional balance, health and productivity (IHM Webpage 1997; emphasis in original).

Later, we are told that we can 'Fine tune and power-up what you, as a woman, have naturally – your intuition and your heart intelligence' Alongside the text, too, there are ECG traces. These are labelled as 'frustration' (a messy trace) and 'appreciation' (an altogether neater one). Reading the electronic traces now takes on the task of bringing together the metaphors of pumping machine and lovesick seat of the emotions.

Here, then, is the heart *as* actor, and as actor which can be fine-tuned for 'peak performance', rather in the way that discourses of immunity now emphasise the need to tune up the immune system (Martin 1994). It is, moreover, an actor that is clearly gendered in this text.

Now the heart-as-pump is typically portrayed as being similar in all of us, no respecter of social categories. Even if the illustrations of body outlines in medical or biological books tend to be largely male, white and young, the internal organs bear no such obvious representation. But when we start to see the heart in medical discourses and practices as an actor, along with the appropriate machines, then it is no longer such an innocent organ.

5. AT THE HEART OF THE MATTER

I have endeavoured to sketch out some of the myriad ways in which metaphors of the heart litter our cultural heritage. Apart from the deep symbolism of the moral/emotional imagery of the heart, there are the equally rich narratives of biomedical discourse. But what matters is not the variety of stories these tell, but the power of these narratives to structure practice. It is precisely the plumbing metaphor that so powerfully constructs how we view heart transplants (or at least, how we are supposed to) that discourse is explicitly mobilised by medical personnel in their dealings with 'heart' patients.

Learning to think about one's body as a collection of body parts is, moreover, facilitated by the structure and division of labour in hospitals and other medical settings. Staff mobility ensures that knowledge about patients and their bodies is disrupted (May 1992; Lupton. 1994); that, in turn, encourages reliance of the scientific discourse of the pump. This, too, is a question that theorists need to address; how are discourses mobilised in different contexts? How do these processes of mobilisation affect the practices of the clinic?

The heritage of other images lurks in the shadows, however. The heart is, culturally, much more than 'just' a pump. As I have tried to show, it carries with it a plethora of other meanings, and a history deeply entwined with contested power. To understand the experiences of heart patients, to understand the practices of the clinic or the hospital, we need to unravel further these intertwined strands of meanings.

Unravelling such strands has implications for our theorising. Mechanical metaphors are certainly encouraged by medical personnel (who are heavily invested in the scientific discourses of biomedicine), and by the practices of the clinic or hospital. But they are also encouraged by the new feminist and other theorising about the body. This theoretical work does so precisely because it has so insistently focused on the exterior of the body – the body as inscriptive surface, the body as a means of performance. To think about the inside, we seem to have to fall back on to the mechanical metaphors. We have also inherited the metaphors of the breakable heart, the seat of emotions; but we do not usually use it to think about what goes on inside our bodily selves. Rather, if we think about it at all, the mechanical model surfaces. Yet isn't that model itself a cultural inscription on (or in) the body? It seems to me that we succeed only in perpetuating mind-body dualism if our emerging theories continue to relegate the inside – including the heart – to the realms of biomedicine.

Unravelling the meanings also has significant implications for our experiences of embodiment, particularly for those people who have experienced heart disease in any form. The gap between the medical discourses of the body as machinery and the experiences of patients with their own perceptions of health/disease and of bodily parts is immense. Having severe pains in the chest is a terrible experience; it frightens us, and can be the harbinger of disability.[16] This experience is not helped by talk of problems with the plumbing, for such talk fails to address the embodied experiences of people for whom the heart carries much more symbolic power than 'simply a pump'. We cannot, after all, exist without it.

Yet the two sets of metaphors remain entwined. Doctors themselves are, of course, heirs to that cultural history; the quotation from Christian Barnard at the beginning of this chapter testifies to his use of more popular metaphors of the heart. Lay people (most patients), too, learn the dispassionate language of the body-machine. To accept the prospect of heart surgery means that one must learn to speak about the heart as a pump (which may not mean accepting that language). For patients, as well as for medical personnel, the clinic or hospital is a site of complex negotiations of meanings. Patients must learn how, and when, to refer to the plumbing. In turn, theoretical analyses of the clinic need to pay more heed to the complexities of those negotiations.

Thinking about the entwined metaphors and their implications for clinical practice reminded me of a time, a few years ago, when I was hospitalised with terrible chest pains (which turned out to be pleurisy). When I first experienced the pains, I went to the GP's surgery; I was crying with the pain (and, no doubt, the fear). The doctor who saw me (not my own GP) said he could find nothing wrong with my heart or lungs: 'It must be boyfriend trouble,' he suggested. Apart from his heterosexist assumptions, he had to conclude that the pain resulted from my emotional heart; the pump appeared to be working.

My scientific training, of course, tells me too to think of pumps. At times, I must still speak that language. Yet my heritage in an English-speaking country also reminds me that I can lose my heart, can have it broken, can give it. The power of those other cultural metaphors should not be underestimated: they lie, I suspect, at the heart of many medical practices.

NOTES

1. Barnard, 1996: quoted in BBC television documentary, *A Knife to the Heart*, Part I: 30 April.
2. Perhaps less so in accounts that develop a phenomenonology of the body, which focus on, for example, the experiencing of pain. However, even though this literature acknowledges the materiality of the body, the body's insides remain largely untheorised, except by biomedicine. See Bendelow and Williams, 1995, for discussion of the phenomenology of the body and pain.
3. Classification of disease has changed considerably over time. A focus on the individual as sick or well shifted towards a conceptualisation of diseases as moving through the body. The shift to a focus on diseased organs or tissues began in the nineteenth century. Jewson (1993) notes how the 'sick man' disappeared from medical cosmology between 1770 and 1870; accordingly, bedside medicine was gradually replaced by laboratory medicine, he argues.
4. Illustration from the iconographic collection, Wellcome Centre for Medical Science; not surprisingly, the woman is white, bringing to mind Richard Dyer's analyses of the construction of 'whiteness' through lighting in visual images (Dyer 1997).
5. These are babies in whom the central nervous system has not developed normally. As a result, the brain is largely missing above the

brainstem at the top of the spinal cord. Such babies are usually born 'alive' in the sense that they are breathing and have a beating heart, because it is the brainstem, not the higher brain, that coordinates these activities. They cannot, however, live beyond a few days, and some doctors and ethicists have argued that they should not, therefore, be classed as fully human or even fully alive. Here, it is the possession of a functional brain that becomes the definition of life. Following this argument means that they could be used as donors for organ transplants (see Lamb 1990).

6. Kantrowitz, BBC television, 'A Knife to the Heart', Part II, 14 May 1996.

7. Davis and Park are writing for a lay audience. The metaphors in more academic medical texts are less overt. But most people gain their understanding of the body from the 'popularising' accounts, which in turn draw their concepts and metaphors from the medical text books.

8. Scientists have carried out some tests on other primate species, receiving hearts from pigs. The procedure has not yet been tried on humans. Without the chemical alteration brought about by inserting human genes, the human body would reject the pig organ very swiftly in what is called the hyperacute rejection; the heart goes black and dies.

9. The association between hybridity and monsters has a long history; see Davidson 1991 and his analysis of monsters (human–animal hybrids) in medieval cosmology.

10. Bruno Latour (1993) suggests that these twin moves are constitutive of modernity: that is, the word 'modern' covers two sets of practices. One is the mixing of things through 'translation' (for example, our understanding of networks of association involving molecules, people and institutions contributes to how we know 'the upper atmosphere'). The other move is purification; the establishment and maintenance of a boundary between human and non-human, between the 'natural' world and the social world. In *We Have Never Been Modern*, Latour argues that the second has made the first possible: 'the more we forbid ourselves to conceive of hybrids, the more possible their interbreeding becomes' (1993: 12). So, while culturally we might prefer to keep things apart – including ourselves and other animals – their literal interbreeding becomes possible precisely through the technologies of separation and reduction.

11. William Harvey was the sixteenth-century physician whose experiments demonstrated that blood circulates. Prior to that, doctors believed that it ebbed and flowed. Once the idea of circulation is established, then the need for a pump becomes clear.

12. Lest critics say that this is an example of a popularising text, but is not 'real' science, I will ask: Surely 'real scientists' (myself included)

have all read such 'popular' texts at times, perhaps in our youth? How sure can you be that 'real science' is not also, covertly, contaminated by the coarse fabric of such metaphors? The history of modern science is replete with examples of just such 'contamination'.

13. British Telecom are running an advertisement at the time of writing, picturing a foetal scan. The doctor is at a London children's hospital, the text informs us, while the mother is in the Isle of Wight, many miles away.

14. Actor Network Theory developed, partly, out of work in the sociology of scientific knowledge. ANT looks at the ways in which particular identities serve the goals of others. Such identities or roles might then be enrolled, or enlisted to serve those goals. But, what is significant about ANT is that non-humans can count as identities; these might be animals, nature, or even technological artefacts. Scientists thus recruit nature (a particular species of marine life, say) as allies in their accounts.

15. Which I found at: http://www.webcom.com/hrtmath/IHM/Womens Empower.html.

16. In the sense that 'heart patients' may become much less able to carry out everyday tasks than previously, and may have their mobility impaired. I recognise that there are many definitions of disability.

REFERENCES

Basch, S. H. (1973) 'The Intrapsychic Integration of a New Organ: a Clinical Study of Kidney Transplantation', *Psychoanalytic Quarterly* 42: 364–84.

Beck, U. (1986) *The Risk Society*, London: Sage.

Bendclow, G. and Williams, S. J. (1995) 'Transcending the Dualisms? Towards a Sociology of Pain', *Sociology of Health and Illness* 17, 2: 139–65.

Calnan, M. and Williams, S. (1992) 'Images of Scientific Medicine', *Sociology of Health and Illness* 14, 2: 233–54.

Classen, C. (1993) *Worlds of Sense: Exploring the Senses in History and across Cultures*, London: Routledge.

Davidson, A. I. (1991) 'The horror of monsters' in J. Sheehan and M. Sosna (eds) *The Boundaries of Humanity: Humans, Animals, Machines*, Berkeley: University of California Press.

Davis, G. P. and Park, E. (1984) *The Heart: The Living Pump*, New York: Torstar Books.

Douglas, M. (1966) *Purity and Danger*, London: Ark.

Dyer, R. (1997) *White*, London: Routledge.

Falk, P. (1994) *The Consuming Body*, London: Sage.

Gatens, M. (1996) *Imaginary Bodies: Ethics, Power and Corporeality*, London: Routledge.

Grosz, E. (1994) *Volatile Bodies: Towards a Corporeal Feminism*, Bloomington: Indiana University Press.

Guerrini, A. (1989) 'The Ethics of Animal Experimentation in Seventeenth-century England', *Journal of the History of Ideas* 50: 391–408.

Haraway, D. (1991) *Simians, Cyborgs and Women*, London: Free Association Books.

Haraway, D. (1997) *Modest_Witness@Second_Millennium. FemaleMan_Meets_OncoMouse*, London: Routledge.

Horigan, S. (1990) *Nature, Culture and Western Discourses*, London: Routledge.

Houser, R. and Konstam, V. and Konstam, M. (1992) 'Transplantation; Implications if the Heart Transplantation Process for Rehabilitation Counsellors', *Journal of Applied Rehabilitation Counseling* 23: 38–43.

Jeffreys, D. (1996) 'Have these patients inherited the donors' characteristics?' *Daily Mail*, 4 June: 51.

Jewson, N. D. (1993) 'The Disappearance of the Sick Man from Medical Cosmology, 1770–1870' in A. Beattie, M. Gott, L. Jones and M. Sidell, *Health and Wellbeing: A Reader*, Buckingham: Open University Press.

Joralemon, D. (1995) 'Organ Wars: The Battle for Body Parts' *Medical Anthropology Quarterly*, 9: 335–56.

Kimbrell, A. (1993) *The Human Body Shop: The Engineering and Marketing of Life*, London: HarperCollins.

Lamb, D. (1990) *Organ Transplants and Ethics*, London: Routledge.

Latour, B. (1987) *Science in Action*, Milton Keynes: Open University Press.

Latour, B. (1993) *We Have Never Been Modern*, Hemel Hempstead: Harvester.

Lupton, D. (1994) *Medicine as Culture: Illness, Disease and the Body in Western Societies*, London: Sage.

Martin, E. (1987) *The Woman in the Body*, Milton Keynes: Open University Press.

Martin, E. (1994) *Flexible Bodies: Tracking Immunity in America from the days of Polio to the Age of AIDS*, Boston: Beacon Books.

May, C. (1992) 'Nursing Work, Nurse's Knowledge and the Subjectification of the Patient' *Sociology of Health and Illness* 14: 472–87.

Mohacsi, P. J. Blumer, C.e, Quine, S. and Thompson, J. F. (1995) 'Aversion to Xenotransplantation', *Nature* 378: 434.

Nuffield Council for Bioethics (1996) *Animal to Human Transplants: The Ethics of Xenotransplantation*. Report.

Parmley, W. W. (1979) 'Circulatory function and control' in P. B. Beeson, W. McDermott and J. B. Wyngaarden (eds) *Cecil Textbook of Medicine*, Philadelphia: W. B. Saunders Company.

Plumwood, V. (1993) *Feminism and the Mastery of Nature*, London: Routledge.

Radley, A. (1996) 'The Critical Moment: Time, Information and Medical Expertise in the Experience of Patients Receiving Coronary Bypass

Surgery' in S. J. Williams and M. Calnan (eds) *Modern Medicine: Lay Perspectives and Experiences*, London: UCL Press.

Sauvy, A. (1989) *Le Miroir du Coeur: quatre siècles d'images savantes et populaires*, Paris: CERF.

Scarry, E. (1985) *The Body in Pain*, Oxford: Oxford University Press.

Shapin, S. and Shaffer, S. (1985) *Leviathan and the air-pump: Hobbes, Boyle and the Experimental Life*, Princeton: Princeton University Press.

Shapin, S. (1996) *The Scientific Revolution*, Chicago: University of Chicago Press.

Sharp, L. (1995) 'Organ Transplantation as a Transformative Experience:

Anthropological Insights into the Restructuring of the Self, *Medical Anthropology Quarterly* 9: 357–89.

Synnott, A. (1993) *The Body Social: Symbolism, Self and Society*, London: Routledge.

Young, S. (1992) 'Review: In Praise of Miraculous Plumbing', *New Scientist*, 22 August: 36.

11

Uncertain Thoughts on the Dis/abled Body

JANET PRICE and MARGRIT SHILDRICK

I

AS THE FOCUS OF a new and growing area of academic concern, disability studies is well placed to take advantage of the insights and operational strategies of deconstruction and postmodernism. Apart from its manifestation within biomedical discourse, it is an area of study largely without the baggage of a traditional history that prescribes a convention of right and wrong methodologies, or that delineates fixed disciplinary boundaries. As such, it has the potential to be open to radical new approaches that suggest both a revaluation of existing concepts and a reordering of binary hierarchies, such as ability/disability, health/disease, normal/abnormal. More challenging yet is the opportunity to set out innovative points of departure that go beyond the rearrangement of scholarship around a given materiality – the disabled body – to contest the very notion of any such fixed object of concern. And to open up the issue of uncertainty and vulnerability, as that must, suggests to us the possibility of a reconceived ethics.

What follows is an attempt to interrogate the narratives of/on disability, to explore the process of naming and being named as disabled. As Gareth Williams argues, the '(l)anguage of disability has become the object of political analysis, and it is increasingly difficult to use terms to describe chronic illness and disability innocently' (1996: 194). We want to ask questions about power, discourse and (con)text in the construction and use of the term disabled.

Historically, biomedicine has served a powerful role in establishing and maintaining normative notions of corporeal sameness and difference. Emergent discourses from within the disability rights movement (DRM) have problematised these medical norms whilst simultaneously setting new ones in place. Our aim, however, is not to set up an opposition between the old and the new, between the naturalised disabled body of medicine and the socially constructed oppression theorised by the DRM. Rather, we want to reflect upon the ways in which such power-saturated discourses not only materialise bodies as disabled (or not) through the reiteration of norms, but also produce 'the user of the term as the emblem and vehicle of normalisation' (Butler 1993: 223). Our analysis will be provisional – as are the categories with which we are concerned. The intention is not simply to apply postmodernist theories with the aim of uncovering new directions of abstract inquiry, but to give body to what should be a substantive area of feminist concern. Moreover, it is to address how, in the face of the uncertainty – an uncertainty that we will argue is necessary to any understanding of health, disease and disability – 'deconstruction can offer crucial resources of thought for survival under duress . . .' (Sedgwick 1994: 12).

Despite its potential, the area of disability studies has been suffused hitherto by precisely the same modernist standards that it purports to contest, and it remains rooted in the very binaries such as sameness/difference and self/other that have underwritten the devaluation of those people defined as disabled. To work towards an end to discrimination and for the establishment of clear rights is an important ethical aim. However, it is one that relies on modernist notions of equality, and of difference as identity, that cuts short any understanding of irreducible and multiple differences as the ground for a reconceived ethics. In short, both the disability rights movement and feminism have largely declined to come to terms with the admittedly risky strategies offered by postmodernism, preferring instead to address the issues from within familiar paradigms. In consequence, though there have been clear and positive changes both in attitudes towards those with disabilities, and in the expectations that disabled people may themselves hold, the terms of the debate remain constrained, and substantive development limited. Perhaps it needs to be said that it is not the purpose of this chapter to negate the efforts of others who are already deeply concerned with issues of disability. A deconstructive approach to existing theory and practice is not a matter of uncovering error, but one that, as Spivak puts it, teaches us to look at limits and questions. And what we would stress, as Spivak goes on to remark, is that 'deconstruction suggests there is no absolute justification of *any* position' (1990: 104).

It is perhaps surprising that feminism – despite its longstanding political analysis of and involvement with health concerns in general – has been remarkably silent around the issue of disability. It is not, of course, that the women's health movement has ever attempted to move much beyond reformism in any of its major areas of concern, a point we discuss in the introduction and which has been one of the motivations of the present collection. What matters, rather, is that when it comes to disability issues, there has been a failure to ensure that such concerns should figure prominently at all, even within the agenda of health care.[1] At the same time, the concern of feminism at a more theoretical level with identifying and theorising the effects of difference in women's lives has stopped short of any adequate engagement with the binary of disability and its oppositions. It is an issue that is permanently pending under the rubric of 'and so on' that forecloses the good intentions of inclusivity. And moreover, despite a powerful recuperation of the body as a matter of theoretical as much as practical attention, the epistemic concern to recover the corporeal as a 'source' of meaning has proceeded almost as if there were only healthy/unbroken bodies. As Susan Wendell remarks:

Until feminists criticize our own body ideals and confront the weak, suffering, and uncontrollable body in our theorizing and practice, women with disabilities are likely to feel we are embarassments to feminism (1997: 93).

For the most part, then, it has been left to disability activists to set the terms of a debate, which while it is properly concerned with the social response to corporeal difference, is frequently insensitive to other differences such as gender, sexuality and ethnicity. The concern of many activists rather is to present a unified front against what is seen as a damaging mix of indifference, negative attitudes and inappropriate practice fostered by western biomedical discourse.

Disability has long been construed as a medical issue, and western societal norms of health, illness and disability are largely constituted by the ways in which doctors talk about and treat (or fail to treat) those with 'broken' bodies. The choices routinely made – about whom to save and whom to abandon, whom to 'restructure' to more closely approximate corporeal 'normality', about how and when to offer rehabilitation, and what its aims should be – are all acts and omissions serving to continually reinforce and re-create medical notions of disabled and ablebodied. As a scientific discourse, biomedicine valorises regularity, uniformity and predictability as the supposedly objective grounds of its epistemological claims. In consequence, all variations on the idealised standard body are taken as pathological, and in the diagnostic search for abnormality, disorder and deformity (Hutchison 1989), biomedicine has constituted disability as physical or bodily lack – as inability, incapacity, deprivation, deviation from the normal. The pathological both confirms what is normal, and demands attention to allay the normative anxiety it provokes. It is, then, the part of the practices of health care to control such grossly fleshy disorders, to promote instead the conformity that characterises the bio/logical body, the body whose physical reality may be forgotten, save as the medium of the autonomous subject.

In contrast to that dominant model, the social constructivist model attempts to place an analysis of disability beyond the influence of medical discourse, beyond, that is, a focus on the material disorders of the biological body. Nonetheless, the circumvention it effects simply mirrors biomedicine's own belief in the givenness of the corporeal as something *before* either social or discursive construction, as something ultimately to be transcended. We would argue, then, that such oppositional struggles are always already implicated within that which they seek to undermine or displace, in this case, biomedicine. The disability rights movement (DRM) in particular has urged that the individualistic medical model should be replaced by the social model of disability.[2] The argument is that the former, in being firmly focused upon a disrupted but nonetheless naturally given corpus – the biological body – is constrained to view disability as a personal tragedy arising from a breakdown in the normative morphology of the individual. In contrast, the social model theorises disability as a form of oppression: as Michael Oliver puts it, 'disability is wholly and exclusively social' (1996: 35). It argues that disabled people are oppressed by society's failure to provide adequately for their needs, not simply on an individual basis, but as a consequence of social organisation which systematically discriminates against them as a group. The DRM's approach to redress this discrimination is through self-help, the development of individual and collective identities as disabled, and the acknowledgement of individual and collective responsibility. The disabled identity is seen both as the driving force for, and the consequence of, social action. And the ultimate goals of such action are *rights* and *choices* for disabled people (Oliver 1996: 34), goals that affirm disabled people as active agents in their own right, rather than as innocent and passive victims of misfortune.

What is strange, however, is that the disabled body itself plays a secondary role, inciting prejudice and anxiety in others, but nonetheless disregarded as a site of material experience, constitutive meaning, or differential and evolving selfhood. It is deemed irrelevant to the constitution of the social. Michael Oliver, again, is particularly insistent that '(d)isablement is nothing to do with the body' (1996: 35). His claim relies upon the distinction, widely accepted within the social model of disability, between *impairment* and *disability*. First formulated in the 1970s by the Union of the Physically Impaired against Segregation (UPIAS), and highly influential since for the British DRM, a separation is made between:

impairment – 'lacking part or all of a limb, or having a defective limb, organism or mechanism of the body'; and
disability – 'the disadvantage or restriction of activity caused by a contemporary social organisation which takes little or no account of people who have physical impairments, and thus excludes them from the mainstream of social activities' (UPIAS 1976: 3–4).

In effect a clear boundary is drawn between the material body and its characteristics, and the social response to such a body. We are not suggesting that the DRM is wholly uniform in its approach, but as with biomedical accounts, the body is at most something to be managed into compliance. Nonetheless, the social model has played an immensely powerful role in the lives of some disabled people. Liz Crow exemplifies this when she writes of her discovery of it:

This was the explanation I had sought for years. Suddenly what I had always known, deep down, was confirmed. It wasn't my body that was responsible for all my difficulties, it was external factors, the barriers constructed by the society in which I live . . . Even more important, if all the problems had been created by society, then surely society could uncreate them. Revolutionary! (1996: 206).

Crow goes on, however, to mark what she has come to see as the limitations of the social model:

Instead of tackling the contradictions and complexities of our experiences head on, we have chosen in our campaigns to present impairment as irrelevant, neutral and, sometimes, positive, but never, ever as the quandary it really is (1996: 208).

The social model itself is evolving, and what Crow focuses on is one of the recent moves, i.e. the demand, particularly from disabled feminists, for a reconsideration of the position of the body within disability politics. However, the body they are attempting to reclaim remains a given, morphologically compromised but largely separate from the self. In other words, little account is taken of the bodilyness of being-in-the-world, and questions of ontology or epistemology are scarcely raised, while the issue of the ethical appears to devolve on an unproblematised emphasis on disabled people as moral agents, with all the inherent disembodiment that that implies in modernist terms. From the perspective of a postmodernism that fundamentally seeks to problematise notions such as the subject, the body, rights, or sameness and difference, it is not sufficient simply to reconceive disabled people as morally autonomous persons. The move to a constructivist model has brought the issue of responsibility for insults suffered to the fore, but we resist the view that all difficulties could be resolved by simply re-evaluating the status of disability by either dissolving or, as recent moves have attempted, reformulating the link with what is taken to be a fixed biological body.

In a recent article, Tom Shakespeare and Nicholas Watson make an appeal for increased recognition of the constructivist model, suggesting that:

There is a broad and vigorous consensus around the social model of disability which should be translated into a renewed attempt to achieve understanding and win acceptance and application of the model within wider society (1997: 293).

Like other disability rights campaigners, they would like to resignify the binary opposite of disabled by replacing the term 'able-bodied' – which links to the individualistic medical model – with the term 'non-disabled' – which throws the emphasis on to a social condition. Several problems arise. It is not just that it is unclear where the necessary resignification of the term 'disabled', that such a move signals, is to take place; nor how the shift will occur by which the silent unmarked term that sits alongside 'disabled' becomes, in everyday usage, 'non-disabled' rather than 'able-bodied'. Unanswered questions of this nature are an inevitable feature of any form of radical rethinking, and speculation as a prelude to practical changes is reasonable. What concerns us more is the thought that even if such a move marked a shift in the norms of disability, of health, of disease, of normality itself, whether the replacement model would yield the effects that campaigners would wish for. It is by no means certain that the hierarchical structure of difference that relies on an acceptance of fixed boundaries between 'them' and 'us' would be greatly challenged by resignifying the binary opposite of disabled; at most there might be some realignment of the flow of power. Moreover, what is implied for a present understanding of disability that such a shift should be desired?

Shakespeare and Watson insist upon the necessity and possibility of such change, as though by force of will and repetition it is possible to conceal/obscure/rewrite the constitutive history of the term 'disabled' and, by extension, the histories of other terms that have been used to describe disabled people – handicapped, physically challenged, and so on – and even of 'disease' itself. What their article seems implicitly to suggest is that we can control the traces of these terms, can determine the slide of signification and the specific effects of the unmarked in discourse. Shakespeare and Watson choose not to engage with postmodernism in this context, but even within the unproblematised terms of their own debate there are dangers: the positions, the roles, the very acts of our bodies, the nature of our embodiments are placed under erasure.[3]

How then can we proceed? How can we begin to understand, physically and theoretically, this thing called disability, which has undeniable material effects, and yet slips away from the grasp? Does it help or hinder to try to play out some determinations that are crucial to the DRM analysis? How can we (be compelled to) reiterate the normative sites of disabled/non-disabled/able-bodied and yet disrupt the power of their necessity? Should we/must we distinguish between the two of us?

II

I am disabled

What am I claiming when I say this, what truth am I attempting to convey – about myself, as embodied, subject, agent – and about the world around me?

Why do I choose to say it here – in this book, in a chapter of which I am a co-author – a text in which you will never be able to definitively untangle which are my words and which my co-author's – for we both ask the questions and we both offer the answers?

I wonder if my claim, our text, makes you read this differently.

What constructions do you put on/into the unnamed, (dis)embodied voice?

I am non-disabled

Displaced from my position of positivity, but nonetheless clearly distinct, different, 1 am a member of an identity category which need never be spoken, which knows that its place remains that of the socio-cultural norm. Perhaps in a better, more thoughtfully organised environment from which physical and social obstacles had been removed, you might imagine me not as ablebodied, but as non-disabled and yet physically impaired. But I do not experience myself as disembodied; only as more or less conscious of my (dis)ability according to the physical context.

I am disabled

Do you need to see or hear me to be convinced of the embodied reality of my claim? Do you need to see a 'broken' body? Or do you imagine my body and wonder what is the nature of it that would authorise what I say about myself? And how much does my body matter – my own, individual, unshared, ultimately incommunicable experience of my body? How much is my body to the point?

Recent feminism in particular has been widely concerned with embodiment, and especially with differential embodiment – this book, and many others like it with 'body' in the title, being a case in point. Nonetheless, for all that we want to own our bodies – after years of theoretical neglect – there is still an uneasiness that as women we can be let down by our bodies, shown to be weak and out of control after all. Though the body is perhaps no longer an inconvenience to be transcended[4] in the interests of attaining fully rational subjectivity, the mind/body split of modernism lingers still. It is the young, healthy, well-formed, preferably white male body that is the most acceptable; the 'normal', tractable body, that is, that in drawing no attention to itself can be forgotten. And whilst feminist phenomenologists have been critical of that universalist model, for the most part the critique of the normal has done little to valorise multiple and irreducible differences. As Julia Epstein puts it: 'The *normal*, even when understood to represent a curve or continuum, remains an inchoate conception of a lack of difference, of conformity, of the capacity to blend in invisibly' (1995: 11).

Ironically, for those who don't blend in, for those who are disabled, the experience is often one of being literally and metaphorically overlooked. Following a conference some years ago I wrote:

There was a pervading sense of dis-ease. l was aware I made others uncomfortable by my presence and I was, in many cases, ignored or avoided. I felt, effectively, invisible and/or 'Othered', fixed by a single/ unitary identity that labelled me as 'disabled', as 'wheelchairbound' (1996: 95).[5]

Now, such an experience is clearly commonplace for people in similar situations, and one that is highly frustrating, but the intention here is not to bemoan any lack of sensitivity, but to explore further how a conventional understanding of the body seems to erase morphological irregularity. Insofar as it is taken as the grounding of the autonomous subject of modernity, the body must appear invulnerable, predictable and consistent in form and function, above all free from the possibility of disruption. Peculiarity in whatever configuration threatens to disturb the paradigms of sameness and difference on which western epistemology, ontology and ethics are founded, and must therefore be managed into neutrality.

The regulatory practices of the body of which Foucault speaks are complicit in the construction of just such an embodied self. And as Thomson suggests, that privileging of sameness of form is a feature not just of the logos, but of the common values of modernity which is characterised by '(m)echanized practices such as standardization, mass production, and interchangeable parts' (1996: 11). Among the several discourses supporting such demands, modern biomedicine, as Foucault himself insists, is preeminent in its claim to know the truth of the body, while at the same time subjecting it to disciplinary power. The conventions of health care constitute the body, whether marked by impairment or not, as stable and predictable. The assumption is that the processes of illness or injury act on an essential body, which can be examined, measured and analysed, and managed in the pursuit of the normative standards of health and physical ability. Like femininity itself, the disabled body is positioned as a universalised other, clearly separated from the unmarked ideal of 'wholeness' but nonetheless a uniform categorisation that finesses the interplay of incalculable differences.

The point is well illustrated by the criteria for the British welfare payment of Incapacity Benefit. The compulsory assessment of ability to work consists of a nineteen-page questionnaire (Benefits Agency 1996) followed, in most cases, by a medical examination of up to an hour. The questionnaire contains detailed questions about the respondent's capacity to sit, stand, bend and kneel, lift weights ranging from a paperback book to a 2.5 kg bag of potatoes, and about sight, hearing and toilet needs. The questions bear no relation to the work experience or aspirations of the respondent, but cover a generalised range of bodily comportment deemed necessary to the working role. The assessment relies upon and serves to constitute the notion of a stable universalised working body and the ill or disabled respondent who does not/cannot work is constrained to produce herself as an 'incapable' body through the regulatory norms set in place by the questionnaire. These norms are further reinforced not only by the medical examination which pays attention only to those aspects of the self that are considered relevant to work, but also by the self-regulating gaze of the individual who monitors her own actions and produces herself as a subject incapable of work.[6]

I am non-disabled

Where one of us has her body rendered silent by others, am *I* free to choose the privileged status of disembodiment? Clearly not, for my body, as every woman is aware, is not an unchanging, indifferent corpus, but a dynamic force in complex reciprocity with the constitution of my self. And moreover, the disciplinary power that saturates and shapes being-in-the-world is directed at us both, albeit in sometimes differential forms. I am not constrained to construct myself as a disabled woman, but we are equally constrained to construct ourselves as women where gender is an achievement, not a given.

What is at issue is that just as postmodernist thought has problematised the self-present human subject, so too the unitary and stable condition of the body has been brought into question. On the one hand, the body is the object of disciplinary practices that seek to secure its boundaries, while on the other, the very lack of an essential corpus opens up the possibility/inevitability of transgression. In presenting various conference and seminar papers together, for example, our ability to swap places physically – one at a lecturn perhaps, the other in a wheelchair – has been clearly a shock to listeners.[7] It is a move that, as we note elsewhere, appears 'to disrupt notions of disability and to challenge the safe perception of categories of disabled and able-bodied as fixed, permanent, internally homogeneous, and moreover as oppositional' (1996: 95). In performing this shift, we hope to make manifest the sense in which all bodies, and the identities they support, are in themselves performative.

The postmodernist claim that there is no essential biologically given corpus upon which meaning is inscribed, and no unmediated access to a body prior to discourse, remains contentious. It is not that the materiality of the body is in doubt, but that materiality is a process negotiated through the discursive exercise of what Foucault (1980) calls power/knowledge. To both the biomedical profession with its fantasy of descriptive objectivity, and to the DRM with its investment in the notion that impairment can be separated off from disability, the claim is anathema. While both may subscribe to the view that health-care practices are both normative and normalising, there is little recognition that those practices are also constitutive of the body. As Judith Butler puts it: 'there is no reference to a pure body which is not at the same time a further formation of that body' (1993: 10). What that means is that the physical impairments of the body, and the socially constructed disability, are equally constructs held in place by the regulatory practices that both produce and govern *all* bodies. The process, however, is never complete or certain, but as Liz Grosz puts it:

> The stability of the unified body image, even in the so-called normal subject, is always precarious It cannot be simply taken for granted as an accomplished fact, for it must be continually renewed (1994: 43–4).

I am disabled

Is the *identity* of the disabled woman also dependent on 'the stability of a unified body image'? Can it override the instability of my condition, by incorporating unpredictability as a defining characteristic? And do I only count as disabled if, as Michael Oliver (1996: 5) claims for political reasons, I identify as disabled? But if 'disabled' is used here as just another identity category, a label that might be used to define one of us in all situations, it is difficult to see how that might disturb the boundaries that seem to separate us one from the other. The issue of identity, with its binaries of sameness and difference, of self and other – where difference and otherness are devalued – is fundamental to a conventional understanding of disability, and remains prominent in an unproblematised disability politics. Indeed, it is through appeal to those apparently stable binaries that a sense of definition, and thus of safety, bodily integrity and (self)identity is maintained. In consequence, it seems that identity must reinforce/reiterate distinction by playing into the very hierarchies that postmodernism reveals as normative discursive constructions, optimistically but finally ineffectively ranged against the threat or promise of categorical breakdown.

But what does such an identity demand, what promises does it hold out, and what boundaries or limits does it place around me? Does it offer me any greater freedom, or does it constrain my actions? Both personal identity – the sense of a unified, unchanging and bounded self, a base perhaps from which to demonstrate autonomous agency – and group identity, with its emphasis on knowing who is to count as the same, seem to manifest a nostalgia for the modernist values of separation and exclusion. Perhaps all politicised groupings face the question of counter-identity, which promises the power of solidarity in challenging group devaluation, whilst at the same time demanding the policing of its own boundaries and the marginalisation of difference just as surely as does unmarked identity. Despite his own sometime allegiance to identity politics, Tom Shakespeare critiques an article by disability activist Alan Holdsworth (1993) for developing a polemic about allies and oppressors, dividing the non-disabled world into professional oppressors, liberal oppressors and allies: 'Disabled people were good and non-disabled people could only be counted as good in very specific circumstances' (1996: 108). In other words, the exclusionary/othering process which is usually attributed to the dominant – the 'non disabled' – group alone, is mirrored in radical disability politics.

I am non-disabled

Where does the more characteristic unproblematised approach of the DRM leave me? The intention to claim and demand a counter-identity certainly challenges the standard or norm against which difference is found wanting, but the oppositional move of reassigning value, also reinforces separation, locking us into our differential identities. In endeavouring to contest that approach, we do not want to suggest that there is no distinction to be made between women who experience themselves as disabled, and those who do not. On the contrary, we are committed to the view that some differences just are irreducible, albeit contingent, and that

ethical acuity lies in the recognition of those multiple and local differences rather than in the supposed fixity of unified categorical
difference. In any case, as is becoming clear from a postmodernist
perspective, those categories are always provisional and insecure,
never entirely distinct. What we are contesting, then, are the conventional dichotomies – of health/illness, disabled/non-disabled,
whole/broken, them and us, and so on – that constitute, by acts of
separation, the very ground of our embodied selves.

Even within the disability movement, identity politics is not the
only approach. In the attempt to disrupt the discursive superiority
of the non-disabled norm – which remains the unmarked term of
an implicit binary – a second strategy recently advocated, particularly in the States, is to push the majority into a recognition that
they are merely temporarily abled bodies (TABs). Susan Wendell,
for example, stresses continuously that corporeal conformity to
standards of normality is precarious: 'Under the disciplines of
normality, everyone must fear becoming a member of the subordinated group; everyone who does not die suddenly *will* become a
member of the subordinated group' (1997: 90). As a mark of the
material vulnerability of the healthy body, not least in the process
of aging, the notion of TABs is useful. It introduces the consideration that the difference between one body and the other in terms
of correspondence to a normative ideal is not sustainable over
time. While on the one hand this explains in part the underlying
anxiety and dis-ease that many people feel in the face of disability,
it also suggests the ethical fatuity of the process of othering. More
radically, however, the notion of TABs can be extended to provide
just that thoroughgoing critique of the binaries of health/ill-
health, non-disabled/disabled that a poststructuralist approach
would demand. It is not simply that all and any of us may be repo-
sitioned, but that if the boundaries between the apparently secure
self and those others can be breached, then any response founded
in fixed binary difference is likely to be inadequate. A more radical
politics of disability, then, would disrupt the norms of dis/abled
identity, not by pluralising the conditions of disability, as the
notion of TABs intends, but rather by exposing the failure of those
norms to ever fully and finally contain a definitive standard.

I am disabled

But if it is the acceptance of a specific identity that authorises my
claim, does that mean I make a conscious avowal that coincides

with my existence, that represents me 'as I am'? Can I ever be fully certain what it is I am owning, and can you ever be fully certain you know what I mean? And what further claims does my avowal authorise? Moreover, where are our bodies in this process of (self)naming – not only my body, but our bodies, your body? How do we understand ways of thinking disability that appear to demand the truth of/from our bodies whilst simultaneously excluding our bodies from the realm of truth(telling)? As though truth itself were waiting to be discovered.

In opposing the social constructivist model of disability to the conventional medical model, the problematic of truth is uncovered only to be reconcealed in the interests of political efficacy. Just as feminism quickly discovered the power of an appeal to the politics of experience, so too the DRM has consciously promoted the notion of a unique standpoint. Perhaps identity cannot function properly without an assertion of epistemic privilege, a rallying round some standard of truth that outsiders cannot fully know. The assumption, as with all standpoint positions, is that there is sufficient shared experience unique to that particular group to justify the claim to know differently. Susan Wendell introduces the notion fairly cautiously in her claim that being feminine and disabled creates 'the possibility of different perspectives which have epistemic advantages with respect to certain issues' (1996: 73), and she recognises the danger of overemphasising experience in common. Nonetheless, her acknowledgement of the difficulties does not encompass the fuller critique long since developed within feminism – a critique which marks the extent to which standpoint epistemology masks the differences within any category, and moreover fails to problematise the intention to speak the truth.

It would be inappropriate to criticise Wendell – who has little or no sympathy for postmodernist analysis – for her confidence in the self-present subject, but what is more worrying is the way in which her own limited caveat with regard to standpoint is forgotten in the passion of opposing what she sees as substantive insults to disabled people. On the question of infant euthanasia, for example, she could not be clearer:

There is considerable agreement among disability activists that people who do not have the same disabilities as the newborns are in no moral position to judge whether their lives will be worth living (1996: 157).

But even should such an agreement exist, it is not clear either that activists speak for all disabled people, or how the claim to overridingly superior moral judgement is justified. l have every sympathy for Wendell's exasperation that those who are disabled are infrequently consulted about decisions affecting their own lives, still less empowered to lead decision-making, but it is another thing to buy into the notion that there is some absolute truth of the situation that only disabled people are able to perceive.

I am non-disabled

Should I accept that I have no entitlement to speak about disability? What ontological insecurities are at stake in the closure of standpoint, in the closure of identity?

I am disabled

Rather than respond with the closing of ranks that stances like those of Wendell, Oliver, Watson and, in certain contexts, Shakespeare seem to demand, l prefer to problematise identity in ways suggested by Butler (1993: 229–30). In her essay 'Critically Queer', Butler questions both the appeal to the self-identical subject – which she sees as an imaginary site – and the imposition of a totalising identity category. The exclusionary nature of both such moves, which, nonetheless, in some senses make focused political work possible, marks also the limits of its effectiveness. As soon as a collectivity lays claim to the term 'queer', it must engage in a series of exclusions that in turn are contested by those who might expect representation under that term and who find themselves on the outside. The inherent instability of the category is further emphasised by its need to close down internal differences. And it is in those moments of contestation that overlapping differences such as class, ethnicity or gender find expression. A paraphrase of Butler's remarks makes clear that a similar analysis fits my own position: If identity is a necessary error, then the assertion of the category 'disabled' will be necessary as a term of affiliation, but it will not fully describe those it purports to represent. Butler goes on:

The term will be revised, dispelled, rendered obsolete to the extent that it yields to the demands which resist the term precisely because of the exclusions by which it is mobilized (1993: 229).

What I would add, as Butler herself does, is that the necessity of identity (which I take to mean both that it is inevitable and necessary) should not be allowed to obscure its inherent risk. The realisation that identity may be radically unstable and contingent does not diminish its discursive power.

I am non-disabled

To say that the boundaries which organise us into definable categories are discursively unstable, and that final self-identity must constantly elude the embodied self, raises the question of just how identity may continue to operate.

At the level theorised by Foucault (1977, 1979) – as we remarked earlier – any corporeal identity is an achievement of a series of regulatory and disciplinary practices directed to the body. At its most effective, the medical gaze takes on the form of self-surveillance, such that the individual is incited to become complicit in the process of constituting herself as an embodied subject, be it as disabled, non-disabled or ablebodied. But rather than being experienced as constraints, the deployment of the norms of identity offer a fantasy of self-mastery, an operation not of subjection but of the autonomous subject. It is by just such mechanisms of imaginary control that we attempt to define our bounded selves. And yet, my identification of myself as non-disabled can function only insofar as constant reiteration is needed to secure the contested boundaries between us. The closure of embodied identity is always just beyond grasp, and it is as much a matter of performing that identity as it would be for sex or gender. As we put it elsewhere: 'the "purity" of the "healthy" body must be actively maintained and protected against its contaminated others – disease, disability, lack of control, material and ontological breakdown' (Shildrick and Price 1996: 106). And it is no less the case, that counter-identity is implicated in the maintenance of boundaries.

I am disabled

In offering a brief Foucauldian analysis of corporeal norms, Susan Wendell (1996) surmises that it is the evident *lack* of control of the disabled body that provokes anxiety and hostility in socio-cultural environments that idealise bodily perfection. What she does not consider is that disabled embodiment itself is caught up in/complicit with the illusion of mastery. Despite the explicit apparatus of regulatory norms which seek to manage the bodies of those who are disabled and mark them as other, that otherness is negotiated.

Once the gaze has become internalised, the performative acts of disabled people – that is the claims, desires, comportment and discursive self-representations – serve equally to constitute effects of identity, coherence and control. In my own case, at an uncontested individual level, the deployment of norms gives shape to the categorisation and management of a condition which constantly escapes attempts at diagnostic closure, and which thwarts prognosis. My performance of disabled embodiment fabricates an aura of mastery that defers the radical instability of both self and body. The point here is not that my condition is physically unstable, for in this I am similar to many other disabled people who have relapsing, remitting conditions such as multiple sclerosis (MS) and arthritis, and for whom diagnosis is often delayed or uncertain. Rather it is that the performative acts of a wheelchair user with an apparently stable spinal cord injury as much as those of a person with relapsing, remitting multiple sclerosis serve to continually reinscribe their disabled embodiment(s) and to (re)form their identities.

What we are suggesting is that the performativity of the body is the gesture – rather than the actuality – of self-control. And though control is already evident in the reiteration, repetition and categorisation of symptoms demanded within a biomedical or welfare context,[8] it is particularly clear in some disability forums, where what count as acceptable markers of the condition may be closely policed. For my own condition of ME or chronic fatigue syndrome, for example, the assertion of viral or environmental rather than psychological aetiology is *de rigeur* should I wish to join a self-help group. I would be constrained to 'perform' my disability according to the norms operative within that particular identity category. And the point is not only that the performativity of my condition is never entirely freely chosen, but that disability itself 'is performative in the sense that it constitutes as an effect the very subject that it appears to express' (Butler 1991: 24). Nonetheless, as we suggested earlier, the boundaries of the embodied self are never finally secured.

I am disabled/I am non-disabled

Can we perform what Butler calls 'an enabling disruption', a resignification of the norms which we necessarily occupy, but which fail to determine us completely?

If the operation of the disciplinary regimes which impel normative standards of embodiment is a matter of constant reiteration, it is precisely because the categories it maintains are inherently leaky and unstable. Moreover, the inescapable requirement to reiterate the regulatory processes through which corporeality is constituted simultaneously destabilises the body, revealing that which is excessive to the norm, that which remains uncontainable. It is not that performativity can be posited as some kind of choice – it is indeed compelled – but that in the repeated citation of a set of conventional practices, there is always the inevitability of slippage. And it is in those cracks that the possibility as well as the limits of agency occur. All those things which must be excluded from the normative binary of self and other, which must be silenced and forgotten, may acquire in their dislocation an accumulative force that returns to inhabit the moments of fracture. In any illness or disability, discontinuities continually erupt, queering any imagined correspondence between bodily form, appearance, function and ability: the man with locked-in syndrome, who writes a best-selling book; the woman who uses a wheelchair and padlocks herself to a bus to hold up the traffic;[9] the visually impaired woman who trains as a film director. Such unexpected disruptions not only contest the apparent limits of an impaired body, but mark the instability of the normative identities of those who are blind, deaf, disabled, and so on.

What is important about the imperfect process by which 'acceptable' norms and counter-norms are reiterated is that it opens up a space for ambivalence. Although the notion of intentionality per se remains highly contestable, agency might be exercised by exploiting the flaws in our own performativity, by re-calling a corporeality that is not wholly transcribed by the discursive strategies of power. The issue is not that a *determinate* challenge should or could be mounted to categorical oppressions, but that we should foster awareness of the final indeterminancy of all embodiments. And as far as political contestation goes, Judith Butler reminds us that '(t)he incalculable effects of action are as much part of their subversive promise as those we plan in advance' (1993: 241). For just such reasons, and for all that it is complicit with existing norms, performativity may also evade or exceed normalisation and move instead into transgressive resistance. Speaking of her experience of breast cancer, Eve Sedgwick captures that moment when she writes of hurling her major energies outward 'to inhabit the very farthest of the loose ends where representation, identity, gender, sexuality and the body can't be made to line up neatly together' (1994: 13).

I am non/disabled

If the attributes of our own embodied being 'can't be made to line up', how then could it be possible to continue in our separation and distinction one from the other? Or are we both, in the saying and the being, text and subject, so closely tied up with each other that we continually remake each other?

The issue, as we see it, is not so much that the leakiness of the boundaries of the embodied self grounds a movement between categories, as that separation is at best maintained precariously by performative reiterations. On the one hand those reiterations are constitutive of the very bodies that they manifest, but on the other they fail to inscribe an excessive domain of what Butler calls 'unintelligibility'. Yet once again, that domain cannot be seen as merely oppositional. On the contrary it is itself the necessary outside which both makes possible and limits the normative subject. As Butler puts it, the process of exclusion 'produces a constitutive outside to the subject, an abjected outside, which is, after all, "inside" the subject as its own founding repudiation' (1993: 3). And in a similar way, the bodies that don't matter – including those which are disabled – both define and haunt the bodies that do matter. What is perhaps less clear from Butler's analysis is that the operation of necessary exclusion pertains to any/body governed by a set of norms. Effectively the identity of disabled and non-disabled selves alike is secured – provisionally – by the reiterated abjection of those things or other selves which do not fit.

What remains, then, is the irreducible trace, the spectre of the other who is at the same time the self. At the very moment of defining identity through exclusion, of creating oppositional categories which rely on the suppression of the trace, the ontological and corporeal security of the self is shown to be precarious. To acknowledge that all bodies carry within the trace of the other is to admit that neither separation nor final closure is possible. Though the otherness of the excluded may speak for an ideal of a fixed and unified corporeality, the boundaries between self and other, inside and outside, disabled and non-disabled are crossed by the absent presence that poses the risk of indifferentiation. And it is the liminality of the spectre, its refusal to stay in the place of the other that generates its transgressive and transformative nature.

III

So what is the point of our asking such questions, and where might our querying of notions of disability take us? We would reiterate that the purpose of this chapter is not to expose the error of either biomedicine or the DRM in relation to disability, and nor is it to offer any ultimate political solutions. We want to problematise our political affiliations and commitments, not by denying those of others or by rejecting strategic action, but by refusing the possibility of totalising answers, by insisting on the necessity of disturbing our ways of thinking. In short we want to complicate Michael Oliver's plea in respect of the social model of disability that 'because it cannot explain everything, we should neither seek to expose its inadequacies, which are more a product of the way we use it, nor abandon it before its usefulness has been fully exploited' (1996: 41). We too would advocate its use, but at the same time demand an unsettling of its certainties, of the fixed identities with which it is bound up. In short, we would argue that our questioning both forefronts difference(s) – through the reiteration and disruption of norms – and that it makes a difference, that it is not simply empty theorising but has material effects for embodied subjects.

Deconstruction offers a way of thinking that refuses, by exposing the inevitable failure of self-presence, to be totally consumed by an/y identity. The question to which we return is this: if I am aware that identity is not all encompassing, that is, if I am cognisant – as opposed to unaware – of the inevitable non-presence within identity, how might that change things? I have lived with chronic fatigue syndrome (CFS) for eight years – an illness that is characterised by, above all things, material instability. I do not/cannot 'know' my body, this body that has been so marked by illness. I cannot keep pace with its/my twists and turns, my sudden surges are dips of energy, my fevers and rashes and pain. As a feminist of the late 1970s and early 1980s – a member of women's health groups – I prided myself on my knowledge of my body, on my ability to read its cycles and interpret the signs it gave me. Yet I look back now and question my complicity in creating the idea of a body that was stable, safe and ultimately knowable. I wonder what I had to silence in order to achieve this fantasy of intimate knowledge, of bodily transparency, of potential control. What I have gained since by letting go of such notions is a differing set of abilities, which enable me to negotiate the day-to-day experiences of illness and of disability, of my immanent bodilyness, without being destroyed by my failure to ever fully meet normative expectations.

In this chapter, we have outlined some of the differing ways in which subject/bodies – both non-disabled and disabled – have been constituted: the identity politics of the DRM which sets in place boundaries between those who are and those who are not disabled; the normative constructions and performativity of health and illness, disabled and non-disabled; the disciplinary regimes of health and welfare systems; and the gaze of the medical profession. All these instances of power/knowledge serve to inscribe us as embodied subjects who are complicit in our ongoing constitution. Yet I can escape from feelings of despair in the face of an unpredictable illness, in part because I know that none of those norms can contain me, that there is always a necessary excess. Whilst knowing that I cannot (re)determine or resist such norms from *outside* the forcefields of power/knowledge – as Foucault argues, 'resistance is never in a position of exteriority in relation to power' (1979: 95) – I can exploit the gaps in my complicity. Even in the reiterative and normative process of questionnaires used to assess welfare entitlement, there is always a necessary slippage which it is possible to utilise. I can, for example, refuse to respond to detailed questions, in a standardised questionnaire assessing my need for assistance, about how I manage my toilet needs and menstruation. Such questions provide no additional information regarding my condition but serve to constitute me as a universalised disabled body. It is not a case of directly opposing power, for that would be to actively reaffirm its authority, but of problematising its claim to speak the truth. I am/not what I seem.

The question of how awareness of non-identity might change things inevitably demands that we engage with considerations of theory and practice, of knowing and doing. New ways of thinking through the subject/body in turn make a difference in that they open up spaces for action. Nonetheless, we do not appeal to a simple theory: practice binary, but argue rather that, at the very simplest level, theory-making just is a form of practice, of necessity a material act. It creates space for the previously unthinkable, and unlocks new possibilities of contesting regimes of power. But that is not to say that theory and practice can be neatly equated, collapsed into each other, but that there is, as Spivak argues, a 'necessary crisis between theory and practice that marks deconstruction' (1992: 152). And the deconstructive move that subverts the opposition between the real and the text of representation, simultaneously undermines the contentious binary of activist/academic, as operative in disability politics as elsewhere.

This tension between knowing and doing has been taken up again by Spivak in a commentary on the standard translation of Foucault's concept of *pouvoir/savoir*. She argues that the English translation of *pouvoir/savoir* 'monumentalizes Foucault unnecessarily', rendering a description of an active process into a given thing – power/knowledge. She suggests a further reading of *pouvoir/ savoir* – 'being able to *do* something, only as you are able to *make sense* of it' (Spivak 1992: 158; our italics) – that holds on to the differentiation between the two acts whilst demonstrating how they are actively bound up in creating each other. This strikes us as a valuable formulation for it speaks to the ongoing and always insecure process of our becoming subject/bodies – a process in which we are deeply involved, in which we exercise agency but are never autonomous. The differing ways in which people respond to bodily changes that affect their mobility can serve as an example. In the face of apparently similar physical changes, some people will use a wheelchair, others will adopt the use of crutches or sticks – decisions affected not by any simple understanding of the changed physical capacities of their body but by how they make sense of mobility. The norms of medical rehabilitation – to maintain the individual as close to 'normality' as possible, in terms of gait and posture, and within which recourse to a wheelchair could be seen as a sign of defeat – are at odds with some views within the disability movement which would perceive rather the use of a wheelchair as an acknowledgement of disability and a challenge to the standards of mobility set by non-disabled people. The situation faced by people who have to relearn ways of being mobile is obviously far more complex than this simple opposition suggests; but what is clear is that the range of options open to them is influenced simultaneously by the limited ways in which they 'know' their changing bodies, and by the ways in which the process of making sense further changes those bodies.

Just saying no to the insults of the body is not an option. Rather, what is demanded is an affirmation – in Derrida's terms, a double affirmation. He speaks of the need to say yes to that against which one struggles, and yes to that which one advocates. For the disability rights movement, this must involve an ongoing negotiation with biomedicine, rather than a simple and unsustainable rejection of it. For us, as authors of this chapter, it necessitates not only an engagement with biomedicine and with disability politics, but also with the biological body as a pre-given biological entity. We cannot simply reject its materiality, as many postmodernist authors have been accused of doing, nor reclaim it through an appeal to modernist values. Rather, we must recognise that we reaffirm its reality even as we struggle against its 'givenness'. Such complicity does not equate with collusion, but marks rather, the 'refusal of a space beyond or outside, the refusal of the fantasy of a position safe or insulated from what it criticizes and disdains' (Grosz 1997: 77). What the outcomes of such impure struggles may be we cannot predict, nor can we know what exactly we risk when we engage with such uncertainty. Clearly the risk, feared by those who advocate the social model of disability as the one true way, is a reincorporation within biomedicine. That fear foresees a reduction of their struggles to the simple matter of broken bodies, in the context of prior experiences of the ways in which those bodies *do not matter*.

There is no reassuring answer to such anxieties, and neither can they be discounted. The postconventional approach that we have outlined here is not intended as a successor analysis, but as a pluralisation of the ways in which we might come to fear the instabilities of our bodies less. To see every form of embodiment not as a fixed category, but as a fluid, shifting set of conditions, frees us from the grasp of pre-given and stable identity categories that slot all too easily into oppositional binaries. The failure of feminism in general to respond adequately to issues around disability reflects both a continuing wariness about the uncontrollable body, and the difficulty of thinking beyond the binary of sameness and difference. But if, as Spivak recommends, we can see deconstruction 'as a radical acceptance of vulnerability' (1990: 18), it becomes clear that vulnerability is not the special case of disabled people, but the condition of all of us. The reconfiguration of fixed difference as the flow of boundless and irreducible differences moves away from a politics of liberal tolerance towards an ethical openness to the disruptive otherness both without and within. What a postmodernist account suggests finally is that our 'responsibility to the trace of the other' (Spivak 1992: 162) is inseparable from an acceptance of our own vulnerability. To forego our fantasies of control and face uncertainty is to take up afresh the question of ethics.

NOTES

1. In defiance of non-disabled feminism's apparent disinterest, there is a growing body of work by disabled feminists. Notable examples include Nasa Begum (1992), Lois Keith (1994), Jenny Morris (1993,

1996), Rosemarie Garland Thomson (1997), Susan Wendell (1996) and, in the UK, the newsletter *Boadicea*, published by the Greater London Association of Disabled People. The present authors together have previously written on postmodernist aspects of disability (1996), as well as separately and with others (Potts and Price 1995, Price 1996, Shildrick 1997).

2. The disability rights movements in the UK has referred to the social model as its 'big idea'. There are clear differences between the disability rights movement in the UK and, for example, in the USA, both in terms of the legislative background against which they are working and in relation to the analyses of the origins and causes of disability they advocate. This article refers to the British disability rights movement, unless otherwise indicated.

3. In contrast to this article, which appears to make a plea for fixed identities and an unwavering adherence to the social model, in a chapter entitled 'Disability, Identity and Difference' Shakespeare problematises notions of identity and suggests that poststructuralist approaches might be of use to disability studies. He expresses a tension when he says, 'the political demands of the disability movement may not allow space for *seemingly* irrelevant diversions' (1996: 110; our italics). We would suggest that it is over the failure to take on board such seemingly irrelevant diversions that feminism experienced such internal difficulties in the 1980s.

4. In contrast to most feminist moves which challenge notions of transcendence, Susan Wendell views it as a potentially positive move. She uses the term transcendence to describe the process by which some disabled people separate their sense of self from the pain or discomfort they experience, strategies of disembodiment from the body's suffering which, she argues, 'increase the freedom of consciousness' (1996: 178).

5. In the examples used in the article we draw upon our experience of disability, which for one of us encompasses being a wheelchair user. This is the image that most clearly signifies 'disabled' for many people, but the point of our examples is not further to cement this as the categorical representation of disability. Rather, it is to offer ways of problematising such fixed significations.

6. For a more detailed analysis of the way in which the disciplinary practices of biomedicine and welfare policy construct the disabled body, see 'Breaking the Boundaries of the Broken Body' 99–107 (Shildrick and Price 1996).

7. The point here is not that we are sometimes physically able to do this but rather that it is one of a wide variety of possible moves that breaks the fixed norms of disability.

8. For an analysis of the specific performativity of the disabled body see note 6.

9. The protests of groups such as DAN (Direct Action Network) have played a major role in highlighting the inaccessibility of public transport systems through, for example, traffic blockades.

REFERENCES

Begum, Nasa (1992) 'Disabled Women and the Feminist Agenda', *Feminist Review* 40: 70–84.

Benefits Agency (1996) *Incapacity for work questionnaire*, Department of Social Security.

Butler, Judith (1991) 'Imitation and Gender Insubordination' in Diana Fuss (ed.) *Inside/Out: Lesbian Theories, Gay Theories*, London: Routledge.

Butler, Judith (1993) *Bodies That Matter: On the Discursive Limits of 'Sex'*, London: Routledge.

Crow, Liz (1996) 'Including All of Our Lives: Renewing the Social Model of Disability' in J. Morris (ed.) *Encounters with Strangers: Feminism and Disability*, London: The Women's Press.

Epstein, Julia (1995) *Altered Conditions: Disease, Medicine, and Storytelling*, London: Routledge.

Foucault, Michel (1979) *History of Sexuality, Vol. 1*, trans, R. Hurley, London: Allen Lane.

Foucault, Michel (1980) *Power/Knowledge: Selected Interviews and Other Writings (1977–1984)*, ed. Colin Gordon, Brighton: Harvester Press.

Grosz, Elizabeth (1994) *Volatile Bodies*, Bloomington: Indiana University Press.

Grosz, Elizabeth (1997) 'Ontology and Equivocation: Derrida's Politics of Sexual Difference' in Nancy J. Holland (ed.) *Feminist Interpretations of Jacques Derrida*, Pennsylvania: Pannsylvania State University.

Holdsworth, A. (1993) 'Our Allies Within', *Coalition*, June: 4–10.

Hutchison's Clinical Methods (1989), 19th edition, ed. Michael Swash, London: Bailliere Tindall.

Keith, Lois (1994) *Mustn't Grumble*, London: The Women's Press.

Morris, Jenny (1993) 'Feminism and Disability', *Feminist Review* 43: 57–70.

Morris, Jenny (ed.) (1996) *Encounters with Strangers: Feminism and Disability*, London: The Women's Press.

Oliver, M. (1996) *Understanding Disability: From Theory to Practice*, London: Macmillan Press.

Potts, Tracey and Price, Janet (1995) 'Out of the Blood and Spirit of Our Lives: The Place of the Body in Academic Feminism' in L. Morley and V. Walsh (eds) *Feminist Academics: Creative Agents for Change*, London: Taylor and Francis.

Price, Janet (1996) 'The Marginal Politics of Our Bodies? Women's Health, the Disability Movement, and Power' in Beth Humphries (ed.) *Critical Perspectives on Empowerment*, Birmingham: Venture Press.

Sedgwick, Eve Kosofsky (1994) *Tendencies*, London: Routledge.

Shakespeare, Tom (1996) 'Disability, Identity and Difference' in C. Barnes and G. Mercer (eds) *Exploring the Divide: Illness and Disability*, Leeds: The Disability Press.

Shakespeare, Tom and Watson, Nicholas (1997) 'Defending the Social Model', *Disability and Society*, 12, 2: 293–300.

Shildrick, Margrit (1997) *Leaky Bodies and Boundaries. Feminism, Postmodernism and (Bio)ethics*, London: Routledge.

Shildrick, Margrit and Price, Janet (1996) 'Breaking the Boundaries of the Broken Body', *Body and Society*, 2, 4.

Spivak, Gayatri Chakravorty (1990) *The Post-colonial Critic: Interviews, Strategies, Dialogues,* ed. Sarah Harasym, London: Routledge.

Spivak, Gayatri Chakravorty (1992) 'More on Power/Knowledge' in T. Wartenberg (ed.) *Rethinking Power.* Albany: SUNY Press.

Thomson, Rosemarie Garland (ed.) (1996) *Freaks: Cultural Spectacles of the Extraordinary Body*, New York: New York University Press.

Thomson, Rosemarie Garland (1997) *Exceptional Bodies: Figuring Physical Disability in American Literature and Culture*, New York: Columbia University Press.

UPIAS (1976) *Fundamental Principles of Disability*, London: Union of the Physically Impaired Against Segregation.

Wendell, Susan (1996) *The Rejected Body: Feminist Philosophical Reflections on Disability*, London: Routledge.

William, G. (1996) 'Representing Disability: Some Questions of Phenomenology and Politics' in C. Barnes and G. Mercer (eds) *Exploring the Divide: Illness and Disability*, Leeds: The Disability Press.

Contributors' Notes

Sara Ahmed undertook her doctoral research on feminism and post-modernism at the Centre for Critical and Cultural Theory, Cardiff University, 1991–4. She has been a lecturer at the Institute for Women's Studies, Lancaster University, since 1994. She teaches courses on gender, race and colonialism, and on feminism, psychoanalysis and deconstruction. Her first book entitled *Differences that Matter: Feminist Theory and Postmodernism* (Cambridge Universily Press, 1998) is based on her PhD, and she begun work on another book provisionally entitled *Strange Encounters: Embodied Others in Post-Coloniality*. She has articles published in journals including *Hypatia*, *Australian Feminist Studies*, *Social and Legal Studies* and *New Formations*.

Lynda Birke is a biologist, now working in science studies/women's studies at the University of Lancaster. Her research focuses on the interface between biological and social theory, particularly in relation to ideas about the body. Her previous books include: *Women, Feminism and Biology* Wheatsheaf, 1986); *Feminism, Animals and Science* (Open University, 1994); and (with Ruth Hubbard) *Reinventing Biology* (Indiana University Press, 1995). She is Series Editor for Edinburgh University Press's forthcoming series on Gender, Science and Technology.

Roma Chatterji is Lecturer in Sociology at The University of Delhi. She has published several papers on popular performances based on her fieldwork in Prurulia and on aging based upon her fieldwork in the Netherlands.

Sangeeta Chattoo completed her doctoral dissertation on 'A Sociological Study of Certain Aspects of Disease and Death: A Case Study of Muslims of Kashmir' in 1992. She is currently based in Pune.

Sheba Chhachhi was born in 1958 in Harar, Ethiopia, and educated in Delhi, Calcutta and Ahmedabad in India. A photographer, sculptor, writer, graphic designer and feminist activist since 1980, she began work with multimedia installations in 1993. She has since created a series of works which investigate and articulate the history, experience and power of feminine consciousness. Her work has been shown in India, the UK, Canada, China and France. She has also contributed to a number of seminars and publications. She lives and works in New Delhi. Recent major works include *Raktpushp (Blood Flower)* on the postcolonial female body in India (1997, France), *A Box of Shards/The Mermaid's Mirror: memories of Meena Kumari Naaz*, on the construction of femininity and romantic love in popular Hindu cinema (1996, New Delhi), and the series *Wild Mothers, Parts I and II* on the mythological, historical and contemporary traditions of female power (1993/4, UK, Canada, New Delhi).

Veena Das is a Professor of Sociology at the University of Delhi and Professor of Social Anthropology at the New School for Social Research. Her most recent book is *Critical Events: An Anthropological Perspective on Contemporary India* (Oxford University Press, 1995).

Lisa L. Diedrich is working on her doctorate at the Institute for Women's Studies at Emory University in Atlanta, Georgia. She is looking at images of illness in contemporary culture.

Rosalyn Diprose teaches Philosophy at the University of New South Wales in Sydney. She is the author of *The Bodies of Women: Ethics, Embodiment and Sexual Difference* (Routledge, 1994), editor (with Robyn Ferrell) of *Cartographies: Poststructuralism and the Mapping of Bodies and Spaces* (Allen and Unwin, 1991) and is currently completing a book entitled *Corporeal Generosity: Ethics, Erotics, Community.*

Camilla Benolirao Griggers is Distinguished Chair of Women's Studies at Carlow College in Pittsburgh. She is the author of *Becoming-Woman* (University of Minnesota Press, 1997) and founding editor of the e-journal *Cultronix* on the World-Wide Web. She has produced and directed several videos including *Alienations of the Mother Tongue* (1995), *The Micropolitics of Biosychiatry* (1996), and *Memories of a Forgotten War* (in progress).

Sonia Jabbar is a writer and graphic designer who has published in *India International Centre Quarterly* and *India Magazine*. She has recently been working more with the camera and has collaborated with Sheba Chhachhi on photos for *Notes to the Body*.

Janet Price is an Honorary Fellow at the Liverpool School of Tropical Medicine, England, though unemployed due to ill-health. She teaches and publishes on feminist health issues and her experience of illness and disability has led her to become increasingly involved in addressing where

251

and how bodies fit into feminist theorising and practice. She collaborates with Margrit Shildrick whenever possible. They are co-editing a forth-coming reader on Feminist Theory and the Body for Edinburgh University Press.

Margrit Shildrick is a Research Fellow in Sociology at Staffordshire University, and an Honorary Research Fellow at the University of Liverpool. She has published extensively in the area of feminist philosophy and bioethics, and is now working on monstrosity and vulnerability. Her first book is *Leaky Bodies and Boundaries: Feminism, Postmodernism and (Bio)ethics* (Routledge, 1997).

Ailbhe Smyth is a feminist activist, writer and researcher. She is Director of the Women's Education, Research and Resource Centre (WERRC) at University College Dublin, where she teaches Women's Studies. She co-edits *f/m* (feminist magazine) and *Women's Studies International Forum*, and has published widely on feminist politics, culture and the state.

Cathryn Vasseleu is a Vice-Chancellor's Research Fellow in Philosophy at the University of New South Wales. She is the author of *Textures of Light: Vision and Touch in Irigaray, Levinas and Merleau-Ponty* (Routledge, 1998).

Lorna Weir is associate professor in the Department of Sociology, York University, Toronto, Canada. She has published on social movements, assisted human reproduction and reproductive rights organising. She is currently working on a book manuscript, 'The Government of Pregnancy', and has previously edited *Governing Medically assisted Human Reproduction* (University of Toronto Press, 1996) and co-edited *Beyond Political Correctness: The Future of the Canadian Academy* (University of Toronto Press, 1995).

Index

Index

Index

poststructuralism, 78, 80, 96
post-traumatic stress syndrome, 133, 135–7, 140, 141–2
Potts, T. and Price, J., 7
power, 134
  /knowledge, 245
pregnancy, 78–9, 80
Price, M., 79
projection of body, 39, 40, 42
Prozac, 133, 143
psychoanalysis, 151, 161–2, 168n.
psychopathology, 135, 137–9, 142
psychopharmacology, 133–45
psychosis, 133, 136, 137–8, 139
psychotherapy, 133, 139
puberty, 108–11
purity/pollution, 106–29, 209–10

race, 140, 242, 246
Radley, A., 207
Rajan, R. S., 11
Rapp, R., 79
regulatory practices see Foucault
resistance, 37
  see also hysteria
rest cure, 150, 152
reterritorialisation, 135
Rivers, W. H. R., 153, 154–5, 156, 161–2, 164, 168n.
rot, 70, 75
Rothman, B. K., 89–90
Russo, M., 165n.

Samvarta Samhita, 110
Sassoon, S., 156, 158, 163–4, 167n.
Sauvy, A., 202–3
scar, 47–8
Scarry, E., 199
scientific discourse, 199, 204–5, 210, 237
  experimental model, 212–13, 214–15
scopic economy, 85
Sechehaye, M., 132
Sedgwick, E. Kosofsky, 9, 167n.
seduction, tool of, 71
self-regulation, 38
sexual abuse, 135, 141
sexuality, 60, 106–29
  ambiguous relation between bodies, 38–40, 42
  clinical encounter, 30–42
  definition, 31, 38
  deployment of, 31–3
  medical discourse, 30, 31–3, 36
  normalisation, 31–3, 36
Shakespeare, T., 235, 247n.
  and Watson, N., 229–30
Shapiro, S. and Dominiak, G., 137, 138, 141
Sharp, L., 208
shell-shock, 146–64, 165n.
  see also hysteria
Sherwin, S., 6
Shildrick, M., 3
Showalter, E., 154, 162, 164
signification, 133

signifier, 134
Sinha, M., 111
skin, 24, 27, 37, 40, 45–64
  as boundary, 47–52
  as mirror, 51, 55–6
Smith-Rosenberg, C., 149, 150
sonogram, foetal, 78–97
space, 67–71, 134
  intimate, 67
Spivak, G. C., 11, 52, 226, 244–6
Stacey, J., 9
standpoint, 237
Strathern, M., 79, 86, 95
subject, chemical prosthetic, 133
subjectivisation, 133, 134
Suleri, S., 47
suppression, 136, 139, 141
surge, 134–5, 136–7, 139, 141–2
  suppressor, 139

Taittriya Samhita, 116–17
tanning, 57–63
teeth, loss of, 69, 75
texts, 1
Thomson, R., 232
touch, 24, 37, 38, 40, 51, 48, 49, 67, 69, 74
transcendence, 231
transplantation, 53
trauma, 141, 143
truth, 10–11, 13, 18, 32, 36, 41, 48, 50, 53, 56, 237, 244
  regime, 81

ultrasound, 67, 78–97
  'entertainment' ultrasound, 82
uncertainty, 224, 237, 246
universalism/ity, 47
UPIAS, 228

Vietnam War, 167n.
voice, 178–80
  and silence, 191–2
vulnerability, 224, 236, 246
Vyasa Samhita, 108

Walsh, V., 5
Watney, S., 33
Wendell, S., 226, 237–9, 247n.
whiteness, 52–3, 58–9
Williams, G., 224
Williamson, J., 60–2
Winterson, J., ii
Woolf, V., 151
  Mrs Dalloway, 155, 158–8, 161, 163–4, 167–8n.
World War I, 146–8, 152–64
  women's participation in, 157–8, 167n.

xenotransplantation, 207–10, 216

Yealland, L., 160
Young, I. M., 8
Young, S., 205

256